Portuguese

at your Fingertips

Other titles in this series

French at your Fingertips
Greek at your Fingertips
Spanish at your Fingertips

Portuguese

at your Fingertips

compiled by

LEXUS

with

Hugh O'Donnell, Miguel Athayde Marques,
Maria dos Santos and Peter Terrell

Routledge & Kegan Paul
London

First published in 1986
by Routledge & Kegan Paul plc

14 Leicester Square, London WC2H 7PH, England

Set in Linotron Baskerville
by Morton Word Processing Ltd, Scarborough
and printed in Great Britain
by Guernsey Press

British Library Cataloguing in Publication Data

French at your fingertips.—(Fingertips)

1. Portuguese language—Conversation and phrase books
I. Lexus   II. O'Donnell, Hugh   III. Series
469.83'421   PC5073

ISBN 0-7102-0727-1

Contents

PORTUGUESE PRONUNCIATION

Because you are likely to want to speak most of the Portuguese given in this book, rather than just to understand its meaning, an indication of the pronunciation has been given in square brackets. If you pronounce this as though it were English, the result will be clearly comprehensible to a Portuguese person.

In some cases, however, we have decided it was not necessary to give the entire pronunciation for a word or phrase. This may be because it would more or less duplicate the ordinary Portuguese spelling, or because the pronunciation of a particular word or words has already been given within the same entry. In these cases we have simply shown how to pronounce the problematic parts of the word or phrase.

Some comments on the pronunciation system used:

VOWELS

a	as in 'hat'
ah	as in 'father'
ay	as in 'day'
e	as in 'men'
eh	like the 'ay' in 'day'
i or ih	as in 'bit'
o	as in 'dog'
oh	as in 'ore'
oo	as in 'boot'

CONSONANTS

sh	like the 's' in 'leisure'
r	always pronounced, never silent as in English

Where the print for a letter (or two letters) is in bold type this means that this part of the word should be stressed. It is very important to get the stress right when speaking Portuguese.

English – Portuguese

A

a um, uma *[oong, ooma]*; **200 escudos a bottle** 200 escudos cada garrafa *[kada garrahſa]*
about: about 25 mais ou menos 25 *[mahiz oh mehnoosh]*; **about 6 o'clock** por volta das seis *[poor volta]*; **is the manager about?** o gerente está por aqui? *[shtah poor akee]*; **I was just about to leave** ia mesmo agora a sair *[ee-a meh-sнmoo agora a sa-eer]*; **how about a drink?** que tal uma bebida? *[kih tahl ooma bibeeda]*
above em cima *[aing seema]*; **above the village** por cima da vila *[poor seema da veela]*
abroad no estrangeiro *[noo shtran-sнayroo]*
abscess um abscesso *[absh-sehssoo]*
absolutely: it's absolutely perfect é ideal! *[eed-yahl]*; **you're absolutely right** tem toda a razão *[taing tohda a razowng]*; **absolutely!** com certeza! *[kong sirtehza]*
absorbent cotton o algodão *[ahlgoodowng]*
accelerator o acelerador *[assiliradohr]*
accept aceitar *[assay-tahr]*
accident um acidente *[asseedent]*; **there's been an accident** houve um acidente *[ohv]*; **sorry, it was an accident** desculpe, foi sem querer *[fohy saing kirehr]*
accommodation(s) o alojamento *[aloosнamentoo]*; **we need accommodation(s) for four** precisamos de alojamento para quatro pessoas *[prisseezamoosh d-yaloosнamentoo]*
accurate exacto *[eezahtoo]*
ache: I have an ache here doi-me aqui *[doy-mih akee]*; **it aches** faz doer *[fahsh dwehr]*
across: across the street do outro lado da rua *[doo ohtroo lahdoo da roo-a]*

actor o actor *[ahtohr]*
actress a actriz *[ahtreesh]*
adapter um adaptador *[—ohr]*
address o endereço *[aingdirehssoo]*; **what's your address?** qual é o seu endereço? *[kwahl e oo seh-oo]*
address book o livro de moradas *[leevroo dih moorahdash]*
admission: how much is admission? quanto custa a entrada? *[kwantoo kooshta a aingtrahda]*
adore: I adore ... adoro ... *[adoroo]*
adult adulto *[adooltoo]*
advance: I'll pay in advance pago adiantado *[pahgoo ad-yantahdoo]*
advert um anúncio *[anoons-yoo]*
advise: what would you advise? o que me aconselha? *[oo kih m-yahkonssehlya]*
affluent rico *[reeko]*
afraid: I'm afraid of heights tenho medo de altitudes *[taing-nyoo mehdoo dih]*; **don't be afraid** não tenha medo *[nowng tehn-ya]*; **I'm not afraid** não tenho medo; **I'm afraid I can't help you** sinto, mas não posso ajudá-lo *[seentoo, mash nowng possoo asнoodah-loo]*; **I'm afraid so** lamento que sim *[lamentoo kih seeng]*; **I'm afraid not** lamento que não
after: after you você primeiro *[vosseh preemay-roo]*; **after 9 o'clock** depois das nove horas *[dipoh-ish]*; **not until after 9 o'clock** só depois das nove horas *[saw]*
afternoon a tarde *[tahrd]*; **in the afternoon** à tarde *[ah]*; **good afternoon** boa tarde *[boh-a]*; **this afternoon** esta tarde *[eshta]*
aftershave o aftershave
after sun cream uma loção para depois do sol *[loossowng para dipoh-ish doo sol]*
afterwards depois *[dipoh-ish]*
again outra vez *[ohtra vehsh]*
against contra

age a idade *[eedahd]*; **under age** menor *[minor]*; **not at my age!** na minha idade não! *[na meen-ya eedahd nowng]*; **it takes ages** leva muito tempo *[mweengtoo tempoo]*; **I haven't been here for ages** não venho aqui há muito tempo *[nowng vehn-yoo akee ah]*

agency uma agência *[ashens-ya]*

aggressive agressivo *[agrisseevoo]*

ago: a year ago há um ano *[ah oong anoo]*; **it wasn't long ago** ainda não foi há muito tempo *[a-eenda nowng fohy ah mweengtoo tempoo]*

agony: it's agony é um tormento *[oong toormentoo]*

agree: do you agree? concorda?; **I agree** concordo *[kongkordoo]*; **port doesn't agree with me** o vinho do Porto não me cai bem *[nowng mih k-eye baing]*

AIDS SIDA *[seeda]*

air o ar; **by air** de avião *[dih av-yowng]*

air-conditioning o ar condicionado *[kondees-yoonadoo]*

air hostess a hospedeira de bordo *[ohshpiday-ra dih bordoo]*

airmail: by airmail por via aérea *[poor vee-a a-air-ya]*

airmail envelope um envelope de avião *[aing-vilop d-yav-yowng]*

airplane o avião *[av-yowng]*

airport o aeroporto *[a-airoopohrtoo]*

airport bus o autocarro para o aeroporto *[owtookahroo para oo a-airoopohrtoo]*

airport tax as taxas de aeroporto *[tahshas d-ya-airoopohrtoo]*

alarm o alarme

alarm clock o despertador *[dishpirtadohr]*

alcohol o álcool *[ahlkwol]*

alcoholic: is it alcoholic? tem álcool? *[taing ahlkwol]*

alive vivo *[veevoo]*; **is he still alive?** ainda está vivo? *[a-eenda shtah]*

all: all the hotels todos os hotéis *[tohdooz ooz ohtaysh]*; **all my friends** todos os meus amigos *[oosh meh-ooz amee-goosh]*; **all my money** todo o meu dinheiro *[tohdoo meh-oo deen-yay-roo]*; **all of it** todo; **all of them** todos *[tohdoosh]*; **all right** está bem *[shtah baing]*; **I'm all right** estou bem *[shtoh]*; **that's all** é tudo; **it's all changed** tudo está mudado *[shtah moodahdoo]*; **thank you**

— not at all obrigado — não tem de quê *[nowng taing dih keh]*

allergic: I'm allergic to ... sou alérgico a ... *[soh alair-sнeekoo a]*

allergy uma alergia *[alirsнee-a]*

all-inclusive tudo incluído *[toodoo eenklweedoo]*

allowed permitido *[pirmeeteedoo]*; **is it allowed?** é permitido?; **I'm not allowed to eat salt** estou proibido de comer sal *[shtoh prweebeedoo dih koomehr]*

almost quase *[kwahz]*

alone só *[saw]*; **are you alone?** está só? *[shtah]*; **leave me alone** deixe-me em paz *[daysh-mih aing pahsh]*

already já *[sнah]*

also tambén *[tambaing]*

alteration *(to plans)* uma alteração *[ahltirassowng]*; *(to clothes)* uma emenda *[eemenda]*

alternative: is there an alternative? não tem outra coisa? *[nowng taing ohtra kohiza]*; **we had no alternative** não tivemos outra hipótese *[nowng teev-emooz ohtra eepotizih]*

alternator um alternador *[ahltirnadohr]*

although embora *[aingbora]*

altogether totalmente *[tootahlment]*; **what does that come to altogether?** quanto é tudo? *[kwantoo e toodoo]*

always sempre

a.m.: at 8 a.m. às oito da manhã *[ahz oh-itoo da man-yang]*

amazing *(surprising)* espantoso *[shpantohzoo]*; *(very good)* estupendo *[shtoopendoo]*

ambassador o embaixador *[aingbah-ishadohr]*

ambulance a ambulância *[amboolans-ya]*; **get an ambulance!** chame uma ambulância *[sham]*

America a América do Norte *[doo nort]*

American americano *[amireekanoo]*

American plan a pensão completa *[pensowng komplehta]*

among entre

amp: a 15-amp fuse um fusível de 15 amperes *[foozeevel dih keenz amperish]*

an(a)esthetic um anestético *[anishteteekoo]*

ancestor um antepassado *[antipassahdoo]*

anchor uma âncora *[ankoora]*

anchovies umas anchovas *[anshovash]*
ancient antigo *[anteegoo]*
and e *[ee]*
angina angina *[ansнeena]*
angry zangado *[zangahdoo]*; **I'm very angry about it** estou muito zangado por causa disso *[shtoh mweengtoo zangahdoo poor kah-wza deessoo]*
animal um animal *[aneemahl]*
ankle o tornozelo *[toornoozehloo]*
anniversary: it's our (wedding) anniversary é o nosso aniversário (de casamento) *[oo nossoo aneevirsahr-yoo (dih kazamentoo)]*
annoy: he's annoying me ele está a aborrecer-me *[ehl shtah aboorrissehr-mih]*; **it's so annoying** que maçada! *[kih massahda]*
anorak um anoraque *[anoorahk]*
another: can we have another room? pode dar-nos outro quarto? *[pod dahr-nooz ohtroo kwahrtoo]*; **another bottle, please** outra garrafa, por favor *[ohtra garrahfa, poor favohr]*
answer: there was no answer não houve resposta *[nowng ohv rishposhta]*; **what was his answer?** qual foi a sua resposta? *[kwahl fohy a soo-a]*
ant: ants umas formigas *[foormeegash]*
antibiotics os antibióticos *[anteebyoteekoosh]*
anticlimax uma desilusão *[dizeeloozowng]*
antifreeze o anticongelante *[anteekonsнilant]*
anti-histamines os anti-histamínicos *[antee-eeshtameeneekoosh]*
antique: is it an antique? é uma antiguidade? *[ooma anteegweedahd]*
antique shop uma casa de antiguidades *[kahza d-yanteegweedahdish]*
antisocial: don't be antisocial não seja antipático *[nowng seh-sнa anteepahteekoo]*
any: have you got any rolls/milk? tem carcaças/leite? *[taing]*; **I haven't got any** não tenho *[nowng taing-nyoo]*
anybody: can anybody help? alguém pode ajudar? *[ahlgaing pod asнoodahr]*; **there wasn't anybody there** não estava lá ninguém *[nowng shtahva lah neenggaing]*
anything qualquer coisa *[kwahlkair koh-

iza]*; **I don't want anything** não quero nada *[nowng kairoo]*; **don't you have anything else?** é só o que tem? *[oo kih taing]*
apart from além de *[alaing dih]*
apartment um andar *[oong andahr]*
aperitif um aperitivo *[apireeteevoo]*
apology: please accept my apologies peço-lhe que me desculpe *[pessoo l-yih kih mih dishkoolp]*
appalling insuportável *[eensoopoortahvel]*
appear: it would appear that ... parece que ... *[paress kih]*
appendicitis a apendicite *[apendeesseet]*
appetite o apetite *[apiteet]*; **I've lost my appetite** perdi o apetite
apple uma maçã *[massang]*
apple pie uma torta de maçã *[dih massang]*
application form uma ficha de inscrição *[feesha deenshkreessowng]*
appointment: I'd like to make an appointment queria marcar uma entrevista *[kiree-a ... entriveeshta]*; *(medical)* queria marcar uma consulta *[konsoolta]*
appreciate: thank you, I appreciate it obrigado, fico muito reconhecido *[ohbreegahdoo, feekoo mweengtoo rikoon-yisseedoo]*
approve: she doesn't approve ela não concorda com isso *[nowng kongkorda kong eessoo]*
apricot o damasco *[damahshkoo]*
April Abril
aqualung garrafas de oxigénio *[garrahfash d-yoksee-sнen-yoo]*
Arab árabe
archaeology a arqueologia *[arkyooloosнee-a]*
are *see page 117*
area: I don't know the area não conheço a região *[nowng koon-yehsso a risн-yowng]*
area code o código *[kodeegoo]*
arena *(sport)* a arena *[arehna]*
arm o braço *[brahssoo]*
around *see about*
arrangement: will you make the arrangements? você encarrega-se dos preparativos? *[vosseh enkarregassih doosh priparateevoosh]*
arrest prender *[prendehr]*; **he's been

arrested foi preso [fohy prehzoo]
arrival a chegada [shigahda]
arrive: when do we arrive? a que horas chegamos? [a k-yorash shigamoosh]; **has my parcel arrived yet?** a minha encomenda já chegou? [a meen-ya enkoomenda sнah shigoh]; **let me know as soon as they arrive** avise-me assim que eles chegarem [aveez-mih asseeng k-yehlsh shigahraing]; **we only arrived yesterday** só chegámos ontem [shigamooz ontaing]
art a arte
art gallery a galeria de arte [galiree-a]
arthritis a artrite [artreet]
artificial artificial [arteefees-yahl]
artist (painter) um pintor [peentohr]
as: as fast as you can tão depressa quanto possível [towng dipressa kwantoo poosseevel]; **as much as you can** tanto quanto puder [tantoo kwantoo poodair]; **as you like** como quiser [kohmoo keezair]; **as it's getting late** visto que está a fazer-se tarde [veeshtoo kishtah a fazehr-sih tahrd]
ashore: to go ashore desembarcar [dizaing-barkahr]
ashtray um cinzeiro [seenzay-roo]
aside from além de [alaing dih]
ask (question) perguntar [pirgoontahr]; (for something) pedir [pideer]; **that's not what I asked for** isso não é o que pedi [eessoo nowng e oo kih pidee]; **could you ask him to phone me back?** importa-se lhe pedir que volte a telefonar? [eemporta-sih dih l-yih pideer kih volt a tilifoonahr]
asleep: he's still asleep ainda está a dormir [a-eenda shtah a doormeer]
asparagus o espargo [shpahrgoo]
aspirin uma aspirina [ashpeereena]
assault: she's been assaulted ela foi assaltada [ela fohy assahltada]; **indecent assault** um ataque sexual [atahk sekswahl]
assistant (in shop) o empregado [aingprigahdoo]
assume: I assume that ... suponho que ... [soopohn-yoo kih]
asthma a asma [ahsнma]
astonishing espantoso [shpantohzoo]

at: at the cafe no café [noo ka-fe]; **at the hotel** no hotel [noo ohtel]; **at 3 o'clock** às três horas [ahsh]; **see you at dinner** vemo-nos ao jantar [vehmoo-nooz ow sнantahr]
Atlantic o Atlântico [atlanteekoo]
atmosphere o ambiente [amb-yent]
attractive: you're very attractive você é muito atraente [vosseh e mweengtoo atra-ent]
aubergine uma beringela [bireensнela]
auction um leilão [lay-lowng]
audience o público [poobleekoo]
August Agosto [agohshtoo]
aunt: my aunt a minha tia [meen-ya tee-a]
au pair (girl) a au-pair
Australia a Austrália [owshtrahl-ya]
Australian australiano [owshtral-yanoo]
Austria a Áustria [owshtr-ya]
authorities as autoridades [owtooreedahdish]
automatic (car) automático [owtoomahteekoo]
automobile o automóvel [owtoomovel]
autumn o outono [ohtohnoo]; **in the autumn** no outono [noo]
available: when will it be available? quando estará disponível? [kwandoo shtarah dishpooneevel]; **when will he be available?** quando é que ele está livre? [e k-yehl shtah leevrih]
avenue a avenida [avineeda]
average: the average Portuguese o português médio [poortoogehsh medyoo]; **an above average hotel** um hotel acima da média [asseema da med-ya]; **a below average hotel** um hotel de baixa qualidade [dih bah-isha kwaleedahd]; **the food was only average** a comida não era grande coisa [a koomeeda nowng era grand koh-iza]; **on average** em média [aing med-ya]
awake: is she awake yet? ela já acordou? [ela sнah akoordoh]
away: is it far away? fica longe? [feeka lonsн]; **go away!** vá-se embora! [vasse-embora]
awful horrível [ohrreevel]
axle o eixo [ay-shoo]

B

baby o bébé [beb-**e**]
baby-carrier o porta-bébés [—beb-**esh**]
baby-sitter a baby-sitter; **can you arrange a baby-sitter for us?** pode arranjar-nos uma baby-sitter? [pod arrans**h**ahr-noosh]
bachelor solteiro [sohlt**ay**-roo]
back: **I've got a bad back** tenho problemas com as minhas costas [ta**i**ng-nyoo proobl**eh**mash kong ash m**ee**n-yash koshtash]; **at the back** atrás [atr**ah**sh]; **in the back of the car** na traseira do carro [na traz**ay**-ra do k**ah**rroo]; **I'll be right back** volto já [v**o**ltoo s**h**ah]; **when do you want it back?** quando precisa dele? [kw**a**ndoo priss**ee**za dehl]; **can I have my money back?** posso reaver o meu dinheiro? [p**o**ssoo r-yav**e**hr oo meh-oo deen-y**ay**-roo]; **come back!** volte!; **I go back home tomorrow** volto para casa amanhã [v**o**ltoo pra k**ah**za ahman-yang]; **we'll be back next year** voltamos no próximo ano [v**o**ltamosh noo pr**o**sseemoo anoo]; **when is the last bus back?** a que horas é o último autocarro de volta? [a k-y**o**raz e oo **oo**lteemoo owtook**ah**rroo dih v**o**lta]; **he backed into me** ele fez marcha-atrás e bateu-me [ehl fesh m**ah**rsh-ahtr**ah**sh ee bat**eh**-oomih]
backache uma dor de costas [dohr dih koshtash]
back door a porta das traseiras [dash traz**ay**-rash]
backpack uma mochila [moosh**ee**la]
back seat o assento traseiro [ass**e**ntoo traz**ay**-roo]
back street uma ruela [rw**e**la]
bacon o bacon; **bacon and eggs** bacon com ovos [kong **o**voosh]
bad (quality) mau (má); **this meat's bad** esta carne está estragada [**e**shta kahrn shtah shtrag**ah**da]; **a bad headache** uma dor de cabeça forte [f**o**rt]; **it's not bad**

não é mau [nowng e m**ah**-oo]; **too bad!** paciência! [pas-y**e**ns-ya]
badly: **he's been badly injured** ele está muito ferido [ehl shtah mw**ee**ngtoo f**i**ree-doo]
bag uma mala
baggage a bagagem [bag**ah**-s**h**aing]
baggage allowance o peso de bagagem permitido [p**eh**zoo dih bag**ah**-s**h**aing pirmeet**ee**doo]
baggage check o depósito de bagagem [dipos**ee**too dih bag**ah**-s**h**aing]
baker o padeiro [pahd**ay**-roo]
balcony a varanda; **a room with a balcony** um quarto com varanda [kw**a**rtoo kong]; **on the balcony** na varanda
bald careca [kar-**e**ka]
ball a bola
ballet o ballet
ball-point pen a caneta esferográfica [shf**i**roo-gr**ah**feeka]
banana a banana
band (mus) a banda
bandage a ligadura [leegad**oo**ra]; **could you change the bandage?** importa-se de mudar a ligadura? [eemp**o**rta-sih dih mood**ah**r]
bandaid um penso [pensoo]
bank (money) o banco [bankoo]; **when are the banks open?** a que horas abrem os bancos? [a k-y**o**raz **ah**braing]
bank account a conta bancária [bankahr-ya]
bar o bar; **let's meet in the bar** vamo-nos encontrar no bar [vam**oo**nooz aingkon-tr**ah**r]; **a bar of chocolate** uma tablete de chocolate [tabl**eh**t dih shookool**ah**t]
barbecue uma churrascada [shoorashk**ah**da]
barber o barbeiro [barb**ay**-roo]
bargain: **it's a real bargain** é uma pechincha [pish**ee**nsha]

barmaid a empregada de balcão [bahlkowng]

barman o barman

barrette o gancho [ganshoo]

bartender o barman

basic: the hotel is rather basic o hotel é muito simples [oo ohtel e mweengtoo seemplish]; **will you teach me some basic phrases?** pode ensinar-me umas frases simples? [pod aingseenahrmih oomash frahzish]

basket um cesto [sehshtoo]

bath um banho [ban-yoo]; **can I take a bath?** posso tomar banho? [possoo toomahr ban-yoo]; **could you give me a bath towel?** pode dar-me uma toalha de banho? [pod dahrmih ooma twahl-ya dih]

bathing costume um fato de banho [fahtoo dih ban-yoo]

bathrobe um roupão [rohpowng]

bathroom a casa de banho [kahza dih ban-yoo]; **a room with a private bathroom** um quarto com casa de banho [kwahrtoo kong]; **can I use your bathroom?** posso ir à casa de banho? [possoo eer ah]

bath salts os sais de banho [sah-ish dih ban-yoo]

battery (for cassette etc) a pilha [peel-ya]; **the battery's flat** (car) a bateria está gasta [a batiree-a shtah gahshta]

bay a baía [ba-ee-a]

be ser [sehr]; **be reasonable** seja razoável [sehsнa razwahvel]; **don't be lazy** nao seja preguiçoso [nowng sehsнa prigeessohzoo]; **where have you been?** onde tem estado? [ond taing shtahdoo]; **I've never been to ...** nunca estive em ... [noonka shteev aing] see page 117

beach a praia [pry-a]; **on the beach** na praia; **I'm going to the beach** vou à praia [voh]

beach ball bola de praia [dih pry-a]

beach cafe o café [ka-fe]

beachmat um colchão de praia [kohlshowng dih pry-a]

beach towel uma toalha de praia [twahl-ya dih pry-a]

beach umbrella um chapéu de sol [shap-e-oo]

beads (necklace) as contas [kontash]

beans uns feijões [fay-sнoingsh]; **runner**

beans uns feijões verdes [fay-sнoingsh vehrdsh]; **broad beans** umas favas [oomas fahvash]

beard a barba

beautiful (person, food) maravilhoso [maraveel-yohzoo]; (beach, weather) bonito [booneetoo]; **thanks, that's beautiful** obrigado, é perfeito [pirfay-too]

beauty salon um salão de beleza [salowng dih bilehza]

because porque [poorkih]; **because of the weather** por causa do tempo [poor kah-ooza doo tempoo]

bed a cama; **single bed** cama individual [eendeeveedwahl]; **double bed** cama de casal [dih kazahl]; **you haven't made my bed** não fez a minha cama [nowng fehz a meen-ya kama]; **I'm going to bed** vou para a cama [voh prah kama]; **he's still in bed** ele ainda está na kama [a-eenda shtah]

bed and breakfast cama e pequeno almoço [ee pikehnoo ahlmohssoo]

bed clothes a roupa de cama [rohpa]

bed linen a roupa de cama [rohpa]

bedroom um quarto de dormir [kwahrtoo dih doormeer]

bee uma abelha [abehl-ya]

beef a carne de vaca [kahrn]

beer a cerveja [sirvay-sнa]; **two beers, please** duas cervejas, por favor [doo-ash sirvay-sнash]

before: before breakfast antes do pequeno almoço [antish doo]; **before I leave** antes de eu sair [antish d-yeh-oo sa-eer]; **I haven't been here before** nunca aqui estive antes [noonka akee shteev antish]

begin: when does it begin? quando é que começa? [kwandoo e kih koomessa]

beginner um principiante [preenseepyant]; **I'm just a beginner** sou apenas um principiante [soh apehnash]

beginning: at the beginning no início [noo eenees-yoo]

behaviour o comportamento [kompoortamentoo]

behind atrás [atrahsh]; **the driver behind me** o condutor atrás de mim [kondootohr atrahsh dih meeng]

beige cor de café com leite [kohr dih ka-fe kong layt]

Belgian belga

Belgium a Bélgica [belsнeeka]

believe: I don't believe you não acredito *[nowng akrideetoo]*; **I believe you** acredito

bell *(door)* a campainha *[kampa-een-ya]*; *(church)* o sino *[seenoo]*

belly-flop um chapão *[shapowng]*

belong: that belongs to me isso pertence-me *[eessoo pirtensih-mih]*; **who does this belong to?** a quem pertence isto? *[a kaing pirtens eeshtoo]*

belongings: all my belongings todos os meus pertences *[tohdooz oosh meh-oosh pirtensish]*

below abaixo *[abah-ishoo]*

belt um cinto *[seentoo]*

bend *(in road)* uma curva *[koorva]*

berries as bagas *[bahgash]*

berth um beliche *[bileesh]*

beside: beside the church junto da igreja *[sнoontoo da eegreh-sнa]*; **sit beside me** sente-se ao pé de mim *[sentih-sih ow pe dih meeng]*

besides: besides that para além disso *[prahlaing deessoo]*

best o melhor *[mil-yor]*; **the best hotel in town** o melhor hotel da cidade *[ohtel da seedahd]*; **that's the best meal I've ever had** é a melhor refeição que jamais comi *[e a mil-yor rifay-sowng kih sнamah-ish koomee]*

bet: I bet you 500 escudos aposto 500 escudos *[aposhtoo]*

better melhor *[mil-yor]*; **that's better** assim é melhor *[asseeng]*; **are you feeling better?** está melhor? *[shtah]*; **I'm feeling a lot better** sinto-me muito melhor *[seentoomih mweengtoo]*; **I'd better be going now** é melhor ir andando agora *[eer andandoo agora]*

between entre

beyond para além de *[prahlaing dih]*

bicycle uma bicicleta *[beeseeklehta]*

bidet o bidet

big grande *[grand]*; **a big one** um grande; **that's too big** é grande demais *[dimah-ish]*; **it's not big enough** não é suficientemente grande *[nowng e soofees-yentiment]*

bigger maior *[ma-yor]*

bike uma bicicleta *[beeseeklehta]*

bikini um bikini

bill a conta; **could I have the bill, please?** a conta, por favor

billfold uma carteira *[kartay-ra]*

billiards o bilhar *[beel-yahr]*

bingo o bingo *[beengoo]*

bird um pássaro *[pahssaroo]*

biro *(tm)* uma esferográfica *[shfiroo-grahfeeka]*

birthday o dia de anos *[dee-a d-yanoosh]*; **it's my birthday** é o meu dia de anos *[oo meh-oo]*; **when is your birthday?** quando é o teu dia de anos? *[kwandoo e oo teh-oo]*; **happy birthday!** feliz aniversário! *[fileez aneevirsahr-yoo]*

biscuit uma bolacha *[boolahsha]*

bit: just a little bit for me para mim, só um pouco *[para meeng, saw oong pohkoo]*; **a big bit** um pedaço grande *[pidahssoo grand]*; **a bit of that cake** uma fatia desse bolo *[fatee-a dehss bohloo]*; **it's a bit too big for me** é um pouco grande para mim *[pohkoo grand para meeng]*; **it's a bit cold today** está um pouco frio hoje *[shtah oong pohkoo free-oo ohsн]*

bite *(by flea etc)* uma picada; **I've been bitten** *(by insect)* fui picado *[fwee peekahdoo]*; **do you have something for bites?** tem alguma coisa para picadas de insectos? *[taing ahlgooma koh-iza para peekahdash deensettoosh]*

bitter *(taste etc)* amargo *[amahrgoo]*

black preto *[prehtoo]*

black and white (photograph) a preto e branco *[a prehtoo ee brankoo]*

blackout: he's had a blackout ele desmaiou *[ehl disнma-yoh]*

bladder a bexiga *[bisheega]*

blanket um cobertor *[koobirtohr]*; **I'd like another blanket** queria mais um cobertor *[kiree-a mah-iz oong]*

blast! bolas! *[bolash]*

blazer um blazer

bleach *(for loo etc)* a lexívia *[lisheev-ya]*

bleed sangrar *[sang-grahr]*; **he's bleeding** ele está a sangrar *[ehl shtah]*

bless you! santinho! *[santeen-yoo]*

blind cego *[sehgoo]*

blinds as persianas *[as pirs-yanash]*

blind spot um local de pouca visibilidade *[lookahl dih pohka vizibeeleedahd]*

blister uma empola

blocked *(road)* cortada *[koortahda]*; *(pipe)* entupido *[aingtoopeedoo]*

block of flats um edifício *[ideefees-yoo]*

blond louro *[lohroo]*
blonde uma loura *[lohra]*
blood o sangue *[sang-gih]*; **his blood group is ...** o grupo de sangue dele é ... *[oo groopoo dih sang-gih dehl]*; **I have high blood pressure** tenho a tensão arterial alta *[taing-nyoo a tensowng artir-yahl ahlta]*
bloody mary um bloody mary
blouse uma blusa *[blooza]*
blue azul *[azool]*
blusher um blusher
board: full board pensão completa *[pensowng komplehta]*; **half-board** meia-pensão *[may-a pensowng]*
boarding house uma pensão *[pensowng]*
boarding pass a carta de embarque *[d-yembahrk]*
boat um barco *[bahrkoo]*
body o corpo *[kohrpoo]*
boil (*on skin*) um furúnculo *[fooroon-kooloo]*; **to boil the water** ferver a água *[firvehr a ahgwa]*
boiled egg um ovo cozido *[ohvoo koozee-doo]*
boiling hot muito quente *[mweengtoo kent]*
bomb uma bomba *[bom-ba]*
bone um osso *[oh-soo]*
bonnet o capot *[kapo]*
book um livro *[leevroo]*; **I'd like to book a table for two** queria reservar uma mesa para dois *[kiree-a rizirvahr ooma mehza]*
bookshop, bookstore a livraria *[leevraree-a]*
boot uma bota; (*of car*) o porta-bagagem *[bagah-sнaing]*
booze a bebida; **I had too much booze** bebi demais *[bibee dimah-ish]*
border (*of country*) a fronteira *[frontay-ra]*
bored: I'm bored estou chateado *[shtoh shat-yahdoo]*
boring maçador *[massadohr]*
born: I was born in ... nasci em ... *[nash-see]*
borrow: may I borrow ...? posso pedir ... emprestado? *[possoo pideer em-prishtahdoo]*
boss o patrão *[patrowng]*
both ambos *[amboosh]*; **I'll take both of them** levo os dois *[levoosh doh-ish]*; **we'll both come** vimos os dois *[veemooz*

oosh doh-ish]
bother: sorry to bother you desculpe incomodá-lo *[dishkoolp eenkoo-moodahloo]*; **it's no bother** não maça nada *[nowng mahssa nahda]*; **it's such a bother** é uma maçada tão grande *[massahda towng grand]*
bottle uma garrafa; **a bottle of wine** uma garrafa de vinho *[veen-yoo]*; **another bottle, please** mais uma garrafa, por favor *[mah-izooma]*
bottle-opener um abre-garrafas *[abrigarrahfash]*
bottom (*of person*) o traseiro *[trazay-roo]*; **at the bottom of the hill** no sopé do monte *[noo soo-pe doo mont]*
bottom gear a primeira mudança *[preemay-ra moodansa]*
bouncer um gabarola
bowels os intestinos *[eentishteenoosh]*
bowling (*ten pin*) o bowling
bowling green o campo de bowling *[kampoo]*
bowls (*game*) os bowls
box uma caixa *[kah-isha]*
box lunch um almoço embalado *[ahlmohsoo aing-balahdoo]*
box office a bilheteira *[beel-yitay-ra]*
boy um rapaz *[rapahsh]*
boyfriend: my boyfriend o meu namorado *[meh-oo namoorahdoo]*
bra um soutien *[soot-yang]*
bracelet uma pulseira *[poolsay-ra]*
brake o travão *[travowng]*; **there's something wrong with the brakes** os travões estão defeituosos *[oosh tra-voingsh shtowng difay-twozoosh]*; **I had to brake suddenly** tive de travar de repente *[teev dih travahr dih ripent]*
brake fluid o líquido para os travões *[oo leekeedo para oosh travoingsh]*
brake lining o revestimento de travões *[oo rivishteementoo dih travoingsh]*
brandy o brandy
brave corajoso *[koorasн-ohzoo]*
bread o pão *[powng]*; **could we have some bread and butter?** queríamos pão e manteiga por favor *[kiree-amoosh powng ee mantay-ga]*; **some more bread, please** mais pão, por favor *[mah-ish powng]*; **white bread** o pão branco *[brankoo]*; **brown bread** pão escuro *[shkooroo]*; **wholemeal bread** o pão

integral [eentigrahl]; **rye bread** o pão de centeio [dih sentay-oo]

break partir [parteer]; **I think I've broken my ankle** acho que parti o tornozelo [ahshoo kih partee oo toornoozehloo]; **it keeps breaking** está sempre a partir-se [shtah sempra parteersih]

breakdown uma avaria [avaree-a]; **I've had a breakdown** tive uma avaria [teev]; **nervous breakdown** um colapso nervoso [koolapsoo nirvohzoo]

breakfast o pequeno almoço [pikehnoo ahlmohsoo]; **English/full breakfast** o pequeno almoço inglês [eenglehsh]; **continental breakfast** o pequeno almoço continental

break in: somebody's broken in a casa foi assaltada [a kahza fohy assahltahda]

breast o peito [pay-too]

breast-feed dar de mamar a [dahr dih]

breath a respiração [rishpeerasowng]; **out of breath** sem fôlego [saing fohligoo]

breathe respirar [rishpeerahr]; **I can't breathe** não consigo respirar [nowng konseegoo]

breathtaking (view etc) de tirar o fôlego [dih teerahr oo fohligoo]

breeze a brisa [breeza]

breezy (fresh, cool) fresco [frehshkoo]

bridal suite a suite nupcial [noops-yahl]

bride a noiva [noh-iva]

bridegroom o noivo [noh-ivoo]

bridge a ponte; (card game) o bridge

brief breve [brev]

briefcase uma pasta [pahshta]

bright (light etc) brilhante [breel-yant]; **bright red** vermelho vivo [veevoo]

brilliant (idea, person) brilhante [breel-yant]

bring trazer [trazehr]; **could you bring it to my hotel?** pode trazer-mo ao hotel? [pod trazehrmoo ow ohtel]; **I'll bring it back** trago isto de volta [trahgoo eeshtoo dih volta]; **can I bring a friend too?** posso trazer um amigo? [possoo trazehr]

Britain a Grã-Bretanha [grang britan-ya]

British británico [breetaneekoo]

Britisher um británico [breetaneekoo]

brochure um folheto [fool-yehtoo]; **do you have any brochures on ...?** tem folhetos sobre ...? [taing fool-yehtoosh sohbrih]

broke: I'm broke estou falido [shtoh fa-leedoo]

broken partido [parteedoo]; **you've broken it** partiu-o [partee-oo]; **it's broken** está partido [shtah]; **broken nose** o nariz partido [nareesh]

brooch um alfinete [ahlfeeneht]

brother: my brother o meu irmão [meh-oo eermowng]

brother-in-law: my brother-in-law o meu cunhado [meh-oo koon-yahdoo]

brown castanho [kashtan-yoo]; (suntanned) bronzeado [bronz-yahdoo]; **I don't go brown** eu não me consigo bronzear [eh-oo nowng mih konseegoo bronz-yahr]

brown paper o papel de embrulho [papel deembrool-yoo]

browse: may I just browse around? posso só dar uma vista de olhos? [possoo saw dahr ooma veeshta d-yol-yoosh]

bruise uma contusão [kontoozowng]

brunette uma morena [moorehna]

brush uma escova [shkohva]; (artist's) um pincel [peensel]

Brussels sprouts as couves de Bruxelas [ash kohvish dih brooselash]

bubble bath um banho de espuma [banyoo dishpooma]

bucket um balde [bahld]

buffet um bufete [boofeht]

bug (insect) um insecto [eensetoo]; **she's caught a bug** ela apanhou um vírus [apan-yoh oong veeroosh]

building um edifício [ideefees-yoo]

bulb uma lâmpada; **we need a new bulb** precisamos de uma lâmpada nova [priseezamoosh dooma]

bull um touro [tohroo]

bull fight uma tourada [tohrahda]

bull fighter um toureiro [tohray-roo]

bull ring a arena [arehna]

bump: I bumped my head bati com a cabeça [batee kong a kabehssa]

bumper o pára-choques [pahra-shoksh]

bumpy (road) uma estrada má [shtrahda mah]

bunch of flowers um ramo de flores [ramoo dih florish]

bungalow um bungalow

bunion um calo [kahloo]

bunk um beliche [bileesh]

bunk beds beliches [bileeshish]

buoy uma bóia [boy-a]

burglar um ladrão *[ladrowng]*

burn: do you have an ointment for burns? tem uma pomada para queimaduras? *[taing ooma poomahda para kaymadoorash]*

burnt: this meat is burnt esta carne está queimada *[eshta kahrn shtah kaymahda]*; **my arms are so burnt** os meus braços estão muito queimados *[shtowng mweengtoo kay-mahdoosh]*

burst: a burst pipe um cano rebentado *[kanoo ribentahdoo]*

bus um autocarro *[owtookahroo]*; **is this the bus for …?** este autocarro vai para …? *[ehsht owtookahroo vahy]*; **when's the next bus?** a que horas é o próximo autocarro? *[a k-yoraz e oo prosseemoo]*

bus driver o condutor *[kondootohr]*

business os negócios *[nigos-yoosh]*; **I'm here on business** estou aqui em negócios *[shtoh akee aing]*

bus station a estação dos autocarros *[shtassowng dooz owtookahrroosh]*

bus stop a paragem *[parah-sHaing]*; **will you tell me which bus stop I get off at?** pode dizer-me em que paragem devo sair? *[pod deezehrmih aing kih parahsHaing dehvoo sa-eer]*

bust o peito *[pay-too]*

bus tour uma viajem de autocarro *[v-yahsHaing d-yowtookahroo]*

busy (*street*) movimentado *[moovee-mentahdoo]*; (*restaurant etc*) frequentado *[frikwentahdoo]*; **I'm busy this evening** esta noite estou ocupado *[eshta noh-it shtoh ohkoopahdoo]*; **the line was busy** a linha estava ocupada *[a leen-ya shtahva]*

but mas *[mash]*; **not … but …** não … mas …

butcher o talho *[tahl-yoo]*

butter a manteiga *[mantay-ga]*

butterfly uma borboleta *[boorboolehta]*

button um botão *[bootowng]*

buy: I'll buy it levo este *[levoo ehsht]*; **where can I buy …?** onde posso comprar …? *[ond possoo komprahr]*

by: by train/car/plane de comboio/carro/avião *[komboy-oo/kahrroo/av-yowng]*; **who's it written by?** quem é o autor? *[kaing e oo owtohr]*; **it's by Picasso** é um Picasso; **I came by myself** vim só *[veeng saw]*; **a seat by the window** um lugar à janela *[loogahr ah sHanela]*; **by the sea** à beira-mar *[ah bay-ra mahr]*; **can you do it by Wednesday?** pode fazê-lo para quarta-feira? *[pod fazehloo para kwahrta fay-ra]*

bye-bye adeus *[adeh-oosh]*

bypass (*road*) uma estrada de circunvalação *[shtrahda dih seerkoonvalassowng]*

C

cab (*taxi*) um táxi

cabaret o cabaret

cabbage uma couve *[kohv]*

cabin um camarote *[kamarot]*

cable (*elec*) o cabo *[kahboo]*

cafe o café *[ka-fe]*

caffeine a cafeína *[a ka-fe-eena]*

cake um bolo *[bohloo]*; **a piece of cake** uma fatia de bolo *[fatee-a]*

calculator uma calculadora *[kahlkooladohra]*

calendar um calendário *[kalendahr-yoo]*

call: what is this called? como é que isto se chama? *[kohmoo e keeshtoo sih shama]*; **call the police!** chame a polícia *[sham a poolees-ya]*; **call the manager!** chame o gerente *[sham o sHirent]*; **I'd like to make a call to England** queria telefonar para Inglaterra *[kiree-a tilifoonahr]*; **I'll call back later** (*come back*) volto mais tarde *[voltoo mah-ish tahrd]*; (*phone back*) volto a telefonar mais tarde *[tilifoonahr]*; **I'm expecting a call from London** estou à espera de um telefonema de Londres *[shtoh a shpaira doong tili-foonehma]*; **would you give me a call at 7.30 tomorrow morning?** importa-se de me chamar amanhã às 7.30 da manhã? *[eemporta-sih dih mih shamahr ahman-yang]*; **it's been called off** foi cancelado *[fohy kanssilahdoo]*

call box uma cabina telefónica *[kabeena tilifoneeka]*

calm a calma *[kahlma]*

calm down! acalme-se! *[akahlmih-sih]*

Calor gas (*tm*) o gás Cidla *[oo gash seedla]*

calories as calorias *[kalooree-ash]*

camera uma máquina fotográfica *[mahkeena footoograhfeeka]*

camp: is there somewhere we can camp? há lá algun sítio onde se possa acampar *[ah lah ahlgoong seet-yoo ond sih possah kampahr]*; **can we camp here?** podemos acampar aqui? *[poo-dehmooz akampahr akee]*

campbed cama de campanha *[kama dih kampan-ya]*

camping o campismo *[kampeesнmoo]*

campsite um parque de campismo *[oom pahrk dih kampeesнmoo]*

can uma lata; **a can of beer** uma lata de cerveja *[sirvay-sнa]*

can: can I ...? posso ...? *[possoo]*; **can you ...?** (*singular polite form*) pode ...? *[pod]*; **can he ...?** pode ...?; **can we ...?** podemos ...? *[poodehmoosh]*; **can they ...?** podem ...? *[podaing]*; **I can't ...** não posso ... *[nowng possoo]*; **he can't ...** ele não pode ... *[ehl nowng pod]*; **can I keep it?** posso ficar com ele? *[possoo feekahr kong ehl]*; **if I can** se eu puder *[s-yeh-oo poodair]*; **that can't be right** isto não pode estar certo *[eeshtoo nowng pod shtahr sehrtoo]*

Canada o Canadá

Canadian canadiano *[kanad-yanoo]*

canal um canal

cancel cancelar; **can I cancel my reservation?** posso cancelar a minha reserva? *[possoo kansilahr a meen-ya rizairva]*; **can we cancel dinner for tonight?** podemos cancelar o jantar desta noite? *[poodehmoosh kansilahr oo sнantahr deshta noh-it]*; **I cancelled it** cancelei-o *[kansilay-oo]*

cancellation um cancelamento *[oong kansilamentoo]*

candle uma vela

candy uns rebuçados *[oongsh riboosah-doosh]*; **a piece of candy** um rebuçado

canoe uma canoa

can-opener um abre-latas *[abrilahtash]*

cap (*yachting etc*) um boné *[boo-ne]*; (*of bottle, radiator*) una tampa; (*bathing*) uma touca *[tohka]*

capital city a capital *[kapeetahl]*

capital letters as letras grandes *[ash letrash grandish]*

capsize: it capsized soçobrou *[soosoo-broh]*

captain o comandante *[koomandant]*

car um carro *[kahroo]*

carafe uma garrafa

carat: is it 9/14 carat gold? é ouro de 9/14 quilates? *[ohroo dih 9/14 keelahtish]*

caravan uma roulote *[roolot]*

caravan site um parque para roulotes *[pahrk para roolotsh]*

carbonated gaseificado *[gazeh-eefee-kahdoo]*

carburettor carburador *[karbooradohr]*

card: do you have a (business) card? tem um cartão? *[taing oong kartowng]*

cardboard box uma caixa de papelão *[kah-isha dih papilowng]*

cardigan uma camisola *[kameezola]*

cards as cartas *[kahrtash]*; **do you play cards?** você joga cartas? *[vossеh sнoga]*

care: goodbye, take care adeus, tome cuidado consigo *[adeh-oosh tom kweedahdoo kongseegoo]*; **will you take care of this for me?** toma-me conta disto por favor? *[tomamih konta deestoo]*; **care of ...** ao cuidado de ... *[ow kwee-dahdoo dih]*

careful: be careful tenha cuidado *[tehn-ya kweedahdoo]*

careless: that was careless of you isso foi um descuido seu *[fohy oong dishkweedoo seh-oo]*; **careless driving** a condução descuidada *[kondoossowng dish-kweedahda]*

car ferry o ferry-boat

car hire o aluguer de automóveis *[aloo-gair d-yowtoomovaysh]*

car keys as chaves do carro *[shahvsh doo kahroo]*

carnation um cravo *[krahvoo]*

carnival o carnaval

car park o parque de automóveis *[pahrk d-yowtoomovaysh]*

carpet uma carpete

car rental (*shop*) uma loja de aluguer de automóveis *[losнa d-yaloogair d-yowtoomovaysh]*

carrot uma cenoura *[sinoнra]*

carry levar *[livahr]*; **could you carry this for me?** importa-se de me levar isto? *[eemportasih dih mih livahr eeshtoo]*

carry-all um saco *[sahkoo]*

carry-cot um porta-bébés *[porta-beb-esh]*

car-sick: I get car-sick eu enjoo de automóvel *[eh-oo ensнoh-oo d-yowtoomovel]*

carton (*of cigarettes*) um pacote *[pakot]*; **a carton of milk** uma embalagem de leite *[embalah-sнaing dih layt]*

carving uma talha *[tahl-ya]*

carwash a lavagem automática *[lavah-sнaing owtoomahteeka]*

case (*suitcase*) uma mala; **in any case** de qualquer modo *[dih kwahlkair modoo]*; **in that case** nesse caso *[nehss kahzoo]*; **it's a special case** é um caso especial *[kahzoo shpis-yahl]*; **in case he comes back** não vá ele voltar *[nowng vah ehl vohltahr]*; **I'll take two just in case** levo dois, talvez sejam necessários *[levoo dohish tahlvehsh seh-sнowng nisisahr-yoosh]*

cash o dinheiro *[deen-yay-roo]*; **I don't have any cash** não tenho dinheiro *[nowng taing-nyoo deen-yay-roo]*; **I'll pay cash** pago em dinheiro *[pahgoo aing deen-yay-roo]*; **will you cash a cheque/ check for me?** pode trocar-me um cheque? *[pod trookahrm-yoong shek]*

cashdesk a caixa *[kah-isha]*

cash dispenser o autobanco *[owtoobankoo]*

cash register a caixa *[kah-isha]*

casino o casino *[kazeenoo]*

cassette uma cassette

cassette player, cassette recorder um gravador de cassettes *[gravadohr]*

castle um castelo *[kashteloo]*

casual: casual clothes roupa desportiva *[rohpa dishpoorteeva]*

cat um gato *[gahtoo]*

catamaran um catamaran

catastrophe uma catástrofe *[katahsh-*

troofih]

catch: the catch has broken o fecho está partido *[fehshoo shtah parteedoo]*; **where do we catch the bus?** onde podemos apanhar o autocarro? *[ond podehmooz apan-yahr oo owtookahroo]*; **he's caught some strange illness** ele apanhou uma doença esquisita *[apan-yoh ooma dwensa shkeezeeta]*

catching: is it catching? é contagioso? *[kontasн-yohzoo]*

cathedral uma catedral *[katidrahl]*

Catholic católico *[katoleekoo]*

cauliflower uma couve-flor *[kohv flohr]*

cause a causa *[kah-ooza]*

cave a caverna *[kavairna]*

caviar o caviar

ceiling o tecto *[tettoo]*

celebrations as celebrações *[silibrassoingsh]*

celery o alho francês *[ahl-yoo fransehsh]*

cellophane o papel celofane *[siloofan]*

cemetery o cemitério *[simeetair-yoo]*

center o centro *[sentroo]* *see also* **centre**

centigrade centígrado *[senteegradoo]* *see page 121*

centimetre, centimeter um centímetro *[senteemitroo]* *see page 119*

central central; **we'd prefer something more central** preferiamos algo mais central *[prifiree-amooz ahlgoo mah-ish sentrahl]*

central heating o aquecimento central *[akesseementoo]*

central station a estação central *[shtassowng]*

centre o centro *[sentroo]*; **how do we get to the centre?** como é que vamos para o centro? *[kohmoo e kih vamoosh para oo sentroo]*; **in the centre** (*of town*) no centro *[noo sentroo]*

century o século *[sekooloo]*; **in the 19th century** no século XIX

ceramics as cerâmicas *[sirameekash]*

certain certo *[sehrtoo]*; **are you certain?** tem a certeza? *[taing a sirtehza]*; **I'm absolutely certain** tenho a certeza absoluta *[taing-nyoo a sirtehza absooloota]*

certainly certamente *[sehrtament]*; **certainly not** certamente que não *[kih nowng]*

certificate uma certidão *[sirteedowng]*; **birth certificate** certidão de nascimento

[nash-seementoo]
chain (*for bike*) uma corrente [koorrent];
(*around neck*) um fio [fee-oo]
chair uma cadeira [kaday-ra]
chalet um chalet
chambermaid a criada de quarto
[kr-yahda dih kwahrtoo]
champagne o champanhe [shampan-yih]
chance: quite by chance por acaso [poor
akahzoo]; **no chance!** nem pensar nisso!
[naing pensahr neessoo]
**change: could you change this into
escudos?** pode trocar isto em escudos?
[pod trookahr eeshtoo]; **I haven't any
change** não tenho troco [nowng taing-
nyoo trohkoo]; **can you give me change
for a 1,000 escudo note?** pode trocar-
me uma nota de 1000 escudos? [pod
trookahrmih]; **do we have to change?**
(*trains*) temos de mudar? [tehmoosh dih
moodahr]; **for a change** para variar
[para var-yahr]; **you haven't changed
the sheets** os lençois não foram mudados
[oosh lensoish nowng fohrowng
moodahdoosh]; **the place has changed
so much** está muito mudado [shtah
mweengtoo moodahdoo]; **do you want
to change places with me?** quer trocar
de lugar comigo? [kair trookahr dih loogahr koomeegoo]; **can I change this
for ...?** posso trocar isto por ...? [possoo
trookahr eeshtoo poor]
changeable (*person, weather*) inconstante
[eenkonshtant]
channel: the English Channel o canal da
Mancha [mansha]
chaos o caos [kah-oosh]
chap o rapaz [rapahsh]; **the chap at reception** o tipo da recepção [rissessowng]
chapel uma capela
charge: is there an extra charge? há
alguma taxa adicional? [ahlgooma
tahsha adees-yoonahl]; **what do you
charge?** quanto é que leva? [kwantoo e
kih leva]; **who's in charge here?** quem é
o responsável? [kaing e oo rishponsahvel]
charming (*person*) encantador [enkanta-
dohr]
chart uma carta
charter flight um voo fretado [voh-oo
fritahdoo]
chassis o chassis [shasseesh]
cheap barato [barahtoo]; **do you have**

something cheaper? tem alguma coisa
mais barata? [taing ahlgooma koh-iza
mah-ish]
cheat: I've been cheated fui enganado
[fwee enganahdoo]
check: will you check? pode verificar?
[pod virifeekahr]; **will you check the
steering?** pode verificar a direcção?
[deeressowng]; **will you check the bill?**
pode verificar a conta?; **we checked in** já
nos registámos [sнah noosh
risнeeshtahmoosh]; **we checked out**
saímos [sa-eemoosh]; **I've checked it** eu
verifiquei [eh-oo virifeekay]
check (*money*): **will you take a check?**
aceita cheques? [assay-ta sheksh]
check (*bill*): **may I have the check
please?** a conta por favor
checkbook o livro de cheques [oo leevroo
dih sheksh]
checked (*shirt etc*) aos quadrados [owsh
kwadrahdoosh]
checkers as damas [damash]
check-in (*at airport*) o check-in
checkroom o vestiário [visht-yahr-yoo]
cheek o descaramento [dishkaramentoo];
what a cheek! que descaramento!
cheeky descarado [dishkarahdoo]
cheerio adeuzinho! [adeh-oozeen-yoo]
cheers (*thank you*) obrigado [ohbree-
gahdoo]; (*toast*) saúde [sa-ood]
cheer up! anime-se [aneemisih]
cheese o queijo [kay-sнoo]
cheesecake um bolo de queijo [bohloo
dih kay-sнoo]
chef o cozinheiro [koozeen-yay-roo]
chemist a farmácia [farmahs-ya]
cheque o cheque [shek]; **will you take a
cheque?** aceita cheques? [assay-ta
sheksh]
cheque book o livro de cheques [oo
leevroo dih sheksh]
cheque card o cartão de garantia [oo
kartowng dih garantee-a]
cherry uma cereja [sireh-sнa]
chess o xadrez [shadrehsh]
chest o peito [pay-too]
chewing gum uma pastilha elástica
[pashteel-ya eelahshteeka]
chicken um frango [frang-goo]
chickenpox a varicela [vareesela]
child uma criança [kree-ansa]
children as crianças [ash kree-ansash]

child minder uma ama

child minding service serviço de baby sitter [sirveeso]

children's playground um parque para crianças [pahrk para kree-ansash]

children's pool uma piscina infantil [ooma peesh-seena eenfanteel]

children's portion uma dose para crianças [dohz para kree-ansash]

children's room o quarto de brinquedos [kwahrtoo dih breenkehdoosh]

chilled (wine) fresco [frehshkoo]; **it's not properly chilled** não está suficientemente fresco [nowng shtah soofees-yentiment]

chilly (weather) frio [freeoo]

chimney uma chaminé [shamee-ne]

chin o queixo [kay-shoo]

china a porcelana [poorsilana]

chips umas batatas fritas [oomash batahtash freetash]

chiropodist um calista [kaleeshta]

chocolate o chocolate [shookoolaht]; **a chocolate bar** uma tablete de chocolate [tableht]; **a box of chocolates** uma caixa de chocolates [kah-isha]; **hot chocolate** um chocolate quente [kent]

choke (car) o ar

choose: it's hard to choose é dificil a escolha [e difeeseel a shkohl-ya]; **you choose for us** escolha você! [shkohl-ya vosseh]

chop: pork/lamb chop uma costeleta de porco/de carneiro [kooshtilehta dih pohrkoo/karnay-roo]

Christian name o nome próprio [nom propr-yoo]

Christmas o Natal [na-tahl]; **merry Christmas** feliz Natal [fileesh]

church a igreja [eegray-sha]; **where is the Protestant/Catholic Church?** onde fica a igreja Protestante/Católica? [ond feeka]

cider a cidra [seedra]

cigar um charuto [sharootoo]

cigarette um cigarro [seegahrroo]; **plain/tipped cigarettes** cigarros sem filtro/com filtro [saing feeltroo/kong feeltroo]

cigarette lighter um isqueiro [ishkay-roo]

cine-camera uma máquina de filmar [mahkeena dih feelmahr]

cinema o cinema [seenehma]

circle um círculo [seerkooloo]; (theatre: seats) plateia [platay-a]

citizen cidadão [seedadowng]; **I'm a British/American citizen** sou um cidadão Britânico/Americano [soh]

city a cidade [seedahd]

city centre, city center o centro [sentroo]

claim (insurance) uma reclamação [riklamassowng]

claim form (insurance) um impresso de reclamação [eemprehsoo dih riklamassowng]

clarify clarificar

classical clássico [klahsseekoo]

clean limpo [leempoo]; **may I have some clean sheets?** pode mudar os lençois, por favor [pod moodahr oosh lensoish]; **our apartment hasn't been cleaned today** hoje o apartamento não foi limpo [ohsh oo apartamentoo nowng fohy leempoo]; **it's not clean** não está limpo [nowng shtah]; **can you clean this for me?** (clothes) pode limpar esta roupa? [pod leempahr eshta rohpa]

cleansing cream o creme de limpeza [oo krem dih leempehza]

clear: it's not very clear não é muito claro [nowng e mweengtoo klahroo]; **ok, that's clear** (understood) ah, sim percebo [pirsehboo]

clever esperto [shpairtoo]

cliff um rochedo [rooshehdoo]

climate o clima [kleema]

climb: it's a long climb to the top é uma grande subida até ao cimo [e ooma grand soobeeda a-te ow seemoo]; **we're going to climb ...** vamos subir ... [vamoosh soobeer]

clinic a clínica

cloakroom (for coats) o vestiário [vishtyahr-yoo]; (WC) a casa de banho [kahza dih ban-yoo]

clock um relógio [rilosh-yoo]

close: is it close? é perto? [pairtoo]; **close to the hotel** perto do hotel [dwotel]; **close by** perto; (weather) abafado [abafahdoo]

close: when do you close? a que horas fecha? [a k-yorash fehsha]

closed fechado [fishahdoo]; **they were closed** estavam fechados [shtahvowng]

closet um armário [armahr-yoo]

cloth (*material*) o tecido [*tiseedoo*]; (*rag etc*) pano [*panoo*]

clothes a roupa [*rohpa*]

clothes line o estendal [*shtendahl*]

clothes peg, clothespin a mola de roupa [*mola dih rohpa*]

cloud uma nuvem [*noovaing*]; **it's clouding over** está a ficar enevoado [*shtah feekahr inivwahdoo*]

cloudy enevoado [*inivwahdoo*]

club o clube [*kloob*]

clubhouse o clube [*kloob*]

clumsy desastrado [*dizashtrahdoo*]

clutch (*car*) a embraiagem [*embra-yahsHaing*]; **the clutch is slipping** a embraiagem patina [*pateena*]

coach o autocarro [*owtookahroo*]

coach party um grupo de excursionistas [*groopoo dishkoors-yooneeshtash*]

coach trip uma excursão [*shkoorsowng*]

coast a costa [*koshta*]; **at the coast** à beira-mar [*ah bay-ramahr*]

coastguard a guarda costeira [*gwahrda kooshtay-ra*]

coat (*overcoat*) o sobretudo [*sohbritoodoo*]; (*jacket*) o casaco [*kazahkoo*]

coathanger um cabide [*kabeed*]

cobbled street estrada empedrada [*shtrahda empidrahda*]

cobbler um sapateiro [*sapatay-roo*]

cockroach uma barata

cocktail o cocktail

cocoa (*drink*) o cacau

coconut o coco [*kohkoo*]

cod o bacalhau [*bakal-yahoo*]

code: what's the (dialling) code for ...? qual é o indicativo de ...? [*kwahl e oo eendeekateevoo dih*]

coffee o café [*ka-fe*]; **white coffee** um café com leite [*kong layt*]; **black coffee** um café sem leite [*saing layt*]; **two coffees, please** dois cafés por favor [*doh-ish ka-fesh*]

coin uma moeda [*mweda*]

Coke (*tm*) uma coca-cola

cold frio [*free-oo*]; **I'm cold** tenho frio [*taing-nyoo*]; **I have a cold** estou constipado [*shtoh konshteepahdoo*]

coldbox (*for food*) uma geleira [*sHilay-ra*]

cold cream o creme de limpeza [*krem dih leempehza*]

collapse: he's collapsed desmaiou [*disHma-yoh*]

collar o colarinho [*koolareen-yoo*]

collar bone a clavícula [*klaveekoola*]

colleague: my colleague o meu colega [*meh-oo koolega*]; **your colleague** o seu colega [*oo seh-oo*]

collect: I've come to collect ... vim buscar ... [*veeng booshkahr*]; **I collect ...** (*stamps etc*) colecciono [*kooless-yonoo*]; **I want to call New York collect** queria fazer uma chamada para Nova Iorque paga no destinatário [*kiree-a fazehr ooma shamahda para nova york pahga noo dishteenatar-yoo*]

collect call uma chamada paga no destinatário [*shamahda pahga noo dishteenatahr-yoo*]

college o colégio [*koolesH-yoo*]

collision o choque [*shok*]

cologne (*eau de ...*) água de colónia [*ahgwa dih koolon-ya*]

colour, color a cor [*kohr*]; **do you have any other colours?** há mais cores? [*ah mah-ish kohrish*]

colo(u)r film filme colorido [*feelm koolooreedoo*]

comb um pente [*pent*]

come vir [*veer*]; **I come from London** eu sou de Londres [*eh-oo soh dih londrish*]; **where do you come from?** donde é? [*dond-ye*]; **when are they coming?** quando é que vêm? [*kwandoo e kih vaing-aing*]; **come here** venha cá [*vehn-ya kah*]; **come with me** venha comigo [*vehn-ya koomeegoo*]; **come back!** volte aqui! [*volt akee*]; **I'll come back later** volto mais tarde [*voltoo mah-ish tahrd*]; **come in!** entre!; **it just came off** saltou [*sahltoh*]; **he/it's coming on very well** (*improving*) está a progredir bastante [*shtah proogrideer bashtant*]; **come on!** venha! [*vehn-ya*]; **do you want to come out this evening?** quer sair esta noite? [*kair sa-eer eshta noh-it*]; **these two pictures didn't come out** estas duas fotos não saíram bem [*eshtash doo-ash fotoosh nowng sa-eerowng baing*]; **the money hasn't come through yet** o dinheiro ainda não chegou [*oo deen-yay-roo a-eenda nowng shigoh*]

comfortable: it's not very comfortable não é muito confortável [*nowng e mweengtoo konfoortahvel*]

Common Market o Mercado Comum

[mirkahdoo koomoong]
company *(firm)* uma companhia *[kompan-yee-a]*
comparison: there's no comparison não há comparação possível *[nowng ah komparassowng pooseevel]*
compartment *(train)* o compartimento *[komparteementoo]*
compass uma bússola *[boosoola]*
compensation uma indemnização *[eendimneezassowng]*
complain reclamar *[riklamahr]*; **I want to complain about my room** quero reclamar sobre o meu quarto *[kairoo riklamahr sohbroo meh-oo kwahrtoo]*
complaint uma reclamação *[riklamassowng]*
complete completo *[komplehtoo]*; **the complete set** o conjunto completo *[konsHoontoo]*; **it's a complete disaster** é um perfeito desastre! *[pirfay-too dizahshtrih]*
completely completamente *[komplehtamente]*
complicated: it's very complicated é muito complicado *[mweengtoo kompleekahdoo]*
compliment: my compliments to the chef parabéns ao cozinheiro *[parabaingz ow koozeen-yay-roo]*
comprehensive *(insurance)* contra todos os riscos *[kontra tohdooz oosh reeshkoosh]*
compulsory obrigatório *[ohbreegatoryoo]*
computer um computador *[kompootadohr]*
concern: we are very concerned estamos muito preocupados *[shtamoosh mweengtoo pr-yokoopahdoosh]*
concert um concerto *[konsairtoo]*
concussion um traumatismo *[trowmateesHmoo]*
condenser *(car)* o condensador
condition a condição *[kondeesowng]*; **it's not in very good condition** não está em muito boas condições *[nowng shtah aing mweengtoo boh-ash kondeesoingsh]*
conditioner *(for hair)* um creme amaciador *[krem amas-yadohr]*
condom um preservativo *[prizirvateevoo]*
conductor *(rail)* o condutor *[kondootohr]*

conference uma conferência *[konfirensya]*
confirm: can you confirm that? pode confirmar? *[pod konfeermahr]*
confuse: it's very confusing é muito confuso *[mweengtoo konfoozoo]*
congratulations! parabéns! *[parabaingsh]*
conjunctivitis a conjuntivite *[konsHoonteeveet]*
connecting flight o voo de ligação *[vohoo dih leegasowng]*
connection a ligação *[leegasowng]*
connoisseur um conhecedor *[koonyisidohr]*
conscious consciente *[konsh-syent]*
consciousness: he's lost consciousness ele desmaiou *[ehl disHma-yoh]*
constipation a prisão de ventre *[preezowng dih ventrih]*
consul o cônsul
consulate o consulado *[konsoolahdoo]*
contact: how can I contact ...? como posso contactar ...? *[kohmoo possoo]*; **I'm trying to contact ...** estou a tentar contactar *[shtoh]*
contact lenses as lentes de contacto *[lentsh dih kontahktoo]*
contraceptive o contraceptivo *[kontrasipteevoo]*
continent: on the continent no continente *[noo konteenent]*
convenient conveniente *[konvin-yent]*
cook: it's not properly cooked não está bem cozido *[nowng shtah baing koozeedoo]*; **it's beautifully cooked** está muito bem cozinhado *[shtah mweengtoo baing koozeen-yahdoo]*; **he's a good cook** ele é muito bom cozinheiro *[ehl e mweengtoo bong koozeen-yay-roo]*
cooker o fogão *[foogowng]*
cookie uma bolacha *[boolahsha]*
cool fresco *[frehshkoo]*
corduroy o veludo cotelé *[viloodoo kootileh]*
cork a rolha *[rohl-ya]*
corkscrew um saca-rolhas *[sahka-rohl-yash]*
corn *(foot)* um calo *[kahloo]*
corner: on the corner na esquina *[na shkeena]*; **in the corner** no canto *[noo kantoo]*; **a corner table** uma mesa de canto *[mehza dih kantoo]*

cornflakes os cornflakes
coronary um enfarte *[aing-fahrt]*
correct exacto *[eezahtoo]*; **please correct me if I make a mistake** por favor corrija-me se eu me enganar *[koorreesнamih s-yeh-oo menganahr]*
corridor o corredor *[koorridohr]*
corset a cinta *[seenta]*
cosmetics os cosméticos *[koosнmetee-koosh]*
cost: what does it cost? quanto custa? *[kwantoo kooshta]*
cot uma cama de bébé *[kama dih beb-e]*
cotton o algodão *[ahlgoodowng]*
cotton buds os cotonetes *[kootoonehtish]*
cotton wool o algodão em rama *[ahlgoo-downg aing rama]*
couch (*sofa*) o sofá *[soofah]*
couchette o beliche *[bileesh]*
cough a tosse *[toss]*
cough drops umas pastilhas para a tosse *[pashteel-yash para a toss]*
cough medicine o xarope *[sharop]*
could: could you ...? podia ...? *[poodee-a]*; **could I have ...?** queria ... *[kiree-a]*; **I couldn't ...** não seria capaz de ... *[nowng siree-a kapahsнdih]*
country o campo *[kampoo]*; **in the country** no campo
countryside o campo *[kampoo]*
couple (*man and woman*) um casal *[ka-zahl]*; **a couple of ...** um par de ...
courier um guia *[g-ee-a]*
course (*of meal*) o prato *[prahtoo]*; **of course** claro *[klahroo]*
court (*law*) o tribunal *[treeboonahl]*; (*tennis*) o campo de ténis *[kampoo dih tenneesh]*
courtesy bus (*hotel to airport etc*) um auto-carro gratuito *[owtookahroo gratweetoo]*
cousin: my cousin o meu primo *[meh-oo preemoo]*
cover charge o couvert *[koovair]*
cow uma vaca
crab um caranguejo *[karang-gehsнoo]*
cracked: it's cracked está rachado *[shtah rashahdoo]*
cracker uma bolacha de água e sal *[boo-lahsha d-yahgwa ee sahl]*
craftshop uma loja de artesanato *[losнa d-yartizanahtoo]*
cramp (*in leg etc*) uma cãibra *[ka-eembra]*
crankshaft a manivela do motor *[manee-*

**vela doo mootohr]*
crash: there's been a crash houve um acidente de automóvel *[ohv oong asee-dent d-yowtoomovel]*
crash course um curso intensivo *[koor-soo eentenseevoo]*
crash helmet um capacete *[kapasseht]*
crawl (*swimming*) o crawl
crazy doido *[doh-idoo]*
cream (*on milk, on cakes*) as natas *[nahtash]*; (*for skin*) o creme *[krem]*; (*colour*) creme
cream cheese o queijo creme *[kay-sнoo krem]*
creche a creche
credit card o cartão de crédito *[kartowng dih kredeetoo]*
crib (*for baby*) um berço *[bairsoo]*
crisis uma crise *[kreez]*
crisps umas batatas fritas *[batahtash freetash]*
crockery a loiça *[loh-issa]*
crook: he's a crook ele é um aldrabão *[ehl e oong ahldrabowng]*
crossing (*by sea*) a travessia *[travissee-a]*
crossroads o cruzamento *[krooza-mentoo]*
crosswalk a passadeira *[passaday-ra]*
crowd a multidão *[moolteedowng]*
crowded apinhado *[apeen-yahdoo]*
crown (*on tooth*) uma ponte *[pont]*
crucial: it's absolutely crucial é abso-lutamente essencial *[absoolootament eesens-yahl]*
cruise um cruzeiro *[kroozay-roo]*
crutch uma muleta *[moolehta]*; (*of body*) o pélvis *[pelveesh]*
cry chorar *[shoorahr]*; **don't cry** não cho-re *[nowng shor]*
cucumber o pepino *[pipeenoo]*
cuisine a cozinha *[koozeen-ya]*
cultural cultural *[kooltoorahl]*
cup uma chávena *[shahvna]*; **a cup of coffee** uma chávena de café *[kaf-e]*
cupboard um armário *[armahr-yoo]*
cure: can you cure it? pode tratá-lo? *[pod tratah-loo]*
curlers os rolos *[roloosh]*
current a corrente *[koorrent]*
curry o caril *[kareel]*
curtains as cortinas *[koorteenash]*
curve uma curva *[koorva]*
cushion a almofada *[ahlmoofahda]*

custom o hábito *[ahbeetoo]*
Customs a Alfândega *[ahlfándiga]*
cut: I've cut myself cortei-me *[koortay-mih]*; **could you cut a little off here?** pode cortar um pouco aqui? *[pod koortahr oong pohkoo akee]*; **we were cut off** a ligação foi cortada *[a leegassowng fohy koortahda]*; **the engine keeps cutting out** o motor está sempre a falhar *[mootohr shtah sempra fal-yahr]*
cutlery os talheres *[tal-yehrish]*

cutlet uma costeleta *[kooshtilehta]*
cycle: can we cycle there? pode-se ir lá de bicicleta? *[pod-sih eer lah dih beeseeklehta]*
cycling o ciclismo *[seekleesHmoo]*
cyclist o ciclista *[seekleeshta]*
cylinder um cilindro *[seeleendroo]*
cylinder-head gasket a junta da culatra *[sHoonta da koolahtra]*
cynical cínico *[seeneekoo]*
cystitis a cistite *[sishteet]*

D

damage: you've damaged it você estragou-o *[vosseh shtragoh-oo]*; **it's damaged** está estragado *[shtah shtragahdoo]*; **there's no damage** não está estragado *[nowng]*
damn! raios me partam! *[rah-yoosh mih pahrtowng]*
damp húmido *[oomeedoo]*
dance: a Portuguese dance uma dança portuguesa *[dansa poortoogehza]*; **do you want to dance?** quer dançar? *[kair dansahr]*
dancer: he's a good dancer ele dança muito bem *[ehl dansa mweengtoo baing]*
dancing: we'd like to go dancing queríamos ir dançar *[kiree-amooz eer dansahr]*; **traditional dancing** a dança tradicional *[tradeess-yoonahl]*
dandruff a caspa *[kahshpa]*
dangerous perigoso *[pireegohzoo]*
dare: I don't dare não me atrevo *[nowng m-yatrehvoo]*
dark escuro *[shkooroo]*; **dark blue** azul escuro *[azool]*; **when does it get dark?** quando é que escurece? *[kwandoo e kishkooress]*; **after dark** à noitinha *[ah noh-iteen-ya]*
darling querido *[kireedoo]*; (*to woman*) querida *[kireeda]*
darts os dardos *[dahrdoosh]*
dashboard o painel *[pay-nel]*
date: what's the date? qual é a data?

[kwahl e a dahta]; **on what date?** em que data? *[aing kih]*; **can we make a date?** podemos marcar um encontro? *[poodehmoosh markahr oong enkontroo]*
dates (*to eat*) as tâmaras *[tamarash]*
daughter: my daughter a minha filha *[meen-ya feel-ya]*
daughter-in-law a nora *[nohra]*
dawn a madrugada *[madroogahda]*; **at dawn** de madrugada *[dih]*
day o dia; **the day after** o dia a seguir *[sig-eer]*; **the day before** o dia anterior *[antir-yohr]*; **every day** todos os dias *[tohdooz oosh dee-ash]*; **one day** um dia *[oong]*; **can we pay by the day?** podemos pagar ao dia? *[poodehmoosh pagahr ow dee-a]*; **have a good day!** um bom dia para si! *[oong bong dee-a para see]*
daylight robbery um roubo descarado *[rohboo dishkarahdoo]*
day trip uma excursão de um dia *[shkoorsowng doong dee-a]*
dead morto *[mohrtoo]*
deaf surdo *[soordoo]*
deaf-aid um aparelho para a surdez *[aparehl-yoo para a soordehsh]*
deal (*business*) um negócio *[nigoss-yoo]*; **it's a deal** é negócio fechado *[fishahdoo]*; **will you deal with it?** quer tratar disso? *[kair tratahr deessoo]*
dealer (*agent*) um concessionário *[konsiss-*

yoonahr-yoo]

dear caro *[kahroo]*; *(expensive)* caro; **Dear Sir** Caro Senhor; **Dear Madam** Cara Senhora; **Dear Francisco** Querido Francisco *[kireedoo]*

death a morte *[mort]*

decadent decadente *[dikadent]*

December Dezembro *[dizembroo]*

decent: that's very decent of you isso é muito amável da sua parte *[e mweengtoo amahvel da soo-a pahrt]*

decide: we haven't decided yet ainda não decidimos *[a-eenda nowng diseedee-moosh]*; **you decide for us** decida você para nós *[diseeda vosseh para nosh]*; **it's all decided** já está tudo decidido *[sнah shtah toodoo diseedeedoo]*

decision a decisão *[diseezowng]*

deck o convés *[konvehsh]*

deckchair uma cadeira de lona *[kaday-ra dih lona]*

declare: I have nothing to declare não tenho nada a declarar *[nowng taingnyoo]*

decoration *(in room)* a decoração *[dikoorassowng]*

deduct descontar *[dishkontahr]*

deep fundo *[foondoo]*; **is it deep?** é fundo?

deep-freeze o congelador *[konsнiladohr]*

definitely de certeza *[dih sirtehza]*; **definitely not** de certeza que não *[dih sirtehza kih nowng]*

degree *(university)* a licenciatura *[leesens-yatoora]*; *(temperature)* o grau *[gra-oo]*

dehydrated *(person)* desidratado *[dizee-dratahdoo]*

delay: the flight was delayed o voo foi atrasado *[voh-oo fohy atrazahdoo]*

deliberately de propósito *[dih proopo-zeetoo]*

delicacy: a local delicacy uma especialidade local *[spiss-yaleedahd lookahl]*

delicious delicioso *[dilees-yohzo]*

deliver: will you deliver it? fazem distribuição? *[fahzaing dishtreeb-weessowng]*

delivery: is there another mail delivery? há mais alguma distribuição de correio? *[ah mah-iz ahlgooma dishtreeb-weessowng dih koorray-o]*

de luxe de luxo *[dih looshoo]*

denims calças de ganga *[kahlsash dih gang-ga]*

dent: there's a dent in it tem uma

amolgadela *[taing ooma amohlgadela]*

dental floss o fio dentário *[fee-oo dentahr-yoo]*

dentist o dentista *[denteeshta]*

dentures a dentadura postiça *[dentadoo-ra pooshteesa]*

deny: he denies it ele nega-o *[nega-oo]*

deodorant um desodorizante *[dizohdoo-reezant]*

department store um armazém *[arma-zaing]*

departure a partida *[parteeda]*

departure lounge a sala de espera *[sahla dishpaira]*

depend: it depends depende *[dipend]*; **it depends on …** depende de …

deposit *(downpayment)* um depósito *[di-pozeetoo]*

depressed deprimido *[dipreemeedoo]*

depth a profundidade *[proofoondeedahd]*

description uma descrição *[dishkree-sowng]*

deserted *(beach etc)* vazio *[vazee-oo]*

dessert a sobremesa *[sohbrimehza]*

destination o destino *[dishteenoo]*

detergent o detergente *[ditirsнent]*

detour um desvio *[dishvee-oo]*

devalued desvalorizado *[dishvalohr-eezahdoo]*

develop: could you develop these films? pode revelar estas películas? *[pod rivilahr eshtash pileekoolash]*

diabetic um diabético *[d-yabeteekoo]*

diagram o diagrama *[d-yagrama]*

dialect um dialecto *[d-yalettoo]*

dialling code o indicativo *[eendeekatee-voo]*

diamond um diamante *[d-yamant]*

diaper uma fralda

diarrhoea, diarrhea a diarreia *[d-yarray-a]*; **do you have something to stop diarrhoea?** tem algum anti-laxante? *[taing ahlgoong antee-lashant]*

diary uma agenda *[asнenda]*

dictionary um dicionário *[deess-yoonahr-yoo]*; **a Portuguese/English dictionary** um dicionário português/inglês *[poortoogehsh eenglehsh]*

die morrer *[moorrehr]*; **I'm absolutely dying for a drink** estou a morrer por uma bebida *[shtoh a moorrehr poor ooma bibeeda]*

didn't *see* **not,** *and page 116*

diesel (fuel) gasóleo *[gazol-yoo]*
diet uma dieta *[d-yeta]*; **I'm on a diet**
estou de dieta *[shtoh]*
difference a diferença *[deefirensa]*;
what's the difference between …? qual
é a diferença entre …? *[kwahl]*; **it doesn't
make any difference** tanto faz *[tantoo
fahsh]*
different: they are different eles são
diferentes *[ehlsh sowng deefirentsh]*;
they are very different eles são muito
diferentes *[mweengtoo]*; **it's different
from this one** é diferente deste *[dehsht]*;
may we have a different table? queremos outra mesa *[kirehmooz ohtra
mehza]*; **ah well, that's different** ah
bem, assim é diferente *[baing aseeng e]*
difficult difícil *[difeeseel]*
difficulty uma dificuldade *[difee-
kooldahd]*; **without any difficulty** sem
qualquer dificuldade *[saing kwahlkair]*;
I'm having difficulties with … tenho
dificuldades com … *[taing-nyoo difee-
kooldahdish kong]*
digestion a digestão *[deesнishtowng]*
dinghy um bote de borracha *[bott dih
boorrahsha]*
dining car o vagão-restaurante *[va-
gowng-rishtowrant]*
dining room a sala de jantar *[sнantahr]*
dinner (*evening meal*) o jantar *[sнantahr]*
dinner jacket um smoking
dinner party um jantar *[sнantahr]*
dipped headlights os médios *[med-
yoosh]*
dipstick o medidor de nível *[mideedohr
dih neevel]*
direct directo *[deerettoo]*; **does it go direct?** é directo?
direction a direcção *[deeressowng]*; **in
which direction is it?** em que direcção
fica? *[aing kih deeressowng feeka]*; **is it
in this direction?** fica nesta direcção?
[feeka neshta]
directory: telephone directory a lista
telefónica *[leeshta tilifoneeka]*; **directory enquiries** as informações
[eenfoormassoingsh]
dirt a sujidade *[soosнeedahd]*
dirty sujo *[soosнoo]*
disabled deficiente *[difees-yent]*
disagree: it disagrees with me (*food*) não
me cai bem *[nowng mih kahy baing]*

disappear desaparecer *[dizaparissehr]*;
it's just disappeared desapareceu *[di-
zaparisseh-oo]*
disappointed: I was disappointed fi-
quei desapontado *[feekay dizapon-
tahdoo]*
disappointing desapontante *[dizapon-
tant]*
disaster uma tragédia *[trasнed-ya]*
discharge (*pus*) a supuração *[soopoo-
rassowng]*
disc jockey o disc jockey
disc of film um disco de filme *[deeshkoo
dih feelm]*
disco um disco *[deeshkoo]*
disco dancing o disco dancing
discount um desconto *[dishkontoo]*
disease uma doença *[dwenssa]*
disgusting (*food, smell etc*) nojento
[noosнentoo]
dish um prato *[prahtoo]*
dishcloth um pano de loiça *[panoo dih
loh-issa]*
dishwashing liquid o detergente líquido
[ditirsнent leekeedo]
disinfectant o desinfectante *[di-
zeenfettant]*
dislocated shoulder um ombro deslocado *[ombroo disнlookahdoo]*
dispensing chemist a farmácia
[farmahs-ya]
disposable nappies fraldas de papel
[frahldash dih pa-pel]
distance a distância *[dishtans-ya]*;
what's the distance from … to …? qual
é a distância de … a …? *[kwahl e]*; **in the
distance** ao longe *[ow lonsн]*
distilled water a água destilada *[ahgwa
dishteelahda]*
distributor (*car*) o distribuidor
[dishtreebweedohr]
disturb: the disco is disturbing us a
discoteca está a incomodar-nos *[a
deeshkooteka shtah eenkoomoodahr-
noosh]*
diversion um desvio *[disнvee-oo]*
diving board uma prancha de saltos
[pransha dih sahltoosh]
divorced divorciado *[deevoors-yahdoo]*
dizzy (*feel*) com tonturas *[tontoorash]*;
dizzy spells períodos de tonturas *[piree-
oodoosh]*
do fazer *[fazehr]*; **what shall I do?** que

devo fazer? *[kih dehvoo]*; **what are you doing tonight?** que faz esta noite? *[kih fahz eshta noh-it]*; **how do you do it?** como se faz? *[kohmoo sih fahsh]*; **will you do it for me?** importa-se de mo fazer? *[eemporta-sih dih moo fazehr]*; **who did it?** quem fez isto? *[kaing fehz eeshtoo]*; **the meat's not done** a carne não está bem passada *[a kahrn nowng shtah baing passahda]*; **do you have ...?** tem ...? *[taing]*; **what do you do?** *(job)* o que é que faz? *[oo k-ye kih fahsh]*

docks as docas *[dokash]*

doctor o médico *[medeekoo]*; **he needs a doctor** ele precisa de um médico *[ehl prisseeza doong]*; **can you call a doctor?** pode chamar um médico? *[pod shamahr]*

document um documento *[dookoomentoo]*

dog um cão *[kowng]*

doll uma boneca *[booneka]*

dollar um dólar

donkey um burro *[boorroo]*

don't! não! *[nowng] see page 116*

door *(of room, car)* a porta

doorman o porteiro *[poortay-roo]*

dormobile *(tm)* um carro-caravana *[kahrroo karavana]*

dosage a dosagem *[doozahsʜaing]*

double: double room um quarto duplo *[kwahrtoo dooploo]*; **double bed** uma cama de casal *[kama dih kazahl]*; **double brandy** um brandy duplo; **double r** *(in spelling name)* com dois 'r's *[kong doh-iz errish]*; **it's all double dutch to me** não percebo nada! *[nowng pirsehboo nahda]*

doubt: I doubt it duvido *[dooveedoo]*

douche o duche *[doosh]*

doughnut uma fartura *[fartoora]*

down: get down! para baixo! *[bah-ishoo]*; **he's not down yet** *(out of bed)* ainda não se levantou *[a-eenda nowng sih livantoh]*; **further down the road** nesta rua mais abaixo *[neshta roo-a mah-iz abah-ishoo]*; **I paid 20% down** dei 20% de sinal *[day ... dih seenahl]*

downmarket *(restaurant etc)* barato *[barahtoo]*

downstairs em baixo *[aing bah-ishoo]*

dozen uma dúzia *[dooz-ya]*; **half a dozen** uma meia dúzia *[may-a]*

drain o cano de esgoto *[kanoo disʜgohtoo]*

draughts *(game)* as damas *[damash]*

draughty: it's rather draughty faz muita corrente de ar *[fash mweengta koorrent d-yahr]*

drawing pin um pionés *[p-yoonehsh]*

dreadful horrível *[ohrreevel]*

dream um sonho *[sohn-yoo]*; **it's like a bad dream** é como num pesadelo *[kohmoo noong pizadeloo]*; **sweet dreams** bons sonhos *[bongsh sohn-yoosh]*

dress *(woman's)* um vestido *[vishteedoo]*; **I'll just get dressed** vou-me só mudar *[voh-mih saw moodahr]*

dressing *(for wound)* o penso *[pensoo]*; *(for salad)* o tempero *[tempehroo]*

dressing gown um roupão *[rohpowng]*

drink beber *[bibehr]*; *(noun)* uma bebida *[bibeeda]*; **can I get you a drink?** o que bebe? *[oo kih beb]*; **I don't drink** não bebo *[nowng behboo]*; **a long cool drink** uma bebida fresca *[bibeeda frehshka]*; **may I have a drink of water?** pode dar-me um copo de água? *[pod dahrmih oong kopoo d-yahgwa]*; **drink up!** bebam! *[behbowng]*; **I had too much to drink** bebi demais *[bibee dimah-ish]*

drinkable *(water)* potável *[pootahvel]*

drive: we drove here viemos de carro *[v-yemoosh dih kahrroo]*; **I'll drive you home** eu levo-o a casa de carro *[eh-oo levoo a kahza dih kahrroo]*; **do you want to come for a drive?** quer vir dar uma volta de carro? *[kair veer dahr ooma volta dih kahrroo]*; **is it a very long drive?** é muito longe? *[e mweengtoo longsʜ]*

driver o condutor *[kondootohr]*

driver's license a carta de condução *[kahrta dih kondoossowng]*

drive shaft a árvore de transmissão *[ahrvoorih dih transʜmeesowng]*

drizzle: it's drizzling está a chuviscar *[shtah shooveeshkahr]*

drop: just a drop só um pouco *[oong pohkoo]*; **I dropped it** deixei-o cair *[day-shay-oo ka-eer]*; **drop in some time** apareça! *[aparehssa]*

drown: he's drowning ele está a afogar-se *[ehl shtah afoogahrsih]*

drug um medicamento *[mideekamentoo]*

drugstore a farmácia *[farmahss-ya]*

drunk bêbado *[behbadoo]*

drunken driving condução enquanto

embriagado *[kondoossowng enkwantoo embr-yagahdoo]*

dry seco *[sehkoo]*

dry-cleaning a limpeza a seco *[leempehza a sehkoo]*

dry-cleaner a lavandaria a seco *[lavandaree-a a sehkoo]*

duck um pato *[pahtoo]*

due: when is the bus due? a que horas é o autocarro? *[a k-yoraz e oo owtookahrroo]*

dumb mudo *[moodoo]*; (*stupid*) estúpido *[shtoopeedoo]*

dummy (*for baby*) uma chupeta *[shoopehta]*

durex (*tm*) um durex

during durante *[doorant]*

dust o pó *[paw]*

dustbin o caixote de lixo *[kah-ishot dih leeshoo]*

Dutch holandês *[ohlandehsh]*

duty-free (goods) duty free

duvet o edredão *[idridowng]*

dynamo o dínamo *[deenamoo]*

dysentery a disenteria *[deezentiree-a]*

E

each: each of them cada um deles *[kada oong dehlsh]*; **one for each of us** um para cada um de nós *[oong para kada oong dih nosh]*; **how much are they each?** quanto é cada um? *[kwantoo e]*; **each time** de cada vez *[vehsh]*; **we know each other** nós conhecemo-nos *[koon-yissehmoo-noosh]*

ear a orelha *[ohrehl-ya]*

earache uma dor de ouvidos *[dohr d-yohveedoosh]*

early cedo *[sehdoo]*; **early in the morning** de manhã cedo *[dih man-yang sehdoo]*; **it's too early** é cedo demais *[dimah-ish]*; **a day earlier** um dia mais cedo *[oong dee-a mah-ish]*; **half an hour earlier** meia-hora mais cedo *[may-a ora]*; **I need an early night** preciso de me deitar cedo *[priseezoo dih mih daytahr]*

early riser: I'm an early riser sou madrugador *[soh madroogadohr]*

earring um brinco *[breenkoo]*

earth (*soil*) a terra *[tairra]*

earthenware os barros *[bahrroosh]*

earwig uma bicha-cadela *[beesha-kadela]*

east o leste *[lesht]*; **to the east** ao leste *[ow]*

Easter a Páscoa *[pahshkwa]*

easy fácil *[fahseel]*; **easy with the cream!** chega de creme! *[shehga dih krem]*

eat comer *[koomehr]*; **something to eat** alguma coisa para comer *[ahlgooma kohiza]*; **we've already eaten** já comemos *[shah koomehmoosh]*

eau-de-Cologne água de Colónia *[ahgwa dih koolon-ya]*

eccentric excêntrico *[eesh-sentreekoo]*

edible comestível *[koomishteevel]*

efficient eficiente *[ifees-yent]*

egg um ovo *[ohvoo]*

eggplant uma beringela *[bireensнela]*

Eire a República da Irlanda *[ripoobleeka deerlanda]*

either: either ... or ... ou ... ou ... *[oh]*; **I don't like either of them** não gosto de nenhum deles *[nowng goshtoo dih nin-yoong dehlsh]*

elastic elástico *[eelahshteekoo]*

elastic band um elástico *[eelahshteekoo]*

Elastoplast (*tm*) um penso *[pensoo]*

elbow o cotovelo *[kootoovehloo]*

electric eléctrico *[eelettreekoo]*

electric blanket um cobertor eléctrico *[koobirtohr eelettreekoo]*

electric cooker um fogão eléctrico *[foogowng eelettreekoo]*

electric fire um aquecedor eléctrico *[a-kessidohr eelettreekoo]*

electrician um electricista *[eelettree-seeshta]*

electricity a electricidade *[eelettree-*

seedahd]

electric outlet uma tomada *[toomahda]*
elegant elegante *[eeligant]*
elevator o elevador *[eelivadohr]*
else: something else uma outra coisa *[ooma ohtra koh-iza];* **somewhere else** noutro sítio *[nohtroo seet-yoo];* **let's go somewhere else** vamos a outro sítio *[vamooz a];* **what else?** que mais? *[kih mah-ish];* **nothing else, thanks** mais nada, obrigado *[mah-ish nahda, ohbreegahdoo];* **is there anywhere else to go?** há outro sítio onde se possa ir? *[ah ohtroo seet-yoo ond sih possa eer]*
embarrassed embaraçado *[embarassahdoo]*
embarrassing embaraçoso *[embarassohzoo]*
embassy a embaixada *[embah-ishahda]*
emergency uma emergência *[eemirsHens-ya];* **this is an emergency** isto é uma emergência *[eeshtoo]*
emotional emotivo *[eemooteevoo]*
empty vazio *[vazee-oo]*
end o fim *[feeng];* **at the end of the road** no fim da rua *[noo feeng da roo-a];* **when does it end?** quando acaba? *[kwandoo akahba]*
energetic enérgico *[eenairsHeekoo]*
energy *(of person)* energia *[eenirsHee-a]*
engaged *(toilet)* ocupado *[ohkoopahdoo];* *(telephone)* impedido *[eempideedoo];* *(person)* noivo *[noh-ivoo]*
engagement ring o anel de noivado *[an-el dih noh-ivahdoo]*
engine o motor *[mootohr]*
engine trouble problemas com o motor *[prooblehmash kong oo mootohr]*
England a Inglaterra *[eenglatairra]*
English inglês *[eenglehsh];* **the English** os ingleses *[eenglehzish];* **I'm English** sou inglês *[soh]*
enjoy: I enjoyed it very much gostei imenso *[gooshtay eemensoo];* **enjoy yourself!** divirta-se! *[diveerta-sih]*
enjoyable divertido *[deevirteedoo]*
enlargement *(of photo)* uma ampliação *[ampl-yassowng]*
enormous enorme *[eenorm]*
enough suficiente *[soofees-yent];* **there's not enough ...** não há suficiente ... *[nowng ah];* **it's not big enough** não é suficientemente grande *[nowng e soofees-*

yentiment grand]; **thank you, that's enough** chega, obrigado *[shehga, ohbreegahdoo]*
entertainment os divertimentos *[deevirteementoosh]*
enthusiastic entusiasta *[entooz-yahshta]*
entrance a entrada
envelope um envelope *[aing-vilop]*
epileptic epiléptico *[eepeelepteekoo]*
equipment *(in flat, diving etc)* o equipamento *[eekeepamentoo]*
eraser uma borracha *[boorrahsha]*
erotic erótico *[eeroteekoo]*
error um erro *[ehrroo]*
escalator as escadas rolantes *[shkahdash roolantish]*
especially especialmente *[shpis-yalment]*
espresso *(coffee)* um expresso *[shpressoo]*
essential essencial *[eesens-yahl];* **it is essential that ...** é essencial que ...
estate agent um agente imobiliário *[asHent eemoobeel-yahr-yoo]*
ethnic *(restaurant etc)* típico *[teepeekoo]*
Eurocheque um Eurocheque *[eh-oorooshek]*
Eurocheque card um cartão Eurocheque *[kartowng eh-oorooshek]*
Europe a Europa *[eh-ooropa]*
European europeu *[eh-ooroopeh-oo]*
European plan meia-pensão *[may-a pensowng]*
even: even the British até os britânicos *[a-te oosh breetaneekoosh];* **even if ...** mesmo se ... *[mehsHmoo sih]*
evening a noite *[noh-it];* **good evening** boa noite *[boh-a];* **this evening** esta noite *[eshta];* **in the evening** à noite *[ah];* **evening meal** o jantar *[oo sHantahr]*
evening dress *(general)* o traje de noite *[trahsH dih noh-it];* *(woman's)* um vestido de noite *[vishteedoo]*
eventually no fim *[noo feeng]*
ever: have you ever been to ...? já esteve alguma vez em ...? *[sHah shtehv ahlgooma vehz aing];* **if you ever come to Britain** se vier alguma vez à Grã-Bretanha *[sih v-yair ahlgooma vehz a grang britan-ya]*
every cada; **every day** todos os dias *[tohdooz oosh dee-ash]*
everyone toda a gente *[tohdah sHent]*

everything tudo *[toodoo]*
everywhere em toda a parte *[aing tohdah pahrt]*
exactly! exactamente! *[eezahtament]*
exam o exame *[eezam]*
example um exemplo *[eezemploo]*; **for example** por exemplo *[poor]*
excellent excelente *[ish-silent]*
except excepto *[ish-settoo]*; **except Sunday** excepto ao domingo *[ow]*
exception uma excepção *[ish-sessowng]*; **as an exception** como excepção *[kohmoo]*
excess o excesso *[ish-sessoo]*
excess baggage excesso de bagagem *[ish-sessoo dih bagah-shaing]*
excessive (*bill etc*) excessivo *[ish-sesseevoo]*; **that's a bit excessive** isso é um bocado excessivo *[eessoo e oong bookahdoo]*
exchange (*money*) o câmbio *[kamb-yoo]*; (*telephone*) a central telefónica *[sentrahl tilifoneeka]*; **in exchange** em troca *[aing troka]*
exchange rate: what's the exchange rate? qual é a taxa de câmbio? *[kwahl e a tahsha dih kamb-yoo]*
exciting emocionante *[eemoos-yoonant]*
exclusive (*club etc*) restrito *[rishtreetoo]*
excursion uma excursão *[shkoorsowng]*; **is there an excursion to ...?** há alguma excursão a ...? *[ah ahlgooma]*
excuse me (*to get past etc*) com licença *[kong leesensa]*; (*to get attention*) se faz favor *[sih fahsh favohr]*; (*apology*) desculpe *[dishkoolp]*
exhaust (*car*) o tubo de escape *[tooboo dishkahp]*
exhausted exausto *[eezowshtoo]*
exhibition uma exposição *[shpoozee-ssowng]*
exist: does it still exist? (*cafe etc*) ainda existe? *[a-eenda eezeesht]*
exit a saída *[sa-eeda]*
expect: I expect so assim o espero *[asseeng oo shpairoo]*; **she's expecting** ela está à espera de bébé *[ela shtah shpaira dih beb-e]*

expensive caro *[kahroo]*
experience: an absolutely unforgettable experience uma experiência absolutamente inesquecível *[shpir-yens-ya absoolootament eenishkess-eevel]*
experienced experiente *[shpir-yent]*
expert um perito *[pireetoo]*
expire: it's expired já expirou *[shah shpeeroh]*
explain explicar *[shpleekahr]*; **would you explain that to me?** pode explicar-me isso? *[pod shpleekahr-mih eessoo]*
explore explorar *[shploorahr]*; **I just want to go and explore** eu só quero ir explorar *[eh-oo saw kairoo eer shploorahr]*
export a exportação *[shpoortassowng]*
exposure meter um fotómetro *[footomi-troo]*
express (mail) correio expresso *[koorray-oo shpressoo]*
extra: can we have an extra chair? pode dar-me mais uma cadeira? *[pod dahr-mih mah-iz ooma kaday-ra]*; **is that extra?** isso é extra? *[eessoo e ehshtra]*
extraordinary extraordinário *[shtra-ohrdeenahr-yoo]*
extremely extremamente *[shtrehma-ment]*
extrovert um extrovertido *[shtroovir-teedoo]*
eye um olho *[ohl-yoo]*; **will you keep an eye on it for me?** pode dar uma olhadela nisso por mim? *[pod dahr ooma ol-yadela neessoo poor meeng]*
eyebrow a sobrancelha *[sohbransehl-ya]*
eyebrow pencil um lápis para as sobrancelhas *[lahpsh para ash soh-bransehl-yash]*
eye drops as gotas para os olhos *[gotash para ooz ol-yoosh]*
eyeliner um lápis para os olhos *[lahpsh para ooz ol-yoosh]*
eye shadow uma sombra para os olhos *[ooz ol-yoosh]*
eye witness uma testemunha ocular *[tishtimoon-ya ohkoolahr]*

F

fabulous fabuloso *[faboolohzoo]*
face a cara
face mask os óculos de mergulhar *[okooloosh dih mirgool-yahr]*
face pack uma máscara *[mahshkara]*
facing: facing the sea voltado para o mar *[vohltahdoo para oo mar]*
fact o facto *[fahktoo]*
factory uma fábrica *[fahbreeka]*
Fahrenheit *see page 121*
faint: she's fainted ela desmaiou *[disнma-yoh]*; **I think I'm going to faint** acho que vou desmaiar *[ahshoo kih voh disнma-yahr]*
fair a feira *[fay-ra]*; **it's not fair** não é justo *[nowng e sнooshtoo]*; **OK, fair enough** está bem, certo *[shtah baing, sairtoo]*
fake falso *[fahlsoo]*
fall: he's had a fall ele deu uma queda *[ehl deh-oo ooma keda]*; **he fell off his bike** ele caiu da bicicleta *[ehl ka-ee-oo da beeseeklehta]*; **in the fall** *(season)* no outono *[noo ohtohnoo]*
false falso *[fahlsoo]*
false teeth a dentadura postiça *[dentadoora pooshteesa]*
family a família *[fameel-ya]*
family hotel um hotel familiar *[ohtel fameel-yahr]*
family name o apelido *[apileedoo]*
famished: I'm famished estou cheio de fome *[shtoh shay-oo dih fom]*
famous famoso *[famohzoo]*
fan *(mechanical)* uma ventoinha *[ventween-ya]*; *(hand held)* um leque *[lek]*; *(football etc)* um adepto *[adeptoo]*
fan belt a correia de ventoinha *[koorray-a da vent-ween-ya]*
fancy: he fancies you ele engraçou consigo *[ehl aingrassoh kong-seegoo]*
fancy dress uma máscara *[mahshkara]*
fantastic fantástico *[fantah-shteekoo]*
far longe *[lonsн]*; **is it far?** é longe?; **how far is it to ...?** qual é a distância até ...? *[kwahl e a dishtans-ya a-te]*; **as far as I'm concerned** por mim *[poor meeng]*
fare o bilhete *[beel-yeht]*; **what's the fare to ...?** quanto é o bilhete para ...? *[kwantoo]*
farewell party uma festa de despedida *[feshta dih dishpideeda]*
farm uma quinta *[keenta]*
farther mais longe *[mah-ish lonsн]*; **farther than ...** mais longe do que ...
fashion a moda
fashionable na moda
fast rápido *[rahpeedoo]*; **not so fast** mais devagar *[mah-ish divagahr]*
fastener o fecho *[feh-shoo]*
fat *(adjective)* gordo *[gohrdoo]*; *(on meat)* a gordura *[goordoora]*
father: my father o meu pai *[meh-oo pahy]*
father-in-law o sogro *[sohgroo]*
fathom a braça *[brahssa]*
fattening: it's very fattening engorda muito *[aingorda mweengtoo]*
faucet uma torneira *[toornay-ra]*
fault um defeito *[difay-too]*; **it was my fault** foi culpa minha *[fohy koolpa meen-ya]*; **it's not my fault** a culpa não é minha *[a koolpa nowng e meen-ya]*
faulty estragado *[shtragahdoo]*
favo(u)rite favorito *[favooreetoo]*; **that's my favourite** esse é o meu favorito *[ehss-ye o meh-oo]*
fawn amarelo acastanhado *[amareloo akashtan-yahdoo]*
February Fevereiro *[fiviray-roo]*
fed up: I'm fed up estou farto *[shtoh fahrtoo]*; **I'm fed up with ...** estou farto de ...
feeding bottle um biberão *[beebirowng]*
feel: I feel hot/cold estou com calor/frio *[shtoh kong kalohr/free-o]*; **I feel like a drink** apetece-me beber qualquer coisa

[apitessimih bibehr kwahlkair koh-iza];
I don't feel like it não me apetece; **how
are you feeling today?** como se sente
hoje? *[kohmoo sih sent ohsн]*; **I'm
feeling a lot better** sinto-me muito
melhor *[seentoomih mweengtoo mil-
yor]*

felt-tip (pen) uma caneta de feltro *[ka-
nehta dih feltroo]*

fence uma cerca *[sehrka]*

ferry o ferry-boat; **what time's the last
ferry?** a que horas é o último barco? *[a
k-yoraz e oo oolteemoo bahrkoo]*

festival o festival *[fishteevahl]*

fetch: I'll go and fetch it eu vou buscar
[eh-oo voh booshkahr]; **will you come
and fetch me?** pode vir buscar-me? *[pod
veer booshkahr-mih]*

fever uma febre *[febrih]*

feverish: I'm feeling feverish estou a
sentir-me com febre *[shtoh a senteer-mih
kong febrih]*

few: only a few só alguns *[ahlgoonsh]*; **a
few minutes** alguns minutos *[meenoo-
toosh]*; **he's had a good few** (*to drink*) ele
já teve a sua conta *[ehl sнah tehv a soo-a
konta]*

fiancé: my fiancé o meu noivo *[meh-oo
noh-ivoo]*

fiancée: my fiancée a minha noiva
[meen-ya noh-iva]

fiasco: what a fiasco! mas que fiasco!
[mash kih f-yahshkoo]

field um campo *[kampoo]*

fifty-fifty a meias *[a may-ash]*

fight (*argument*) uma discussão *[dish-
koossowng]*

figs uns figos *[feegoosh]*

figure a figura *[feegoora]*; (*number*) o alga-
rismo *[ahlgareesнmoo]*; **I have to watch
my figure** tenho que vigiar a linha
[taing-nyoo kih visн-yahr a leen-ya]

fill encher *[enshehr]*; **fill her up please**
encha o depósito por favor *[ensha oo
dipozeetoo]*; **will you help me fill out
this form?** importa-se de me ajudar a
preencher este impresso? *[eemporta-sih
dih mih asнoodahr a pree-enshehr ehsht
eemprehssoo]*

fillet um filete *[feeleht]*

filling: it's very filling enche muito
[ensh mweengtoo]; (*in a tooth*) o chumbo
[shoomboo]

filling station uma bomba de gasolina
[bom-ba dih gazooleena]

film (*phot, movie*) o filme *[feelm]*; **do you
have this type of film?** tem este tipo de
filme? *[taing ehsht teepo]*; **16mm film**
um filme de dezasseis milímetros; **35mm
film** um filme de trinta e cinco milímetros

film processing a revelação de filmes *[ri-
vilassowng dih feelmsh]*

filter um filtro *[feeltroo]*

filter-tipped com filtro *[kong feeltroo]*

filthy (*room etc*) nojento *[noosнentoo]*

find encontrar *[enkontrahr]*; **I can't find
it** não consigo encontrar *[nowng kon-
seegoo]*; **if you find it** se o encontrar
[s-yoo]; **I've found a ...** encontrei um ...
[enkontray]

fine: it's fine weather está bom tempo
[shtah bong tempoo]; **a 3,000 escudo
fine** uma multa de três mil escudos
[ooma moolta dih]; **thank you, that's
fine** (*to waiter etc*) está bem, obrigado
[shtah baing, ohbreegahdoo]; **how are
you? — fine, thanks** como está? — bem,
obrigado *[kohmoo shtah — baing
ohbreegahdoo]*

finger um dedo *[dehdoo]*

fingernail uma unha *[oon-ya]*

finish: I haven't finished não terminei
[nowng tirmeenay]; **when I've finished**
quando terminar *[kwandoo tirmeenahr]*;
when does it finish? quando é que
termina? *[kwandoo e kih tirmeena]*;
finish off your drink acabe a sua bebida
[akahb a soo-a bibeeda]

Finland a Finlândia *[feenland-ya]*

fire: fire! fogo! *[fohgoo]*; **may we light a
fire here?** podemos fazer uma fogueira
aqui? *[poodehmoosh fazehr ooma
foogay-ra akee]*; **it's on fire** está a arder
[shtah ahrdehr]; **it's not firing
properly** a corrente não está a chegar às
velas *[a koorrent nowng shtah shigahr
ahsh velash]*

fire alarm um alarme de incêndios
[alahrm deensend-yoosh]

fire brigade, fire department os
bombeiros *[bombay-roosh]*

fire escape uma saída de emergência *[sa-
eeda deemirsнens-ya]*

fire extinguisher um extintor *[shteen-
tohr]*

firm (*company*) uma firma *[feerma]*

first primeiro *[preemay-roo]*; **I was first** eu estava primeiro *[eh-oo shtahva]*; **at first** ao princípio *[ow preenseep-yoo]*; **this is the first time** esta é a primeira vez *[eshta e a preemay-ra vehsh]*

first aid primeiros socorros *[preemayroosh sookorroosh]*

first aid kit a caixa de primeiros socorros *[kah-isha dih preemay-roosh sookorroosh]*

first class *(travel)* primeira classe *[preemay-ra klahs]*

first name o nome próprio *[nom propryoo]*

fish o peixe *[pay-ish]*

fisherman um pescador *[pishkadohr]*

fishing a pesca *[peshka]*

fishing boat um barco de pesca *[bahrkoo dih peshka]*

fishing net a rede de pesca *[rehd dih peshka]*

fishing rod a cana de pesca *[peshka]*

fishing tackle o equipamento para a pesca *[eekeepamentoo para a peshka]*

fishing village uma aldeia de pescadores *[ahlday-a dih pishkadohrish]*

fit *(healthy)* em forma *[aing forma]*; **I'm not very fit** não estou muito em forma *[nowng shtoh mweengtoo]*; **keep fit fanatic** um adepto de fazer exercícios *[adeptoo dih fazehr eezirsees-yoosh]*; **it doesn't fit** não serve *[nowng serv]*

fix: can you fix it? *(arrange)* pode arranjá-lo? *[pod arransнah-loo]*; *(repair)* pode repará-lo? *[riparah-loo]*; **let's fix a time** vamos marcar uma hora *[vamoosh markahr ooma ora]*; **it's all fixed up** já está tudo arranjado *[sнah shtah toodoo arransнahdoo]*; **I'm in a bit of a fix** estou em apuros *[shtoh aing apooroosh]*

fizzy gasoso *[gazohzoo]*

fizzy drink uma bebida com gás *[bibeeda kong gash]*

flab *(on body)* um pneu de gordura *[pnehoo dih goordoora]*

flag uma bandeira *[banday-ra]*

flannel *(for washing)* uma toalha de cara *[twahl-ya dih kahra]*

flash *(phot)* o flash

flashcube o cubo de flash *[kooboo]*

flashlight uma lanterna *[lantairna]*

flashy *(clothes)* vistoso *[veeshtohzoo]*

flat plano *[planoo]*; *(apartment)* um apartamento *[apartamentoo]*; **this beer is flat** esta cerveja está morta *[eshta sirvehsнa shtah morta]*; **I've got a flat (tyre)** tenho um pneu furado *[taing-nyoo oong pnehoo foorahdoo]*

flatterer lisonjeador *[leezonsн-yadohr]*

flatware a baixela *[bah-ishela]*

flavo(u)r o sabor *[sabohr]*

flea uma pulga *[poolga]*

flea powder insecticida para pulgas *[eensetteeseeda para poolgash]*

flexible flexível *[flekseevel]*

flies *(on trousers)* a braguilha *[brageel-ya]*

flight o voo *[voh-oo]*

flippers umas barbatanas *[barbatanash]*

flirt flartar

float flutuar *[flootwahr]*

flood uma incundação *[eenoondassowng]*

floor *(of room)* o chão *[showng]*; *(storey)* o andar *[andahr]*; **on the floor** no chão; **on the second floor** *(UK)* no segundo andar; *(USA)* no primeiro andar

floorshow um espectáculo *[shpettahkooloo]*

flop *(failure)* um falhanço *[fal-yansoo]*

florist uma florista *[flooreeshta]*

flour a farinha *[fareen-ya]*

flower uma flor *[flohr]*

flu a gripe *[greep]*

fluent: he speaks fluent Portuguese ele fala português fluentemente *[ehl fahla poortoogehsh flwentiment]*

fly voar *[vwahr]*; **can we fly there?** pode-se ir de avião até lá? *[pod-sih eer d-yav-yowng a-te lah]*

fly *(insect)* uma mosca *[moshka]*

fly spray insecticida para as moscas *[eensetteeseeda parahsh moshkash]*

foggy: it's foggy está nevoeiro *[shtah nivway-roo]*

fog light o farol de nevoeiro *[nivway-roo]*

folk dancing dança folclórica *[dansa fohl-kloreeka]*

folk music música folclórica *[moozeeka fohl-kloreeka]*

follow seguir *[sig-eer]*; **follow me** siga-me *[seega-mih]*

fond: I'm quite fond of ... *(food)* gosto bastante de ... *[goshtoo bashtant dih]*

food a comida *[koomeeda]*; **the food's excellent** a comida é excelente *[ish-silent]*

food poisoning intoxicação alimentar

[eentokseekassowng aleementahr]
food store uma mercearia *[mirs-yaree-a]*
fool um tolo *[tohloo]*
foolish tolo *[tohloo]*
foot o pé; **on foot** a pé
football o futebol *[footibol]*; *(ball)* uma bola de futebol
for: is that for me? isto é para mim? *[eeshtoo e para meeng]*; **what's this for?** para que serve isto? *[para kih serv eeshtoo]*; **for two days** *(rent etc)* para dois dias *[para doh-isн dee-ash]*; **I've been here for a week** estou aqui há uma semana *[shtoh akee ah ooma simana]*; **a bus for ...** um autocarro para ... *[owtookahrroo]*
forbidden proibido *[prweebeedoo]*
forehead a testa *[teshta]*
foreign estrangeiro *[shtransнay-roo]*
foreigner um estrangeiro *[shtransнayroo]*
foreign exchange as divisas *[diveezash]*
forest a floresta *[flooreshta]*
forget esquecer *[shkessehr]*; **I forget, I've forgotten** esqueci-me *[shkessee-mih]*; **don't forget** não se esqueça *[nowng sishkehssa]*
fork um garfo *[gahrfoo]*; *(in road)* uma bifurcação *[beefoorkassowng]*
form *(document)* um impresso *[eemprehsoo]*
formal *(person)* cerimonioso *[sireemoonyohzoo]*; *(dress)* de cerimónia *[dih sireemon-ya]*
fortnight uma quinzena *[keenzehna]*
fortunately felizmente *[fileesнment]*
fortune-teller uma pessoa que lê a sina *[pissoh-a kih leh a seena]*
forward: could you forward my mail? pode passar a enviar-me o correio? *[pod passahr a aingv-yahrmih oo koorray-oo]*
forwarding address o novo endereço *[nohvoo endirehsoo]*
foundation cream um creme de base *[krem dih bahz]*
fountain uma fonte *[font]*
foyer *(of cinema etc)* o foyer
fracture uma fractura *[frahtoora]*
fractured skull uma fractura do crânio *[frahtoora doo kran-yoo]*
fragile frágil *[frah-sнeel]*
frame *(picture)* uma moldura *[mohldoora]*
France a França *[fransa]*

fraud uma fraude *[frowd]*
free *(no charge)* gratuito *[gratweetoo]*; *(no constraints)* livre *[leevrih]*; **admission free** entrada gratuita
freezer um congelador *[konsнiladohr]*
freezing cold um frio de rachar *[free-oo dih rashahr]*
French francês *[fransehsh]*
French fries batatas fritas *[batahtash freetash]*
Frenchman um francês *[fransehsh]*
Frenchwoman uma francesa *[fransehza]*
frequent frequente *[frikwent]*
fresh fresco *[frehshkoo]*; **don't get fresh with me** não abuse! *[nowng aboozih]*
fresh orange juice sumo natural de laranja *[soomoo natoorahl dih laransнa]*
friction tape a fita isoladora *[feeta eezooladohra]*
Friday sexta-feira *[sehshta fay-ra]*
fridge o frigorífico *[freegoo-reefeekoo]*
fried egg um ovo estrelado *[ohvoo shtrilahdoo]*
friend um amigo *[ameegoo]*
friendly simpático *[seempahteekoo]*
frog uma rã *[rang]*
from: I'm from London eu sou de Londres *[eh-oo soh dih londrish]*; **from here to the beach** daqui até à praia *[dakee a-te a prah-ya]*; **the next boat from ...** o próximo barco de ... *[oo proseemoo bahrkoo dih]*; **as from Tuesday** a partir de terça-feira *[a parteer dih tehrssa fay-ra]*
front a frente *[frent]*; **in front** em frente *[aing]*; **in front of us** à nossa frente; **at the front** à frente
frost a geada *[sн-yahda]*
frozen gelado *[sнilahdoo]*
frozen food comida congelada *[koomeeda konsнilahda]*
fruit a fruta *[froota]*
fruit juice o sumo de fruta *[soomoo dih froota]*
fruit machine uma máquina de jogo *[mahkeena dih sнohgoo]*
fruit salad salada de frutas *[salahda dih frootash]*
frustrating: it's very frustrating é muito frustrante *[mweengtoo frooshtrant]*
fry fritar *[freetahr]*; **nothing fried** nada frito *[nahda freetoo]*
frying pan uma frigideira *[frisнeeday-ra]*

full cheio [sh**ay**-oo]; **it's full of …** está cheio de …; **I'm full** estou cheio [shtoh sh**ay**-oo]
full-board pensão completa [pens**ow**ng kompl**eh**ta]
full-bodied (wine) cheio de corpo [sh**ay**-oo dih k**oh**rpoo]
fun: it's fun é divertido [deevirt**ee**doo]; **it was great fun** foi muito divertido [fohy mw**ee**ngtoo]; **just for fun** só por graça [poor gr**ah**ssa]; **have fun** divirta-se [deev**eh**rta-sih]
funeral o funeral [foonir**ah**l]
funny (strange) estranho [shtr**a**n-yoo];

(comical) engraçado [aingrass**ah**doo]
furniture a mobília [moob**ee**l-ya]
further mais longe [m**ah**-ish lons**H**]; **2 kilometres further** dois quilómetros adiante [ad-y**a**nt]; **further down the road** mais abaixo na rua [m**ah**-iz ab**ah**-ishoo na r**oo**-a]
fuse um fusível [fooz**ee**vel]; **the lights have fused** as luzes fundiram-se [ash l**oo**zish foond**ee**rowng-sih]
fuse wire um fio de fusível [f**ee**-oo dih fooz**ee**vel]
future o futuro [foot**oo**roo]; **in future** no futuro [noo]

G

gale um vendaval [vendav**ah**l]
gallon um galão [gal**ow**ng] see page 121
gallstone um cálculo biliar [k**ah**lkooloo beel-y**ah**r]
gamble jogar [s**H**oog**ah**r]; **I don't gamble** eu não jogo [**eh**-oo nowng s**H**ogoo]
game (sport) o jogo [s**H**ohgoo]; (meat) a caça [k**ah**ssa]
games room a sala de jogos [s**ah**la dih s**H**og**oo**sh]
gammon o fiambre curado [f-y**a**mbrih koor**ah**doo]
garage (repair) uma garagem [gar**ah**-s**H**aing]; (fuel) uma bomba de gasolina [b**o**m-ba dih gazool**ee**na]; (parking) uma garagem de estacionamento [shtas-yoonam**e**ntoo]
garbage o lixo [l**ee**shoo]
garden um jardim [s**H**ard**ee**ng]
garlic o alho [**ah**l-yoo]
gas o gás [g**ah**sh]; (gasoline) a gasolina [gazool**ee**na]
gas cylinder uma bilha de gás [b**ee**l-ya dih g**ah**sh]
gasket uma junta [s**H**oonta]
gas pedal o acelerador [asilirad**oh**r]
gas permeable lenses umas lentes semi-rígidas [lentsh simee-reesh**ee**dash]
gas station uma bomba de gasolina [b**o**m-

ba dih gazool**ee**na]
gas tank (car) o depósito [dip**o**zeetoo]
gate o portão [poort**ow**ng]; (at airport) o portão de embarque [deemb**ah**rk]
gauge (oil) o indicador [eendeekad**oh**r]
gay um homosexual [ohmooseksw**ah**l]
gear (car) a mudança [mood**a**nsa]; (equipment) o equipamento [eekeepam**e**ntoo]; **the gears stick** as mudanças prendem [ash mood**a**nsash pr**e**ndaing]
gearbox: I have gearbox trouble tenho problemas na caixa de velocidades [t**ai**ng-nyoo proobl**eh**mash na k**ah**-isha dih vilooseed**ah**dish]
gear lever, gear shift a alavanca das mudanças [alav**a**nka dash mood**a**nsash]
general delivery a posta restante [p**o**shta risht**a**nt]
generous: that's very generous of you isso é muito generoso da sua parte [**ee**ssoo e mw**ee**ngtoo s**H**inir**oh**zoo da s**oo**-a pahrt]
gentleman: that gentleman over there aquele senhor ali [ak**eh**l sin-y**oh**r al**ee**]; **he's such a gentleman** ele é tão cavalheiro [ehl e towng kaval-y**ay**-roo]
gents a casa de banho dos homens [k**ah**za dih ban-yoo dooz **o**maingsh]
genuine genuíno [s**H**inw**ee**noo]

German alemão *[alimowng]*
German measles a rubéola *[roobay-ola]*
Germany a Alemanha *[aliman-ya]*
get: have you got ...? tem ...? *[taing]*;
how do I get to ...? como vou para ...?
[kohmoo voh para]; **where do I get
them from?** onde é que os arranjo? *[ond-
ye k-yooz arranshoo]*; **can I get you a
drink?** posso arranjar-lhe uma bebida?
[possoo arranshahrl-yih ooma bibeeda];
will you get it for me? pode arranjar-me
isso? *[pod arranshahr-mih eessoo]*;
when do we get there? quando é que
chegamos? *[kwandoo e kih shigamoosh]*;
I've got to go tenho que ir embora
[taing-nyoo kih eer eembora]; **where do
I get off?** onde é que saio? *[ond-ye kih
sah-yoo]*; **it's difficult to get to** é difícil
chegar lá *[difeeseel shigahr lah]*; **when I
get up** (*in morning*) quando me levanto
[kwandoo mih livantoo]
ghastly horroroso *[ohrroor-ohzoo]*
ghost um fantasma *[fantahshma]*
giddy: it makes me giddy faz-me sentir
tonto *[fahsh-mih senteer tontoo]*
gift um presente *[prizent]*
gigantic gigantesco *[sheeganteshkoo]*
gin o gin *[sheeng]*; **a gin and tonic** um
gin-tónico
girl uma rapariga *[rapareega]*
girlfriend a namorada *[namoorahda]*
give dar *[dahr]*; **will you give me ...?**
pode dar-me...? *[pod dahr-mih]*; **I gave
it to him** dei-lhe *[dayl-yih]*; **I'll give you
300 escudos** dou-lhe trezentos escudos
[dohl-yih]; **will you give it back?** pode
devolver-me isto? *[pod divohlvehr
meeshtoo]*; **would you give this to ...?**
pode dar isto a ...? *[pod dahr eeshtoo a]*
glad contente *[kontent]*; **I'm so glad** estou
tão contente *[shtoh towng]*
glamorous vistoso *[veeshtohzoo]*
gland a glândula *[glandoola]*
glandular fever febre glandular *[febrih
glandoolahr]*
glass (*substance*) o vidro *[veedroo]*;
(*drinking*) um copo *[kopoo]*; **a glass of
water** um copo de água *[kopoo d-
yahgwa]*
glasses os óculos *[okooloosh]*
gloves as luvas *[loovash]*
glue a cola
gnat uma melga

go ir *[eer]*; **we want to go to ...** queremos
ir a ... *[kirehmooz eer a]*; **I'm going
there tomorrow** vou lá amanhã *[voh lah
ahman-yang]*; **when does it go?** (*leave*) a
que horas parte? *[a k-yorash pahrt]*;
where are you going? onde vai? *[ond
vy]*; **let's go** vamos *[vamoosh]*; **he's
gone** (*left*) ele foi-se embora *[ehl fohy-sih
eembora]*; **it's all gone** desapareceu tudo
[dizaparisseh-oo toodoo]; **I went there
yesterday** fui lá ontem *[fwee lah
ontaing]*; **a hotdog to go** (*to take away*)
um cachorro quente para levar *[kashoh-
rroo kent para livahr]*; **go away!** vá-se
embora! *[vah-seembora]*; **it's gone off**
(*food*) está estragado *[shtah shtra-
gahdoo]*; **we're going out tonight** vamos sair esta noite *[vamoosh sa-eer eshta
noh-it]*; **do you want to go out tonight?**
quer sair esta noite? *[kair sa-eer]*; **has the
price gone up?** o preço aumentou?
[prehsoo owmentoh]
goal (*sport*) um golo *[gohloo]*
goat uma cabra
goat's cheese o queijo de cabra
[kay-shoo]
God Deus *[deh-oosh]*
gold o ouro *[ohroo]*
golf o golfe
golf clubs os paus de golfe *[pah-oosh]*
golf course um campo de golfe *[kampoo]*
good bom *[bong]*; **good!** bem! *[baing]*;
that's no good não presta *[nowng
preshta]*; **good heavens!** céus! *[se-oosh]*
goodbye adeus *[adeh-oosh]*
good-looking bem parecido *[baing pa-
risseedoo]*
gooey (*food etc*) pegajoso *[pigashohzoo]*
goose um ganso *[gansoo]*
gooseberries as uvas-espins *[oovaz-
ishpeengsh]*
gorgeous estupendo *[shtoopendoo]*
gourmet um gourmet
gourmet food a alta cozinha *[ahlta
koozeen-ya]*
government o governo *[goovehrnoo]*
gradually gradualmente *[gradwahlment]*
grammar a gramática *[gramahteeka]*
gram(me) uma grama
granddaughter a neta
grandfather o avô *[avoh]*
grandmother a avó
grandson o neto *[netoo]*

grapefruit a toranja *[tooransha]*
grapefruit juice um sumo de toranja *[soomoo dih tooransha]*
grapes as uvas *[oovash]*
grass a relva
grateful agradecido *[agradiseedoo]*; **I'm very grateful to you** estou-lhe muito agradecido *[shtohl-yih mweengtoo]*
gravy o molho *[mohl-yoo]*
gray cinzento *[seenzentoo]*
grease (*on food*) a gordura *[goordoora]*; (*for car*) o óleo *[ol-yoo]*
greasy (*cooking*) gorduroso *[goordoorohzoo]*
great grande; (*very good: holiday, hotel etc*) óptimo *[otteemoo]*; **that's great!** isso é óptimo! *[eesoo]*
Great Britain a Grã-Bretanha *[grang britan-ya]*
Greece a Grécia *[gress-ya]*
greedy (*for food*) glutão *[glootowng]*
Greek grego *[grehgoo]*
green verde *[vehrd]*
green card (*insurance*) a carta verde *[kahrta vehrd]*
greengrocer um lugar de vegetais *[loogahr dih vishitah-ish]*
grey cinzento *[seenzentoo]*
grilled grelhado *[gril-yahdoo]*
gristle (*on meat*) a cartilagem *[karteelah-shaing]*
grocer o merceeiro *[mirs-yay-roo]*
ground o chão *[showng]*; **on the ground** no chão *[noo]*; **on the ground floor** no rés-do-chão *[noo resh doo]*
ground beef a carne picada *[kahrn peekahda]*
group um grupo *[groopoo]*
group insurance o seguro de grupo *[sigooroo dih groopoo]*
group leader o chefe do grupo *[shef doo groopoo]*
guarantee uma garantia *[garantee-a]*; **is it guaranteed?** tem garantia? *[taing]*
guardian (*of child*) um tutor *[tootohr]*
guest um convidado *[konveedahdoo]*
guesthouse uma hospedaria *[ohshpidaree-a]*
guest room um quarto de hóspedes *[kwahrtoo d-yoshpidish]*
guide (*tourist*) uma guia *[g-ee-a]*
guidebook um livro-guia *[leevroo g-ee-a]*
guilty culpado *[koolpahdoo]*
guitar uma viola *[v-yola]*
gum (*in mouth*) a gengiva *[shensheeva]*
gun uma pistola *[peeshtola]*
gymnasium o ginásio *[sheenahz-yoo]*
gyn(a)ecologist um ginecologista *[sheenikooloosheeshta]*

H

hair o cabelo *[kabehloo]*
hairbrush uma escova de cabelo *[shkohva dih kabehloo]*
haircut um corte de cabelo *[kort dih kabehloo]*; **just an ordinary haircut, please** só um simples corte de cabelo, por favor *[oong seemplish]*
hairdresser o cabeleireiro *[kabilay-ray-roo]*
hairdryer um secador de cabelo *[sikadohr dih kabehloo]*
hair gel o gel para o cabelo *[shel para oo kabehloo]*
hair grip uma mola para o cabelo *[kabehloo]*
hair lacquer a laca
half a metade *[mitahd]*; **half an hour** meia hora *[may-a ora]*; **a half portion** meia dose *[may-a doz]*; **half a litre** meio litro *[may-oo leetroo]*; **half as much** a metade disso *[mitahd deessoo]*; **half as much again** isso e mais metade *[eessoo ee mah-ish] see page 118*
halfway: halfway to Lisbon a meio caminho de Lisboa *[a may-oo kameen-yoo dih lishboh-a]*

ham fiambre *[f-yambrih]*
hamburger um hamburger *[amboorger]*
hammer um martelo *[marteloo]*
hand a mão *[mowng]*; **will you give me a hand?** pode dar-me uma ajuda? *[pod dahrm-yooma asнooda]*
handbag uma mala de mão *[mahla dih mowng]*
hand baggage a bagagem de mão *[bagah-sнaing dih mowng]*
handbrake o travão de mão *[travowng dih mowng]*
handkerchief um lenço *[lensoo]*
handle (*door*) o fecho *[fehshoo]*; (*cup*) a asa *[ahza]*; **will you handle it?** pode tratar disso? *[pod tratahr deesoo]*
hand luggage a bagagem de mão *[bagah-sнaing dih mowng]*
handmade feito à mão *[fay-too ah mowng]*
handsome bonito *[booneetoo]*
hanger (*for clothes*) um cabide *[kabeed]*
hangover uma ressaca *[rissahka]*; **I've got a terrible hangover** estou com uma ressaca terrível *[shtoh kong ooma rissahka tirreevel]*
happen acontecer *[akontisehr]*; **how did it happen?** como é que aconteceu? *[kohmoo e k-yakontisseh-oo]*; **what's happening?** o que é que está a acontecer? *[oo k-ye kishtah akontisehr]*; **it won't happen again** não voltará a acontecer *[nowng vohltarah]*
happy contente *[kontent]*; **we're not happy with the room** não estamos contentes com o quarto *[nowng shtamoosh kontentsh kong oo kwahrtoo]*
harbo(u)r o porto *[pohrtoo]*
hard duro *[dooroo]*; (*difficult*) difícil *[difeeseel]*
hard-boiled egg um ovo cozido *[ohvoo koozeedoo]*
hard lenses as lentes rígidas *[lentsh reesнeedash]*
hardly mal; **hardly ever** quase nunca *[kwahz noonka]*
hardware store uma loja de ferragens *[losнa dih firrah-sнaingsh]*
harm o mal
hassle: it's too much hassle é demasiada complicação *[dimaz-yahda kompleekassowng]*; **a hassle-free holiday** umas férias sem complicações *[fair-yash saing*

kompleekassoingsh]
hat um chapéu *[sha-pe-oo]*
hatchback (*car*) um carro de dois volumes *[kahrroo dih doh-ish vooloomsh]*
hate: I hate … detesto … *[diteshtoo]*
have ter *[tehr]*; **do you have …?** tem …? *[taing]*; **can I have …?** pode dar-me …? *[pod dahr-mih]*; **can I have some water?** pode dar-me água? *[pod dahrm-yahgwa]*; **I have …** tenho … *[taing-nyoo]*; **I don't have …** não tenho … *[nowng]*; **can we have breakfast in our room?** podemos tomar o pequeno almoço no quarto? *[podehmoosh toomahr o pikehnoo ahlmohsoo noo kwahrtoo]*; **have another** (*drink etc*) tome outro *[tomyohtroo]*; **I have to leave early** tenho que sair cedo *[taing-nyoo kih sa-eer sehdoo]*; **do I have to …?** tenho de …? *[taing-nyoo dih] see page 114*
hay fever a febre dos fenos *[febrih doosh fehnoosh]*
he ele *[ehl]*; **is he here?** ele está aqui? *[shtah akee] see page 112*
head a cabeça *[kabehssa]*; **we're heading for Lisbon** vamos para Lisboa *[vamoosh para lisнboh-a]*
headache uma dor de cabeça *[dohr dih kabehssa]*
headlight o farol
headphones os auscultadores *[owshkooltadohrish]*
head waiter o chefe de mesa *[shef dih mehza]*
head wind um vento contrário *[ventoo kontrahr-yoo]*
health a saúde *[sa-ood]*; **your health!** à sua saúde! *[ah soo-a]*
healthy saudável *[sowdahvel]*
hear: can you hear me? consegue ouvir-me? *[konseg ohveer-mih]*; **I can't hear you** não o consigo ouvir *[nowng oo konseegoo ohveer]*; **I've heard about it** ouvi falar nisso *[ohvee falahr neesoo]*
hearing aid um aparelho para a surdez *[aparehl-yoo para a soordehsh]*
heart o coração *[koorassowng]*
heart attack um enfarte *[aingfahrt]*
heat o calor *[kalohr]*; **not in this heat!** não com um calor destes! *[nowng kong oong kalohr dehstsh]*
heated rollers os rolos *[roloosh]*
heater (*in car*) o aquecedor *[a-kessidohr]*

heating o aquecimento *[a-kesseementoo]*

heat rash uma irritação provocada pelo sol *[eerreetass**ow**ng proov**oo**k**ah**da p**eh**loo sol]*

heat stroke uma insolação *[eensoo-. lass**ow**ng]*

heatwave uma vaga de calor *[v**ah**ga dih kal**ohr**]*

heavy pesado *[piz**ah**doo]*

hectic atarefado *[atarif**ah**doo]*

heel *(of foot)* o calcanhar *[k**ah**lkan-y**ah**r];* **could you put new heels on these?** podia pôr uns saltos novos? *[pood**ee**-a pohr oongsh s**ah**ltoosh n**o**voosh]*

heelbar um balcão para reparações rápidas de sapatos *[bahlk**ow**ng para riparass**o**ingsh r**ah**peedash dih sap**ah**toosh]*

height *(person)* a altura *[ahlt**oo**ra];* *(mountain)* a altitude *[ahlteet**oo**d]*

helicopter um helicóptero *[eeleek**o**ptiroo]*

hell: oh hell! oh diabo! *[d-y**ah**boo];* **go to hell!** vá para o diabo! *[vah para]*

hello! olá; *(on phone)* está *[sht**ah**]*

helmet *(motorcycle)* um capacete *[kapass**eh**t]*

help ajudar *[asHood**ah**r];* **can you help me?** pode ajudar-me? *[pod asHood**ah**rmih];* **thanks for your help** obrigado pela sua ajuda *[ohbreeg**ah**doo p**eh**la soo-a asH**oo**da];* **help!** socorro! *[sook**oh**roo]*

helpful: he was very helpful ele foi muito útil *[ehl fohy mw**ee**ngtoo **oo**teel];* **that's helpful** isso é útil *[ees**oo** e]*

helping *(of food)* uma porção *[poors**ow**ng]*

hepatitis a hepatite *[ipat**ee**t]*

her: I don't know her eu não a conheço *[eh-oo nowng a koon-y**eh**soo];* **will you send it to her?** pode mandar isso a ela? *[pod mand**ah**r ees**oo** a **e**la];* **it's her** é ela *[e];* **with her** com ela *[kong];* **for her** para ela; **that's her suitcase** essa é a mala dela *[m**ah**la d**e**la] see pages 110, 112*

herbs as ervas *[**ai**rvash]*

here aqui *[ak**ee**];* **here you are** *(giving something)* aqui tem *[ak**ee** taing];* **here he comes** aqui vem ele *[ak**ee** vaing ehl]*

hers: that's hers isso é dela *[ees**oo** e d**e**la] see page 113*

hey! eh!

hiccups os soluços *[sool**oo**soosh]*

hide esconder *[shkond**eh**r]*

hideous horroroso *[ohrroor**oh**zoo]*

high alto *[**ah**ltoo]*

highbeam os faróis máximos *[far**oi**sh m**ah**seemoosh]*

highchair *(for baby)* uma cadeira de bébé *[kad**ay**-ra dih beb-**e**]*

highway uma auto-estrada *[owtoosht**rah**da]*

hiking caminhar no campo *[kameen-y**ah**r noo k**ah**mpoo]*

hill o monte *[mont];* **it's further up the hill** é mais acima no monte *[m**ah**-iz ass**ee**ma noo]*

hilly acidentado *[asseedent**ah**do]*

him: I don't know him não o conheço *[nowng oo koon-y**eh**ssoo];* **will you send it to him?** pode mandar isso a ele? *[pod mand**ah**r ees**oo** a ehl];* **it's him** é ele *[e];* **with him** com ele *[kong];* **for him** para ele *see page 112*

hip a anca

hire: can I hire a car? pode-se alugar um carro? *[pods-yaloog**ah**r oong k**ah**rroo];* **do you hire them out?** estão para alugar? *[shtowng para aloog**ah**r]*

his: it's his drink é a bebida dele *[e a bib**ee**da dehl];* **it's his** é dele *see pages 110, 113*

history: the history of Lisbon a história de Lisboa *[eesht**o**r-ya]*

hit: he hit me ele bateu-me *[ehl bat**eh**oomih];* **I hit my head** bati com a minha cabeça *[bat**ee** kong a m**ee**n-ya kab**eh**ssa]*

hitch: is there a hitch? há alguma dificuldade? *[ah ahlg**oo**ma difeekoold**ah**d]*

hitch-hike andar à boleia *[and**ah**r ah bool**ay**-a]*

hitch-hiker uma pessoa que anda à boleia *[piss**oh**-a k-y**a**ndah bool**ay**-a]*

hit record um disco no top *[deeshkoo noo top]*

hole um buraco *[boor**ah**koo]*

holiday as férias *[ash f**ai**r-yash];* **I'm on holiday** estou de férias *[shtoh dih]*

Holland a Holanda *[ohl**a**nda]*

home *(house)* a casa *[k**ah**za];* **at home** em casa *[aing k**ah**za];* *(in my own country)* no meu país *[noo m**eh**-oo pa-**ee**sh];* **I go home tomorrow** eu vou-me embora amanhã *[**eh**-oo voh meemb**o**ra ahman-yang];* **home sweet home!** lar doce lar! *[lahr d**oh**ssih lahr]*

home address a morada de casa *[moo-rahda dih kahza]*
homemade caseiro *[kazay-roo]*
homesick: I'm homesick tenho saudades de casa *[taing-nyoo sa-oodahdsh dih kahza]*
honest honesto *[ohneshtoo]*
honestly? de verdade? *[dih virdahd]*
honey o mel
honeymoon a lua-de-mel *[looa dih mel]*; **it's our honeymoon** é a nossa lua-de-mel; **a second honeymoon** uma segunda lua-de-mel *[sigoonda]*
honeymoon suite a suite nupcial *[sweet noops-yahl]*
hoover *(tm)* um aspirador *[ashpeeradohr]*
hope esperar *[shpirahr]*; **I hope so** espero que sim *[shpairoo kih seeng]*; **I hope not** espero que não *[nowng]*
horn *(car)* a buzina *[boozeena]*
horrible horrível *[ohrreevel]*
hors d'oeuvre os acepipes *[assipeepsh]*
horse um cavalo *[kavahloo]*
horse riding andar a cavalo *[andahr a kavahloo]*
hose *(for car radiator)* um tubo de borracha *[tooboo dih boorrahsha]*
hospital um hospital *[ohshpeetahl]*
hospitality a hospitalidade *[ohshpeeta-leedahd]*; **thank you for your hospitality** obrigado pela sua hospitalidade *[ohbreegahdoo pehla soo-a]*
hostel *(youth etc)* um albergue *[ahlbairg]*
hot quente *[kent]*; *(curry etc)* picante *[peekant]*; **I'm hot** tenho calor *[taing-nyoo kalohr]*; **something hot to eat** algo quente para comer *[ahlgoo kent para koomehr]*; **it's so hot today** está imenso calor hoje *[shtah eemensoo kalohr ohsh]*
hotdog um cachorro quente *[kashohrroo kent]*

hotel um hotel *[ohtel]*; **at my hotel** no meu hotel *[noo meh-oo]*
hotel clerk o recepcionista *[risess-yooneeshta]*
hotplate *(on cooker)* a placa *[plahka]*
hot-water bottle um saco de água quente *[sahkoo d-yahgwa kent]*
hour uma hora *[ora]*; **on the hour** às horas certas *[ahz orash sehrtash]*
house uma casa *[kahza]*
housewife uma dona de casa *[kahza]*
how como *[kohmoo]*; **how many?** quantos? *[kwantoosh]*; **how much?** quanto? *[kwantoo]*; **how often?** quantas vezes? *[kwantash vehzish]*; **how are you?** como está? *[shtah]*; **how do you do?** muito prazer *[mweengtoo prazehr]*; **how about a beer?** que tal uma cerveja? *[kih tahl ooma sirvay-sha]*; **how nice!** que agradável! *[agradahvel]*; **would you show me how to?** podia mostrar-me como é? *[poodee-a mooshtrahr-mih]*
humid húmido *[oomeedoo]*
humidity a humidade *[oomeedahd]*
humo(u)r: where's your sense of humo(u)r? não tem sentido de humor? *[nowng taing senteedoo d-yoomohr]*
hundredweight *see page 120*
hungry: I'm hungry tenho fome *[taing-nyoo fom]*; **I'm not hungry** não tenho fome *[nowng]*
hurry: I'm in a hurry estou com pressa *[shtoh kong]*; **hurry up!** despache-se! *[dishpah-shisih]*; **there's no hurry** não há pressa! *[nowng ah]*
hurt: it hurts dói-me *[doy-mih]*; **my back hurts** doem-me as costas *[daw-aing-mih ash koshtash]*
husband: my husband o meu marido *[meh-oo mareedoo]*
hydrofoil um hydrofoil *[eedro-]*

I

I eu [eh-oo]; **I am English** eu sou inglês [soh eenglehsh]; **I live in Michigan** vivo em Michigan [veevoo] see page 112
ice gelo [sнehloo]; **with ice** com gelo [kong]; **with ice and lemon** com gelo e limão [leemowng]
ice cream um gelado [sнilahdoo]
ice-cream cone um cone de gelado [kon dih sнilahdoo]
iced coffee um café glacé [ka-fe glasseh]
idea uma ideia [eeday-a]; **good idea!** boa ideia! [boh-a]
ideal ideal [eed-yahl]
identity papers os documentos de identificação [dookoomentoosh deedenteefeekassowng]
idiot um idiota [eed-yota]
idyllic idílico [eedeeleekoo]
if se [sih]; **if you possibly could** se pudesse [sih poodess]; **if not** se não [nowng]
ignition a ignição [eegneesowng]
ill doente [dwent]; **I feel ill** sinto-me doente [seentoo-mih]
illegal ilegal [eeligahl]
illegible ilegível [eelisнeevel]
illness uma doença [dwenssa]
imitation (leather etc) uma imitação [eemeetassowng]
immediately imediatamente [eemidyatament]
immigration a imigração [eemeegrassowng]
import importar [eempoortahr]
important importante [eempoortant]; **it's very important** é muito importante [mweengtoo]; **it's not important** não é importante [nowng]
impossible impossível [eempooseevel]
impressive impressionante [eemprisyoonant]
improve: it's improving está a melhorar [shtah mil-yoorahr]; **I want to improve**

my Portuguese quero melhorar o meu português [kairoo mil-yoorahr oo mehoo poortoogehsh]
improvement uma melhoria [mil-yooree-a]
in: in my room no meu quarto [noo mehoo kwahrtoo]; **in the town centre** no centro [sentroo]; **in London** em Londres [aing londrish]; **in one hour's time** dentro de uma hora [dentroo dooma ora]; **in August** em Agosto [agohshtoo]; **in English** em inglês [eenglehsh]; **is he in?** ele está? [ehl shtah]
inch uma polegada [poolgahda] see page 119
include incluir [eenklweer]; **is that included in the price?** isso está incluído no preço? [eesoo shtah eenklweedoo noo prehsoo]
inclusive inclusive [eenkloozee-ve]
incompetent incompetente [eenkompitent]
inconvenient pouco conveniente [pohkoo konvin-yent]
increase um aumento [owmentoo]
incredible incrível [eenkreevel]
indecent indecente [eendisent]
independent independente [eendipendent]
India a Índia [eend-ya]
Indian indiano [eend-yanoo]
indicator um indicador [eendeekadohr]
indigestion a indigestão [eendisнishtowng]
indoor pool uma piscina coberta [peeshseena koobairta]
indoors dentro de casa [dentroo dih kahza]
industry a indústria [eendooshtr-ya]
inefficient ineficiente [eenifees-yent]
infection uma infecção [eenfeks-owng]
infectious infeccioso [eenfeks-yohzoo]
inflammation uma inflamação [eenfla-

massowng]
inflation a inflação *[eenflassowng]*
informal informal *[eenfoormahl]*
information a informação *[eenfoormassowng]*
information desk o balcão de informações *[bahlkowng deenfoormassoingsh]*
information office as informações *[eenfoormassoingsh]*; (*tourist office*) o centro de turismo *[sentroo dih tooreeshmoo]*
injection uma injecção *[eensHeksowng]*
injured ferido *[fireedoo]*; **she's been injured** ela ficou ferida *[feekoh fireeda]*
injury um ferimento *[fireementoo]*
in-law: my in-laws os meus sogros *[oosh meh-oosh sogroosh]*
innocent inocente *[eenoosent]*
inquisitive inquisitivo *[eenkeezeeteevoo]*
insect um insecto *[eensettoo]*
insect bite uma picada de insecto *[peekahda deensettoo]*
insecticide o insecticida *[eensetteeseeda]*
insect repellent um repele-insectos *[ripel-eensettoosh]*
inside: inside the tent dentro da tenda *[dentroo]*; **let's sit inside** vamos sentarnos lá dentro *[vamoosh sentahr-noosh lah dentroo]*
insincere pouco sincero *[pohkoo seensehroo]*
insist: I insist insisto *[eenseeshtoo]*
insomnia a insónia *[eenson-ya]*
instant coffee o café instantâneo *[ka-fe eenshtantaneh-oo]*
instead em vez *[aing vehz]*; **I'll have that one instead** dê-me antes aquele *[dehmih antiz akehl]*; **instead of ...** em vez de ... *[aing vehsh dih]*
insulating tape a fita isoladora *[feeta eezooladohra]*
insulin a insulina *[eensooleena]*
insult um insulto *[eensooltoo]*
insurance um seguro *[sigooroo]*; **write your insurance company here** escreva aqui o nome da sua companhia de seguros *[shkrehv akee oo nom da soo-a kompan-yee-a dih sigooroosh]*
insurance policy a apólice de seguro *[apolees dih sigooroo]*
intellectual um intelectual *[eentilettwahl]*
intelligent inteligente *[eentileesHent]*

intentional: it wasn't intentional não foi de propósito *[nowng fohy dih proopozeetoo]*
interest: places of interest lugares de interesse *[loogahrsh deentrehs]*
interested: I'm very interested in ... estou muito interessado em ... *[shtoh mweengtoo eentrisahdoo aing]*
interesting interessante *[eentrisant]*; **that's very interesting** isso é muito interessante *[eesoo e mweengtoo]*
international internacional *[eentirnasyoonahl]*
interpret interpretar *[eentirpritahr]*; **would you interpret?** podia interpretar? *[poodee-a eentirpritahr]*
interpreter um intérprete *[eentairpritih]*
intersection um cruzamento *[kroozamentoo]*
interval o intervalo *[eentirvahloo]*
into para; **I'm not into that** (*don't like*) não me interesso por isso *[nowng meentiressoo poor eesoo]*
introduce: may I introduce ...? posso apresentar ...? *[possoo aprizentahr]*
introvert um introvertido *[eentroovirteedoo]*
invalid um inválido *[eenvahleedoo]*
invalid chair uma cadeira de rodas *[kaday-ra dih rodash]*
invitation um convite *[konveet]*; **thank you for the invitation** obrigado pelo convite *[ohbreegahdoo pehloo konveet]*
invite convidar *[konveedahr]*; **can I invite you out?** quer sair comigo? *[kair sa-eer koomeegoo]*
involved: I don't want to get involved in it não quero involver-me nisso *[nowng kairoo eenvohlvehrmih neesoo]*
iodine o iodo *[yodoo]*
Ireland a Irlanda *[eerlanda]*
Irish irlandês *[eerlandehsh]*
iron (*for clothes*) um ferro de engomar *[fairroo daing-goomahr]*; **can you iron these for me?** pode engomar-me isto? *[pod aing-goomahrmih eeshtoo]*
ironmonger uma loja de ferragens *[losHa dih firrah-sHaingsh]*
is é, está *see page 117*
island uma ilha *[eel-ya]*; **on the island** na ilha
isolated isolado *[eezoolahdoo]*

it o, a *[oo, a]*; **is it ...?** é ...?, está ...?
[shtah]; **where is it?** onde é?, onde está?
[ond-ye, ond shtah]; **it's her** é ela; **it's
only me** sou só eu *[soh saw eh-oo]*; **it was
...** era ... *[aira]*; **that's just it!** é isso
mesmo! *[eesoo mehsнmoo]*; **that's it**

(*that's right*) é **i**sso *see page 112*
Italian italiano *[eetal-yanoo]*
Italy a Itália *[eetahl-ya]*
itch: it itches faz comichão *[fahsh koo-
meeshowng]*
itinerary o itinerário *[eeteenirahr-yoo]*

J

jack (*for car*) um macaco *[makahkoo]*
jacket um casaco *[kazahkoo]*
jacuzzi uma banheira de massagens *[ban-
yaya-ra dih massah-sнaingsh]*
jam a comp**o**ta; **traffic jam** um engarrafamento *[aing-garrafamentoo]*; **I
jammed on the brakes** eu travei a fundo
[eh-oo travay a foondoo]
January Janeiro *[sнanay-ro]*
jaundice icterícia *[eektirees-ya]*
jaw a maxila *[mahkseela]*
jazz o jazz
jazz club um clube de jazz *[kloob]*
jealous (*in love*) ciumento *[s-yoomentoo]*;
he's jealous ele tem ciúmes *[taing
s-yoomsh]*
jeans uns jeans
jellyfish uma alforreca *[ahlfoorreka]*
jet-setter um membro do jet-set *[mem-
broo]*
jetty o pontão *[pontowng]*
Jew um judeu *[sнoodeh-oo]*
jewel(le)ry a joalharia *[sнwal-yaree-a]*
Jewish judaico *[sнoodah-ikoo]*
jiffy: just a jiffy! só um momentinho!
[saw oong moomenteen-yoo]
job um emprego *[aingprehgoo]*; **just the
job!** mesmo a calhar! *[mehsнmoo a kal-
yahr]*; **it's a good job you told me!**
ainda bem que me disse! *[a-eenda baing
kih mih dees]*
jog: I'm going for a jog vou correr um
bocado *[voh koorrehr oong bookahdoo]*
jogging o jogging
join (*a club*) inscrever-se *[eenshkrivehr-
sih]*; **I'd like to join** eu gostava de me
inscrever *[eh-oo gooshtahva dih

meenshkrivehr]*; **can I join you?** posso
fazer-lhe companhia? *[possoo fazehrl-yih
kompan-yee-a]*; **do you want to join us?**
quer juntar-se a nós? *[kair sнoontahr-sih
a nosh]*
joint (*in bone*) a articulação *[artee-
koolassowng]*; (*to smoke*) uma p**a**ssa
joke uma piada *[p-yahda]*; **you've got to
be joking!** você deve estar a brincar!
[vosseh dev shtahr a breenkahr]; **it's no
joke** não é para brincar *[nowng]*
jolly: it was jolly good estava mesmo
bem *[shtahva mehsнmoo baing]*; **jolly
good!** muito bem! *[mweengtoo]*
journey uma viagem *[v-yah-sнaing]*;
have a good journey! boa viagem!
[boh-a]; **safe journey!** boa viagem!
jug um jarro *[sнahrroo]*; **a jug of water**
um jarro de água *[d-yahgwa]*
July Julho *[sнool-yoo]*
jump: you made me jump você pregou-
me um susto *[vosseh prigoh-mih oong
sooshtoo]*; **jump in!** (*to car*) suba! *[soo-
ba]*
jumper uma camisola *[kameezola]*
jump leads cabos para ligar a bateria
[kahboosh para leegahr a batiree-a]
junction um cruzamento *[kroozamen-
too]*
June Junho *[sнoon-yoo]*
junior: Mr Jones junior o senhor Jones
filho *[feel-yoo]*
junk velharias *[vehl-yaree-ash]*
just: just one só um *[saw oong]*; **just me**
só eu *[eh-oo]*; **just for me** só para mim
[para meeng]; **just a little** só um pouco
[pohko]; **just here** aqui mesmo *[akee

mehsнmoo]; **not just now** agora não [agora nowng]; **he was here just now** ele esteve aqui mesmo há pouco [shtehv akee mehsнmoo ah]; **that's just right** é assim

mesmo [e asseeng]; **it's just as good** é bom na mesma [e bong na mehsнma]; **that's just as well** ainda bem [a-eenda baing]

K

kagul um impermeável de nylon [eempirm-yahvel]

keen: I'm not keen não tenho vontade [nowng taing-nyoo vontahd]

keep: can I keep it? posso ficar com isto? [possoo feekahr kong eeshtoo]; **you can keep it** pode ficar com isso [pod feekahr kong eesoo]; **keep the change** guarde o troco [gwahrd oo trohkoo]; **will it keep?** (food) será que se conserva? [sirah kih sih konsairva]; **it's keeping me awake** não me deixa dormir [nowng mih day-sha doormeer]; **it keeps on breaking** está sempre a partir-se [shtah sempra parteer-sih]; **I can't keep anything down** (food) não consigo reter nada no estômago [nowng konseegoo ritehr nahda noo shtohmagoo]

kerb a borda do passeio [doo passay-oo]

ketchup o ketchup

kettle uma chaleira [shahlay-ra]

key a chave [shahv]

kid: the kids os miúdos [m-yoodoosh]; **I'm not kidding** não estou a brincar [nowng shtoh a breenkahr]

kidneys os rins [reengsh]

kill matar [matahr]

kilo um quilo [keeloo] see page 120

kilometre, kilometer um quilómetro [keelomitroo] see page 119

kind: that's very kind é muito amável [mweengtoo amahvel]; **this kind of ...** esta espécie de ... [eshta shpess-yih dih]

kiss um beijo [bay-sнoo]

kitchen a cozinha [koozeen-ya]

kitchenette uma cozinha pequena [koozeen-ya peekehna]

kleenex (tm) os lenços de papel [lensoosh dih pa-pel]

knackered todo partido [tohdoo parteedoo]

knee o joelho [sнwehl-yoo]

knickers umas cuecas de mulher [oomash kwekash dih mool-yair]

knife uma faca [fahka]

knitting a malha [mahl-ya]

knitting needles as agulhas de malha [agool-yash dih mahl-ya]

knobbly knees joelhos saídos [shwehl-yoosh sa-eedoosh]

knock: there's a knocking noise from the engine o motor tem uma batida [oo mootohr taing ooma bateeda]; **he's had a knock on the head** ele bateu com a cabeça [ehl bateh-oo kong a kabehssa]; **he's been knocked over** ele foi atropelado [fohy atroopilahdoo]

knot (in rope) um nó [naw]

know (somebody) conhecer [koon-yissehr]; (something) saber [sabehr]; **I don't know** não sei [nowng say]; **do you know a good restaurant?** sabe de algum bom restaurante? [sahb dahlgoong bong rishtowrant]; **who knows?** quem sabe? [kaing]; **I didn't know that** não sabia isso [nowng sabee-a eesoo]

L

label (*on clothes*) a etiqueta [*eeteekehta*]; (*on bottles etc*) o rótulo [*rotooloo*]

laces (*shoes*) os atacadores [*atakadohrsh*]

lacquer a laca

ladies' (room) o quarto de banho das senhoras [*kwahrtoo dih ban-yoo dash sin-yohrash*]

lady a senhora [*sin-yohra*]; **ladies and gentlemen!** senhoras e senhores! [*sin-yohraz ee sinyohrsh*]

lager a cerveja [*sirvay-sha*]; **lager and lime** uma cerveja com lima [*kong leema*]

lake um lago [*lahgoo*]

lamb o carneiro [*karnay-roo*]

lamp um candeeiro [*kand-yay-roo*]

lamppost um poste de iluminação [*posht deeloomeenassowng*]

lampshade um quebra-luz [*kebra-loosh*]

land a terra [*tairra*]; **when does the plane land?** a que horas aterra o avião? [*a k-yoraz atairra oo av-yowng*]

landscape a paisagem [*pye-zah-shaing*]

lane (*car*) uma faixa [*fah-isha*]; (*narrow road*) uma viela [*v-yela*]

language a língua [*leeng-gwa*]

language course um curso de línguas [*koorsoo dih leeng-gwash*]

large grande [*grand*]

laryngitis laringite [*lareensheet*]

last o último [*oolteemoo*]; **last year** no ano passado [*anoo passahdoo*]; **last Wednesday** na quarta-feira passada [*kwahrta fay-ra passahda*]; **last night** ontem à noite [*ontaing ah noh-it*]; **when is the last bus?** a que horas é o último autocarro? [*a k-yoraz-e oo oolteemoo owtookahrroo*]; **one last drink** só mais uma bebida [*saw mah-iz ooma bibeeda*]; **when were you last in London?** quando é que esteve da última vez em Londres? [*kwandoo-e kih shtehv da oolteema vehz aing londrish*]; **at last** finalmente! [*feenahlment*]; **how long**

does it last? (*film etc*) quanto tempo dura? [*kwantoo tempoo doora*]

last name o apelido [*apileedoo*]

late: sorry I'm late desculpe o atraso [*dishkoolp oo atrahzoo*]; **don't be late** não chegue atrasado [*nowng shehg atrazahdoo*]; **the bus was late** o autocarro veio atrasado [*oo owtookahrroo vay-oo atrazahdoo*]; **we'll be back late** estaremos de volta tarde [*shtarehmoosh dih volta tahrd*]; **it's getting late** está-se a fazer tarde [*shtah-sih a fazehr tahrd*]; **is it that late!** já é tão tarde! [*shah e towng tahrd*]; **it's too late now** é tarde demais [*tahrd dimah-ish*]; **I'm a late riser** gosto de me levantar tarde [*goshtoo dih mih livantahr tahrd*]

lately ultimamente [*oolteemament*]

later mais tarde [*mah-ish tahrd*]; **later on** mais logo [*mah-ish logoo*]; **I'll come back later** volto mais logo [*voltoo mah-ish logoo*]; **see you later** até logo [*a-te logoo*]; **no later than Tuesday** o mais tardar terça-feira [*oo mah-ish tardahr*]

latest: the latest news as últimas notícias [*az oolteemash nootees-yash*]; **at the latest** o mais tardar [*oo mah-ish tardahr*]

laugh rir [*reer*]; **don't laugh** não ria [*nowng ree-a*]; **it's no laughing matter** não é para rir [*nowng*]

launderette, laundromat uma lavandaria automática [*lavandaree-a owtoo-mahteeka*]

laundry (*clothes*) roupa para lavar [*rohpa para lavahr*]; (*place*) lavandaria [*lavandaree-a*]; **could you get the laundry done?** pode mandar lavar a roupa? [*pod mandahr lavahr a rohpa*]

lavatory os lavabos [*lavahboosh*]

law a lei [*lay*]; **against the law** contra a lei

lawn o relvado [*relvahdoo*]

lawyer um advogado [*advoogahdoo*]

laxative um laxativo [*lashateevoo*]

lay-by uma área de estacionamento *[ahr-ya dishtas-yoonamentoo]*

laze around: I just want to laze around eu só quero descansar *[eh-oo saw kairoo dishkansahr]*

lazy preguiçoso *[prigeesohzoo]*; **don't be lazy!** não seja preguiçoso! *[nowng say-sнa]*; **a nice lazy holiday** umas belas férias sem fazer nada *[oomash belash fair-yash saing fazehr nahda]*

lead *(elec)* o fio *[fee-oo]*; **where does this road lead?** onde é que esta estrada vai ter? *[ond-ye keshta shtrahda vahy tehr]*

leaf uma folha *[fohl-ya]*

leaflet um panfleto *[pamflehtoo]*; **do you have any leaflets on …?** tem alguma informação sobre …? *[taing ahlgooma eenfoormassowng sohbrih]*

leak uma fuga *[fooga]*; **the roof leaks** há uma fuga de água no telhado *[ah ooma fooga d-yahgwa noo til-yahdoo]*

learn: I want to learn … eu quero aprender … *[eh-oo kairoo aprendehr]*

learner: I'm just a learner estou só a aprender *[shtoh saw a aprendehr]*

lease arrendar *[arrendahr]*

least: not in the least de nenhum modo *[dih nin-yoong modoo]*; **at least 50** pelo menos cinquenta *[pehloo mehnoosh]*

leather o cabedal *[kabidahl]*

leave: when does the bus leave? a que horas parte o autocarro? *[a k-yorash pahrt oo owtookahrroo]*; **I leave tomorrow** parto amanhã *[pahrtoo ahman-yang]*; **he left this morning** ele foi-se embora esta manhã *[ehl fohy-seembora eshta man-yang]*; **may I leave this here?** posso deixar isto aqui? *[possoo day-shahr eeshtoo akee]*; **I left my bag in the bar** deixei a minha mala no bar *[day-shay a meen-ya mahla noo bar]*; **she left her bag here** ela deixou aqui a mala *[ela day-shoh akee a mahla]*; **leave the window open please** deixe a janela aberta por favor *[day-sha sнanela abairta]*; **there's not much left** não sobrou muito *[nowng soobroh mweengtoo]*; **I've hardly any money left** quase que já não tenho dinheiro *[kwahz kih sнah nowng taing-nyoo deen-yay-roo]*; **I'll leave it up to you** deixo isso ao seu critério *[day-shoo eesoo ow seh-oo kreetair-yoo]*

lecherous lascivo *[lash-seevoo]*

left esquerdo *[ishkehrdoo]*; **on the left** à esquerda *[ah ishkehrda]*

left hand drive com volante à esquerda *[kong voolant ah shkehrda]*

left-handed canhoto *[kan-yohtoo]*

left luggage (office) o depósito de bagagem *[dipozeetoo dih bagah-sнaing]*

leg a perna *[pairna]*

legal legal *[ligahl]*

legal aid a assistência legal gratuita *[aseeshtens-ya ligahl gratweeta]*

lemon um limão *[leemowng]*

lemonade uma limonada *[leemoonahda]*

lemon tea um chá de limão *[shah dih leemowng]*

lend: would you lend me your …? empresta-me o seu …? *[aing-preshta-mih oo seh-oo]*

lens *(phot)* a objectiva *[ohbsнetteeva]*; *(contact)* a lente *[lent]*

lens cap a tampa da objectiva *[ohbsнetteeva]*

Lent a Quaresma *[kwaresнma]*

lesbian uma lésbica *[lesнbeeka]*

less: less than an hour menos de uma hora *[mehnoosh dooma ora]*; **less than that** menos que isso *[mehnoosh keesoo]*; **less hot** menos quente *[mehnoosh kent]*

lesson uma lição *[leessowng]*; **do you give lessons?** dá lições? *[dah leesoingsh]*

let: would you let me use it? deixa-me usá-lo? *[day-shamih oozahloo]*; **will you let me know?** diz-me depois? *[deesнmih dipoh-ish]*; **I'll let you know** depois digo-lhe *[dipoh-ish deegoolyih]*; **let me try** deixe-me tentar *[day-shimih tentahr]*; **let me go!** largue-me! *[lahrgih-mih]*; **let's leave now** vamo-nos embora agora *[vamoonooz eembora agora]*; **let's not go yet** não vamos ainda *[nowng va-mooz a-eenda]*; **will you let me off at …?** deixa-me sair em …? *[day-shamih sa-eer aing]*; **room to let** um quarto para alugar *[kwahrtoo para aloogahr]*

letter uma carta *[kahrta]*; **are there any letters for me?** há correio para mim? *[ah koorray-oo para meeng]*

letterbox um marco de correio *[mahrkoo dih koorray-oo]*

lettuce uma alface *[ahlfahss]*

level crossing a passagem de nível *[passah-sнaing dih neevel]*

lever uma alavanca
liable responsável [rishponsahvel]
liberated: a liberated woman uma mulher independente [mool-yair eendipendent]
library a biblioteca [beebl-yooteka]
licence, license uma licença [leesensa]
license plate a chapa de matrícula [shahpa dih matreekoola]
lid a tampa
lie (untruth) uma mentira [menteera]; **can she lie down for a while?** ela pode deitar-se por uns momentos? [ela pod day-tahrsih poor oonsh moomentoosh]; **I want to go and lie down** quero ir deitarme [kairoo eer day-tahrmih]
lie-in: I'm going to have a lie-in tomorrow vou levantar-me tarde amanhã [voh livantahr-mih tahrd ahman-yang]
life a vida [veeda]; **not on your life!** de maneira nenhuma! [dih man-ay-ra ninyooma]; **that's life** é a vida [e a veeda]
lifebelt o cinto de salvação [seentoo dih sahlvassowng]
lifeboat o barco salva-vidas [bahrkoo sahlva-veedash]
lifeguard (on beach) o nadador salvador [nadadohr sahlvadohr]
life insurance um seguro de vida [sigooroo dih veeda]
life jacket o colete de salvação [kooleht dih sahlvassowng]
lift (in hotel) o elevador [eelivadohr]; **could you give me a lift?** pode dar-me uma boleia? [pod dahrmih ooma boolay-a]; **do you want a lift?** quer uma boleia? [kair]; **thanks for the lift** obrigado pela boleia [ohbreegahdoo pehla]; **I got a lift** arranjei uma boleia [arransнay]
light a luz [loosh]; (not heavy) leve [lev]; **the light was on** a luz estava acesa [a looz shtahva assehza]; **do you have a light?** tem lume? [taing loom]; **a light meal** uma refeição ligeira [rifay-sowng leesнay-ra]; **light blue** azul claro [azool klahroo]
light bulb uma lâmpada
lighter (cigarette) um isqueiro [shkay-roo]
lighthouse o farol
light meter o fotómetro [footawmitroo]
lightning a trovoada [troovwahda]
like: I'd like a ... queria um ... [kiree-a oong]; **I'd like to ...** queria ... [kiree-a];

would you like a ...? gostaria dum ...? [gooshtaree-a doong]; **would you like to come too?** gostaria de vir também? [gooshtaree-a dih veer tambaing]; **I like it** gosto [goshtoo]; **I like you** gosto de si [goshtoo dih see]; **I don't like it** não gosto [nowng goshtoo]; **he doesn't like it** ele não gosta [ehl nowng goshta]; **do you like ...?** você gosta de ...? [vosseh goshta dih]; **I like swimming** gosto de nadar [goshtoo dih nadahr]; **OK, if you like** se quiser [sih keezair]; **what's it like?** como é? [kohmoo e]; **do it like this** faça assim [fahs ahsseeng]; **one like that** um como esse [oong kohmoo ehss]
lilo (tm) um colchão de ar [kohlshowng d-yahr]
lime cordial um sumo de lima [soomoo dih leema]
lime juice um sumo de lima [soomoo dih leema]
line uma linha [leen-ya]; (of people) uma fila [feela]; (telephone) uma linha; **would you give me a line?** (tel) dá-me uma linha? [dahm-yooma]
linen (for beds) a roupa de cama [rohpa dih kama]
linguist um linguista [leeng-gweeshta]; **I'm no linguist** eu não tenho jeito para línguas [nowng taing-nyoo sнay-too para leeng-gwash]
lining o forro [fohrroo]
lip o lábio [lahb-yoo]
lip gloss o lip gloss
lip pencil um lápis para os lábios [lahpsh para oosh lahb-yoosh]
lip salve um baton para o cieiro [batong para oo s-yay-roo]
lipstick um baton [batong]
liqueur um licor [leekohr]
liquor uma bebida alcoólica [bibeeda ahlkwoleeka]
liquor store uma loja de vinhos [losнa dih veen-yoosh]
list uma lista [leeshta]
listen: I'd like to listen to ... eu gostaria de ouvir ... [eh-oo gooshtaree-a d-yohveer]; **listen!** escute! [shkoot]
liter, litre um litro [leetroo] see page 120
litter o lixo [leeshoo]
little pequeno [peekehnoo]; **just a little, thanks** só um pouco, por favor [saw oong pohkoo]; **just a very little** só muito

pouco [mweengtoo]; **a little cream** um pouco de natas [dih nahtash]; **a little more** um pouco mais [mah-ish]; **a little better** um pouco melhor [mil-yor]; **that's too little** (not enough) é muito pouco [e mweengtoo]

live viver [veevehr]; **I live in Manchester/Texas** eu vivo em Manchester/Texas [eh-oo veevoo aing]; **where do you live?** onde é que vive? [ond-ye kih veev]; **where does he live?** onde é que ele vive? [k-yehl veev]; **we live together** vivemos juntos [veevehmoosh sHoontoosh]

lively animado [aneemahdoo]

liver o fígado [feegadoo]

lizard um lagarto [lagahrtoo]

loaf um pão [powng]

lobby (in hotel) o hall

lobster uma lagosta [lagoshta]

local: a local wine um vinho da região [veen-yoo da risH-yowng]; **a local newspaper** um jornal local [sHoornahl lookahl]; **a local restaurant** um restaurante pertinho [rishtowrant pirteen-yoo]

lock uma fechadura [fishadoora]; **it's locked** está fechado à chave [shtah fishahdoo ah shahv]; **I've locked myself out of my room** fechei o quarto com a chave lá dentro [fishay oo kwahrtoo kong a shahv lah dentroo]

locker (for bags) um cacifo [kasseefoo]

log: I slept like a log dormi como uma pedra [doormee kohmoo ooma pedra]

lollipop um chupa-chupa [shoopa-shoopa]

London Londres [londrish]

lonely solitário [sooleetahr-yoo]; **are you lonely?** sente-se só? [sent-sih saw]

long comprido [kompreedoo]; **how long does it take?** quanto tempo demora? [kwantoo tempoo dimora]; **is it a long way?** é muito longe? [e mweengtoo lonsH]; **a long time** muito tempo; **I won't be long** não me demoro [nowng mih demoroo]; **don't be long** não se demore [sih dimorih]; **that was long ago** isso foi há muito tempo [eesoo fohy ah]; **I'd like to stay longer** gostaria de ficar por mais tempo [gooshtaree-a dih feekahr poor mah-ish]; **long time no see!** não te vejo há muito! [te vay-sHoo ah]; **so long!** até à

vista! [a-te a veeshta]

long distance call uma chamada de longa distância [shamahda dih longa dishtans-ya]

long drink um refresco [rifrehshkoo]

loo: where's the loo? onde é a casa de banho? [ond-ye a kahza dih ban-yoo]; **I want to go to the loo** quero ir à casa de banho [kairoo eer ah]

look: that looks good isso tem bom aspecto [eesoo taing bong aspettoo]; **you look tired** você tem um ar cansado [vosseh taing oom ahr kansahdoo]; **I'm just looking, thanks** estou só a ver, obrigado [shtoh saw a vehr]; **you don't look it** (your age) você não parece [vosseh nowng paress]; **look at him** olhe para ele [ol-yih para ehl]; **I'm looking for ...** procuro ... [prookooroo]; **look out!** cuidado! [kweedahdoo]; **can I have a look?** posso ver? [possoo vehr]; **can I have a look around?** posso dar uma vista de olhos? [possoo dahr ooma veeshta d-yol-yoosh]

loose (handle etc) solto [sohltoo]

loose change uns trocos [trokoosh]

lorry um camião [kam-yowng]

lorry driver um camionista [kam-yooneeshta]

lose perder [pirdehr]; **I've lost my ...** perdi o meu ... [pirdee oo meh-oo]; **I'm lost** estou perdido [shtoh pirdeedoo]

lost property office, lost and found a secção de perdidos e achados [seksowng dih pirdeedooz ee ashahdoosh]

lot: a lot, lots muito [mweengtoo]; **not a lot** não muito [nowng]; **a lot of money** muito dinheiro [deen-yay-roo]; **a lot of women** muitas mulheres [mweengtash mool-yairsh]; **quite a lot cooler** muito mais fresco [mah-ish frehshkoo]; **I like it a lot** gosto imenso [goshtoo eemensoo]; **is it a lot further?** é muito mais longe? [e mweengtoo mah-ish lonsH]; **I'll take the (whole) lot** levo tudo [levoo toodoo]

lotion uma loção [loosowng]

loud alto [ahltoo]; **the music is rather loud** a música está bastante alta [moozeeka shtah bashtant ahlta]

lounge a sala de espera [sahla dishpaira]

lousy péssimo [pesseemoo]

love: I love you amo-te [amootih]; **he's**

fallen in love ele está apaixonado *[ehl shtah apah-ishoonahdoo]*; **I love Portugal** adoro Portugal *[adoroo poortoogahl]*; **let's make love** vamos fazer amor *[vamoosh fazehr amohr]*
lovely encantador *[aing-kantadohr]*
low baixo *[bah-ishoo]*
low beam farois médios *[faroish medyoosh]*
LP um LP *[elpeh]*
luck a sorte *[sort]*; **hard luck!** pouca sorte! *[pohka]*; **good luck!** boa sorte! *[boh-a]*; **just my luck!** que sorte a minha! *[kih*

sort a meen-ya]; **it was pure luck** foi pura sorte *[fohy poora]*
lucky: that's lucky! que sorte! *[kih sort]*
lucky charm um amuleto *[amoolehtoo]*
luggage a bagagem *[bagah-sHaing]*
lumbago o lumbago *[loombahgoo]*
lump um inchaço *[eenshahsoo]*
lunch o almoço *[ahlmohsoo]*
lungs os pulmões *[poolmoingsh]*
Luxembourg o Luxemburgo *[looxemboorgoo]*
luxurious luxuoso *[loosh-wohzoo]*
luxury o luxo *[looshoo]*

M

macho machão *[mashowng]*
mad doido *[doh-idoo]*
madam senhora *[sin-yohra]*
Madeira a Madeira *[maday-ra]*
magazine uma revista *[riveeshta]*
magnificent esplêndido *[shplendeedoo]*
maid (*in hotel*) a criada *[kr-yahda]*
maiden name o nome de solteira *[nom dih sohltay-ra]*
mail: is there any mail for me? há correio para mim? *[ah koorray-oo para meeng]*
mailbox um marco de correio *[mahrkoo dih koorray-oo]*
main principal *[preenseepahl]*; **where's the main post office?** onde é a estação de correio principal? *[ond-ye a shtassowng dih koorray-oo]*; **main road** a rua principal *[roo-a preenseepahl]*; (*in the country*) a estrada principal *[shtrahda preenseepahl]*
male chauvinist pig um machista *[masheeshta]*
make fazer *[fazehr]*; (*type*) a marca; **do you make them yourself?** é você que os faz? *[e vosseh k-yoosh fahsh]*; **it's very well made** está muito bem feito *[shtah mweengtoo baing fay-too]*; **what does that make altogether?** quanto é isso tudo? *[kwantoo e eesoo toodoo]*; **I make it only 520 escudos** pelas minhas contas

são só quinhentos e vinte escudos *[pehlash meen-yash kontash sowng saw]*
make up a maquilhagem *[makeel-yah-sHaing]*
make-up remover um desmaquilhante *[disHmakeel-yant]*
man um homem *[omaing]*
manager o gerente *[sHirent]*; **may I see the manager?** pode chamar o gerente? *[pod shamahr]*
manicure a manicura *[maneekoora]*
many muitos *[mweengtoosh]*
map: a map of ... um mapa de ...; **it's not on this map** não vem neste mapa *[nowng vaing nehsht]*
marble o mármore *[mahrmoorih]*
March Março *[mahrsoo]*
margarine a margarina *[margareena]*
marijuana a marijuana *[mareesH-wana]*
mark: there's a mark on it tem uma mancha *[taing ooma mansha]*; **could you mark it on the map for me?** pode marcar-mo no mapa? *[pod markahr-moo noo mahpa]*
market o mercado *[mirkahdoo]*
marmalade uma compota de laranja *[kompota dih laransHa]*
married: are you married? você é casado? *[vosseh e kazahdoo]*; **I'm married** sou casado *[soh kazahdoo]*

mascara o rímel [*reemel*]

mask (*for diving*) os óculos de mergulho [*okooloosh dih mirgool-yoo*]

mass: I'd like to go to mass eu gostava de ir à missa [*eh-oo gooshtahva deer ah meessa*]

massage uma massagem [*massah-sнaing*]

mast o mastro [*mahshtroo*]

masterpiece uma obra-prima [*preema*]

match (*sport*) o jogo [*sнohgoo*]

matches os fósforos [*foshfooroosh*]

material (*cloth*) o tecido [*tisseedoo*]

matter: it doesn't matter não faz mal [*nowng fahsh mahl*]; **what's the matter?** o que se passa? [*oo kih sih pahssa*]

mattress um colchão [*kohlshowng*]

maximum máximo [*mahsseemoo*]

May Maio [*mah-yoo*]

may: may I have another bottle? pode dar-me mais uma garrafa? [*pod dahr-mih mah-iz ooma garrahfa*]; **may I?** posso? [*possoo*]

maybe talvez [*tahlvehz*]; **maybe not** talvez não [*nowng*]

mayonnaise maionese [*mah-yoonehz*]

me: come with me venha comigo [*vehn-ya koomeegoo*]; **it's for me** é para mim [*meeng*]; **it's me** sou eu [*soh eh-oo*]; **me too** eu também [*tambaing*] *see page 112*

meal: that was an excellent meal a refeição estava excelente [*a rifay-sowng shtahva ish-silent*]; **does that include meals?** isso inclui as refeições? [*eesoo eenklooy ash rifay-soingsh*]

mean: what does this word mean? o que significa esta palavra? [*oo kih seegneefeeka eshta palahvra*]; **what does he mean?** o que quer ele dizer? [*oo kih kair ehl deezehr*]

measles o sarampo [*sarampoo*]

measurements as medidas [*mideedash*]

meat a carne [*kahrn*]

mechanic: do you have mechanic here? há algum mecânico aqui? [*ah ahlgoong mikaneekoo akee*]

medicine um remédio [*rimed-yoo*]

medieval medieval [*mid-yivahl*]

Mediterranean o Mediterrâneo [*mideetirraneh-oo*]

medium médio [*med-yoo*]

medium-dry meio seco [*may-oo sehkoo*]

medium-rare (*steak*) meio passado [*may-oo passahdoo*]

medium-sized da tamanho médio [*dih taman-yoo med-yoo*]

medium sweet meio doce [*may-oo dohss*]

meet: pleased to meet you muito prazer em conhecê-lo [*mweengtoo prazehr aing koon-yiseh-loo*]; **where shall we meet?** onde é que nos vamos encontrar? [*ond-ye kih noosh vamooz aing-kontrahr*]; **let's meet up again** vamos encontrar-nos outra vez [*vamooz aing-kontrahrnooz ohtra vehsh*]

meeting uma reunião [*r-yoon-yowng*]

meeting place um local de encontro [*lookahl d-yaing-kontroo*]

melon um melão [*milowng*]

member um membro [*membroo*]; **I'd like to become a member** gostava de me tornar membro [*gooshtahva dih mih toornahr*]

mend: can you mend this? pode consertar isto? [*pod konsirtahr eeshtoo*]

men's room a casa de banho de homens [*kahza dih ban-yoo d-yomaingsh*]

mention: don't mention it não tem de quê [*nowng taing dih keh*]

menu a ementa [*eementa*]

mess uma porcaria [*poorkaree-a*]

message: are there any messages for me? há algum recado para mim? [*ah ahlgoong rikahdoo para meeng*]; **I'd like to leave a message for ...** gostava de deixar um recado para ... [*gooshtahva dih day-shahr oong rikahdoo*]

metal o metal [*mitahl*]

metre, meter um metro [*metroo*] *see page 119*

midday: at midday ao meio-dia [*ow may-oo dee-a*]

middle: in the middle no meio [*noo may-oo*]; **in the middle of the road** no meio da rua [*da roo-a*]; **in the Middle Ages** na Idade Média [*na eedahd med-ya*]

middle-aged de meia-idade [*dih may-a eedahd*]

midnight: at midnight à meia-noite [*ah may-a noh-it*]

might: I might want to stay another 3 days sou capaz de querer ficar mais uns três dias [*soh kapahsh dih kirehr feekahr mah-iz oongsh trehsh dee-ash*]; **you might have warned me!** podia ter-me

avisado! *[poodee-a tehr m-yaveezahdoo]*
migraine uma enxaqueca *[aing-sha-keka]*
mild suave *[swahv]*; (*weather*) ameno *[amehnoo]*
mile uma milha *[meel-ya]*; **that's miles away!** isso fica muito longe! *[eeso feeka mweengtoo lonsн] see page 119*
military militar *[meeleetahr]*
milk o leite *[layt]*
milkshake um batido *[bateedoo]*
millimetre, millimeter um milímetro *[mileemitroo]*
minced meat a carne picada *[kahrn peekahda]*
mind: I don't mind não me importo *[nowng meemportoo]*; (*either will do etc*) tanto faz *[tantoo fahsh]*; **would you mind if I ...?** importa-se que eu ...? *[eemporta-sih k-yeh-oo]*; **never mind** não faz mal *[nowng fahsh mahl]*; **I've changed my mind** mudei de ideias *[mooday deeday-ash]*
mine: it's mine é meu *[e meh-oo] see page 113*
mineral water água mineral *[ahgwa meenirahl]*
minimum mínimo *[meeneemoo]*
mint (*sweet*) uma pastilha de mentol *[pashteel-ya]*
minus menos *[mehnoosh]*; **minus 3 degrees** três graus negativos *[trehsh grahoosh nigateevoosh]*
minute um minuto *[meenootoo]*; **in a minute** dentro de um momento *[dentroo doong moomentoo]*; **just a minute** só um momento *[saw oong]*
mirror um espelho *[shpehl-yoo]*
Miss a menina *[mineena]*
miss: I miss you tenho saudades tuas *[taing-nyoo sowdahdish too-ash]*; **there is a ... missing** falta um ...; **we missed the bus** perdemos o autocarro *[pirdehmooz oo owtookahrroo]*; **I'm going to miss the boat!** vou perder o barco! *[voh pirdehr oo bahrkoo]*
mist a névoa *[nevwa]*
mistake um erro *[ehrroo]*; **I think there's a mistake here** julgo que há um erro aqui *[sнoolgoo k-yah oong ehrroo akee]*
misunderstanding um mal-entendido *[mahl-aing-tendeedoo]*
mixture uma mistura *[meeshtoora]*

mix-up: there's been some sort of mix-up with ... houve uma certa confusão com ... *[ohv ooma sehrta konfoozowng kong]*
modern moderno *[moodairnoo]*; **a modern art gallery** uma galeria de arte moderna *[galiree-a d-yahrt moodairna]*
moisturizer um creme hidratante *[krem eedratant]*
moment um momento *[moomentoo]*; **I won't be a moment** eu não demoro nada *[eh-oo nowng dimoroo nahda]*
monastery um mosteiro *[mooshtay-roo]*
Monday segunda-feira *[sigoonda fay-ra]*
money o dinheiro *[deen-yay-roo]*; **I don't have any money** não tenho dinheiro nenhum *[nowng taing-nyoo deen-yay-roo nin-yoong]*; **do you take English/American money?** aceita dinheiro inglês/americano? *[assay-ta deen-yay-roo eenglehsh/amireekanoo]*
month um mês *[mehsh]*
monument um monumento *[moo-noomentoo]*; (*statue*) uma estátua *[shtahtwa]*
moon a lua *[loo-a]*
moorings o ancoradouro *[ankoora-dohroo]*
moped uma motorizada *[mootoo-reezahda]*
more mais *[mah-ish]*; **may I have some more?** pode dar-me mais? *[pod dahrmih]*; **more water, please** mais água, por favor *[mah-iz ahgwa]*; **no more** mais nada *[mah-ish nahda]*; **more expensive** mais caro *[mah-ish kahroo]*; **more than 50** mais de 50 *[mah-ish dih]*; **more than that** mais do que isso *[mah-ish doo kih eesoo]*; **a lot more** muito mais *[mweengtoo]*; **not any more** já não *[sнah nowng]*; **I don't stay there any more** já não estou lá *[sнah nowng shtoh lah]*
morning a manhã *[man-yang]*; **good morning** bom dia *[bong dee-a]*; **this morning** esta manhã *[eshta]*; **in the morning** de manhã *[dih]*
mosquito um mosquito *[mooshkeetoo]*
most: I like this one most gosto mais deste *[goshtoo mah-ish dehsht]*; **most of the time/the hotels** a maior parte do tempo/dos hotéis *[a ma-yor pahrt]*
mother: my mother a minha mãe *[meen-*

ya maing]
motif (*patterns*) um motivo *[mooteevoo]*
motor o motor *[mootohr]*
motorbike uma mota
motorboat um barco a motor *[bahrkoo a mootohr]*
motorist um motorista *[mootooreeshta]*
motorway a autoestrada *[owtoo-shtrahda]*
motor yacht um iate a motor *[yaht a mootohr]*
mountain a montanha *[montan-ya]*; **up in the mountains** lá em cima nas montanhas *[lah aing seema nash montan-yash]*; **a mountain village** uma vila de montanha *[veela]*
mouse um rato *[rahtoo]*
moustache um bigode *[beegod]*
mouth a boca *[bohka]*
move: he's moved to another hotel ele mudou-se para outro hotel *[ehl moodoh-sih para ohtroo ohtel]*; **could you move your car?** podia mudar o seu carro? *[poodee-a moodahr oo seh-oo kahrroo]*
movie um filme *[feelm]*; **let's go to the movies** vamos ao cinema *[vamooz ow seenehma]*
movie camera uma máquina de filmar *[mahkeena dih feelmahr]*
movie theater um cinema *[seenehma]*
moving: a very moving tune uma música muito comovente *[moozeeka mweengtoo koomoovent]*
Mr Senhor (Sr.) *[sin-yohr]*
Mrs Senhora (Sra.) *[sin-yohra]*
Ms *no equivalent in Portuguese*
much muito *[mweengtoo]*; **much better** muito melhor *[mil-yor]*; **much cooler**

muito mais fresco *[mah-ish frehshkoo]*; **not much** não muito *[nowng]*; **not so much** não tanto *[nowng tantoo]*
mud a lama
muffler (*on car*) a panela de escape *[dishkahp]*
mug: I've been mugged fui assaltado *[fwee assahltahdoo]*
muggy abafado *[abafahdoo]*
mule uma mula *[moola]*
mumps a papeira *[papay-ra]*
muscle um músculo *[mooshkooloo]*
murals as pinturas murais *[peentoorash moorah-ish]*
museum o museu *[moozeh-oo]*
mushrooms os cogumelos *[koogoomeh-loosh]*
music a música *[moozeeka]*; **guitar music** a música de viola *[v-yola]*; **do you have the sheet music for ...?** tem a pauta de música para ...? *[taing a powta dih moozeeka para]*
musician um músico *[moozeekoo]*
mussels uns mexilhões *[misheel-yoingsh]*
must: I must ... tenho que ... *[taing-nyoo kih]*; **I mustn't drink ...** não devo beber ... *[nowng dehvoo bibehr]*; **you mustn't forget** você não pode esquecer *[vosseh nowng pod shkessehr]*
mustache um bigode *[beegod]*
mustard a mostarda *[mooshtahrda]*
my: my husband o meu marido *[oo meh-oo]*; **my wife** a minha mulher *[a meen-ya]*; **my children** os meus filhos *[oosh meh-oosh]*; **my suitcases** as minhas malas *[ash meen-yash] see page 110*
myself: I'll do it myself eu faço isso por mim *[eh-oo fahsso eesoo poor meeng]*

N

nail (*finger*) a unha *[oon-ya]*; (*wood*) um prego *[prehgoo]*
nail clippers alicate de unhas *[aleekaht d-yoon-yash]*
nailfile uma lima de unhas *[leema*

d-yoon-yash]
nail polish o verniz de unhas *[virneesh d-yoon-yash]*
nail polish remover a acetona *[asitona]*
nail scissors uma tesoura de unhas *[ti-*

zohra d-yoon-yash]
naked nu [noo]; nua [noo-a]
name o nome [nom]; **what's your name?**
como se chama? [kohmoo sih shama];
what's its name? como se chama?; **my
name is ...** o meu nome é ... [meh-oo
nom-ye]
nap: he's having a nap está a fazer uma
sesta [shtah fazehr ooma seshta]
napkin um guardanapo [gwahrda-
nahpoo]
nappy uma fralda [frahlda]
narrow estreito [shtray-too]
nasty (person, weather, taste) mau [mah-oo];
(cut) grave [grahv]
national nacional [nass-yoonahl]
nationality a nacionalidade [nas-yoona-
lidahd]
natural natural [natoorahl]
naturally naturalmente [natoorahlment]
nature a natureza [natoorehza]
naturist um naturista [natooreeshta]
nausea as náuseas [nowzeh-ash]
near: is it near here? é perto daqui?
[pairtoo dakee]; **near the window** perto
da janela [da sнanela]; **do you go near
...?** passa perto de ...? [pahssa pairtoo
dih]; **where is the nearest ...?** onde fica o
... mais próximo? [ond feeka oo ... mah-
ish prosseemoo]
nearby perto [pairtoo]
nearly quase [kwahz]
nearside (wheel etc) do lado direito [doo
lahdoo deeray-too]
necessary necessário [nississahr-yoo]; **is
it necessary to ...?** é necessário ...?; **it's
not necessary** não é necessário [nowng]
neck o pescoço [pishkohsoo]
necklace um colar [koolahr]
necktie uma gravata
need: I need a ... eu preciso de ... [eh-oo
priseezoo dih]; **it needs more salt** precisa de mais sal [priseeza dih mah-ish];
do I need to ...? preciso de ...?; **there's
no need** não há necessidade [nowng ah
nisiseedahd]; **there's no need to shout!**
não é preciso gritar! [nowng e priseezoo
greetahr]
needle uma agulha [agool-ya]
negative (film) o negativo [nigateevoo]
neighbo(u)r o vizinho [vizeen-yoo]
neighbo(u)rhood a vizinhança [vizeen-
yansa]

neither: neither of us nenhum de nós
[nin-yoong dih nosh]; **neither one (of
them)** nenhum deles [dehlsh]; **neither ...
nor ...** nem ... nem ... [naing]; **neither
do I** eu também não [eh-oo tambaing
nowng]
nephew: my nephew o meu sobrinho [oo
meh-oo soobreen-yoo]
nervous nervoso [nirvohzoo]
net (fishing, tennis) a rede [rehd]; **£100 net**
£100 libras sem encargos [saing aing-
kahrgoosh]
nettle as urtigas [oorteegash]
neurotic neurótico [neh-ooroteekoo]
neutral (gear) o ponto morto [pontoo
mohrtoo]
never nunca [noonka]
new novo [nohvoo]
news (TV etc) as notícias [nootees-yash];
is there any news? há novidades? [ah
nooveedahdish]
newspaper um jornal [sнoornahl]; **do
you have any English newspapers?**
tem jornais ingleses? [taing sнoornah-iz
eenglehzish]
newsstand um vendedor de jornais
[vendidohr dih sнoornah-ish]
New Year Ano Novo [anoo nohvoo];
Happy New Year! Feliz Ano Novo! [fi-
leez]
New Year's Eve a véspera do dia de Ano
Novo [veshpira doo dee-a dih anoo
nohvoo]
New York Nova Iorque [nova york]
New Zealand a Nova Zelândia [nova
ziland-ya]
New Zealander Neo-Zelandês [ne-o zi-
landehsh]
next próximo [prosseemoo]; **next to the
post office** próximo dos correios [doosh
koorray-oosh]; **the one next to that** o
próximo; **it's at the next corner** é na
próxima esquina [na prosseema
shkeena]; **next week/next Monday** a
próxima semana/a próxima segunda-
feira [simana/sigoonda fay-ra]
nextdoor na casa ao lado [kahza ow
lahdoo]
next of kin o parente mais próximo [pa-
rent mah-ish proseemoo]
nice agradável [agradahvel]; **that's very
nice of you** é muito simpático da sua
parte [mweengtoo seempahteekoo da

soo-a *pahrt]*; **a nice cold drink** uma
bebida fresca *[bibeeda frehshka]*
nickname a alcunha *[ahlkoon-ya]*
niece: my niece a minha sobrinha *[meen-
ya soobreen-ya]*
night a noite *[noh-it]*; **for one night** por
uma noite *[poor ooma]*; **for three nights**
por três noites *[poor trehsh]*; **good night**
boa noite *[boh-a]*; **at night** à noite *[ah]*
nightcap (*drink*) uma bebida antes de ir
para a cama *[ooma bibeeda antish deer
para kama]*
nightclub uma boite *[bwaht]*
nightdress a camisa de dormir *[kameeza
dih doormeer]*
night flight o voo da noite *[voh-oo dih
noh-it]*
nightie a camisa de noite *[kameeza dih
noh-it]*
night-life a vida nocturna *[veeda nok-
toorna]*
nightmare um pesadelo *[pizadeloo]*
night porter o porteiro da noite *[poortay-
roo da noh-it]*
nit (*bug*) uma lêndea *[lendeh-a]*
no não *[nowng]*; **I've no money** não tenho
dinheiro *[nowng taing-yoo deen-yay-
roo]*; **there's no more** não há mais
[nowng ah mah-ish]; **no more than ...**
não mais de ... *[nowng mah-ish dih]*; **oh
no!** (*upset*) oh não!
nobody ninguém *[neeng-gaing]*
noise o barulho *[barool-yoo]*
noisy barulhento *[barool-yentoo]*; **it's too
noisy** é barulhento demais *[dimah-ish]*
non-alcoholic não alcoólico *[nowng
ahlkwoleekoo]*
none nenhum *[nin-yoong]*; **none of them**
nenhum deles *[dehlsh]*
nonsense um disparate *[dishparaht]*
non-smoking para não fumadores
[nowng foomadohrish]
non-stop (*drive etc*) directo *[deerettoo]*
no-one ninguém *[neeng-gaing]*
nor: nor do I eu também não *[eh-oo

tambaing nowng]*
normal normal *[normahl]*
north o norte *[nort]*; **to the north** ao norte
[ow]
northeast o nordeste *[noordehsht]*; **to the
northeast** ao nordeste *[ow]*
Northern Ireland a Irlanda do Norte
[eerlanda doo nort]
northwest o noroeste *[noorwesht]*; **to the
northwest** ao noroeste *[ow]*
Norway a Noruega *[noorwehga]*
nose o nariz *[nareesh]*
nosebleed uma hemorragia nasal
[eemoorrahsн-ya nazahl]
not não *[nowng]*; **I don't smoke** não fumo
[nowng foomoo]; **he didn't say anything** ele não disse nada *[ehl nowng dees
nahda]*; **it's not important** não tem
importância *[nowng taing eempoortans-
ya]*; **not that one** esse não *[ehss nowng]*;
not for me para mim não *[para meeng
nowng]* *see page 116*
note (*bank note*) uma nota
notebook o bloco de apontamentos
[blohkoo dapontamentoosh]
nothing nada *[nahda]*
November Novembro *[noovembroo]*
now agora; **not now** agora não *[nowng]*
nowhere em parte nenhuma *[aing part
nin-yooma]*
nudist um nudista *[noodeeshta]*
nudist beach uma praia de nudistas
[pry-a dih noodeeshtash]
nuisance: he's being a nuisance está a
incomodar *[shtah eenkoomoodahr]*
numb entorpecido *[entoorpiseedoo]*
number o número *[noomiroo]*; **what
number?** que número? *[kih]*
number plate a chapa da matrícula
[shahpa da matreekoola]
nurse a enfermeira *[aingfirmay-ra]*
nursery o infantário *[eenfantahr-yoo]*
nut uma noz *[nosh]*; (*for a bolt*) uma porca
nutter: he's a nutter é maluco *[maloo-
koo]*

O

oar um remo *[rehmoo]*
obligatory obrigatório *[ohbreegator-yoo]*
oblige: much obliged muito obrigado *[mweengtoo ohbrigahdoo]*
obnoxious detestável *[ditishtahvel]*
obvious: that's obvious isso é óbvio *[eesoo e obv-yoo]*
occasionally de vez em quando *[dih vehz aing kwandoo]*
o'clock *see page 118*
October Outubro *[ohtoobroo]*
octopus o polvo *[pohlvoo]*
odd *(number)* ímpar *[eempahr]*; *(strange)* estranho *[shtran-yoo]*
odometer o conta-quilómetros *[konta-keelomitroosh]*
of de *[dih]*; **the name of the hotel** o nome do hotel *[oo nom doo ohtel]*; **have one of mine** tome um dos meus *[tom-yoong doosh meh-oosh] see page 108*
off: it just broke off partiu-se *[partee-oosih]*; **20% off** menos 20% *[meh-noosh]*; **the lights were off** as luzes estavam desligadas *[ash looziz ishtahvowng disнleegahdash]*; **just off the main road** mesmo ao lado da estrada principal *[mehsнmoo ow lahdoo da shtrahda preenseepahl]*
offend: don't be offended não fique ofendido *[nowng feek ohfendeedoo]*
office o escritório *[shkreetor-yoo]*
officer *(said to policeman)* Senhor Guarda *[sin-yohr gwahrda]*
official um alto funcionário *[ahltoo foons-yoonahr-yoo]*; **is that official?** isso é oficial? *[eesoo e ohfees-yahl]*
off-season fora de estação *[fora dishtassowng]*
off-side *(wheel etc)* do lado esquerdo *[doo lahdoo shkehrdoo]*
often muitas vezes *[mweengtash vehzish]*; **not often** não muitas vezes *[nowng]*

oil *(for car, salad)* óleo *[oleh-oo]*; **it's losing oil** está a perder óleo *[shtah pirdehr]*; **will you change the oil?** pode mudar o óleo? *[pod moodahr]*; **the oil light's flashing** a luz do óleo está a piscar *[a loosh doo oleh-oo shtah peeshkahr]*
oil painting uma pintura a óleo *[peen-toora a oleh-oo]*
oil pressure a pressão do óleo *[prissowng doo oleh-oo]*
ointment uma pomada *[poomahda]*
OK ok; **are you OK?** você está bem? *[vosseh shtah baing]*; **that's OK thanks** está bem obrigado *[ohbreegahdoo]*; **that's OK by me** por mim está bem *[poor meeng]*
old velho *[vehl-yoo]*; **how old are you?** que idade tem? *[kih eedahd taing]*
old-age pensioner um reformado de terceira idade *[rifoormahdoo dih tirsay-ra eedahd]*
old-fashioned antiquado *[antikwahdoo]*
old town a cidade antiga *[seedahd an-teega]*
olive uma azeitona *[azay-tona]*
olive oil azeite *[azayt]*
omelet(te) uma omeleta *[ohmleta]*
on: on the beach na praia *[na prah-ya]*; **on Friday** na sexta-feira *[sehshta fay-ra]*; **on television** na televisão *[tilivee-zowng]*; **I don't have it on me** não o tenho comigo *[nowng oo taing-nyoo koomeegoo]*; **this drink's on me** esta bebida sou eu que pago *[eshta bibeeda soh eh-oo kih pahgoo]*; **a book on Lisbon** um livro sobre Lisboa *[leevroo sohbrih lisнboh-a]*; **the warning light comes on** a luz de aviso acende *[a loosh d-yaveezoo asend]*; **the light was on** a luz estava acesa *[a looz ishtahva asehza]*; **what's on in town?** o que é que há na cidade? *[oo k-ye k-yah na seedahd]*; **it's just not on!** *(not acceptable)* de maneira

nenhuma! *[dih man**ay**-ra nin-y**oo**ma]*
once uma vez *[**oo**ma vehsh]*; **at once** imediatamente *[eemid-yahtam**e**nt]*
one um, uma *[oong, **oo**ma]*; **that one** aquele *[ak**e**hl]*; **the green one** o verde *[oo vehrd]*; **the one with the black dress on** a do vestido preto *[a doo visht**ee**doo pr**e**htoo]*; **the one in the blue shirt** o da camisa azul *[oo da kam**ee**za az**oo**l]*
onion uma cebola *[sib**o**la]*
only: only one só um/uma *[saw oong/**oo**ma]*; **only once** só uma vez *[**oo**ma vehsh]*; **it's only 9 o'clock** ainda só são 9 horas *[a-**ee**nda saw sowng]*; **I've only just arrived** só cheguei mesmo ag**o**ra *[sawshig**ay** m**e**hsнmoo]*
open aberto *[ab**ai**rtoo]*; **when do you open?** quando abre? *[kwandoo **ah**brih]*; **in the open** ao ar livre *[ow ahr l**ee**vrih]*; **it won't open** não abre *[nowng **ah**brih]*
opening times horas de abertura *[**o**rash d-yabirt**oo**ra]*
open top *(car)* descapotável *[dishkapoo-t**ah**vel]*
opera a ópera *[**o**pira]*
operation *(med)* uma operação *[ohpi-rass**ow**ng]*
operator *(tel)* a telefonista *[tilifoon**ee**shta]*
opportunity uma oportunidade *[ohpoor-toon**ee**dahd]*
opposite: opposite the church em frente à igreja *[aing frent ah eegr**ay**-sнa]*; **it's directly opposite** é directamente em frente *[deeretam**e**nt]*
oppressive opressivo *[ohpris**ee**voo]*
optional opcional *[ops-yoon**ah**l]*
or ou *[oh]*
orange *(fruit)* uma laranja *[lar**a**nsнa]*; *(colour)* cor de laranja *[kohr dih]*
orange juice o sumo de laranja *[s**oo**moo dih lar**a**nsнa]*; *(fizzy)* uma laranjada *[la-ransн**ah**da]*
orchestra a orquestra *[ohrk**e**shtra]*
order: could we order now? podemos pedir ag**o**ra? *[pood**e**hmoosh pid**ee**r]*; **I've already ordered** já pedi *[sнah pi-d**ee**]*; **I didn't order that** eu não pedi aquilo *[**e**h-oo nowng pid**ee** ak**ee**loo]*; **it's out of order** *(lift etc)* está estragado *[shtah shtrag**ah**doo]*
ordinary vulgar *[voolg**ah**r]*
organization a organização *[ohrganee-zass**ow**ng]*

organize organizar *[ohrganeez**ah**r]*; **could you organize it?** podia arranjá-lo? *[pood**ee**-a arransн-**ah**loo]*
original original *[ohreesнeen**ah**l]*; **is it an original?** é um original? *[e oong]*
ornament o ornamento *[ohrnam**e**ntoo]*
ostentatious faustoso *[fowsht**oh**zoo]*
other: the other waiter o outro criado de mesa *[oo **oh**troo kr-y**ah**doo dih m**e**hza]*; **the other one** o outro; **do you have any others?** tem mais? *[taing m**ah**-ish]*; *(different ones)* tem outros? *[**oh**troosh]*; **some other time, thanks** noutra altura, obrigado *[noh**t**rahlt**oo**ra]*
otherwise doutro modo *[d**oh**troo m**o**doo]*
ouch! au! *[ow]*
ought: he ought to be here soon deve estar a chegar *[dev shtahr a shig**ah**r]*
ounce *see page 120*
our o nosso *[n**o**ssoo]* *see page 110*
ours nosso *see page 113*
out: he's out *(of building etc)* saiu *[sa-**ee**-oo]*; **get out!** rua! *[r**oo**-a]*; **I'm out of money** já não tenho dinheiro *[sнah nowng t**a**ing-nyoo deen-y**ay**-roo]*; **a few kilometres out of town** uns quilómetros a seguir à cidade *[oongsh keel**o**mitrooz a sig-**ee**r a seed**ah**d]*
outboard *(motor)* um motor fora de bordo *[moot**o**hr f**o**ra dih b**o**rdoo]*
outdoors fora de casa *[f**o**ra dih k**ah**za]*
outlet *(elec)* uma tomada *[toom**ah**da]*
outside: can we sit outside? podemos sentar-nos lá fora? *[pood**e**hmoosh sent**ah**r-noosh lah f**o**ra]*
outskirts: on the outskirts of ... nos arredores de ... *[nooz arrid**o**hrish dih]*
oven o forno *[f**oh**rnoo]*
over: over here aqui *[ak**ee**]*; **over there** ali *[al**ee**]*; **over 100** mais de 100 *[m**ah**-ish dih]*; **I'm burnt all over** estou todo queimado *[shtoh t**oh**doo kay-m**ah**doo]*; **the holiday's over** as férias acabaram *[ash f**ai**r-yaz akab**ah**rowng]*
overcharge: you've overcharged me você vendeu-me mais caro *[voss**e**h vend**e**h-oomih m**ah**-ish k**ah**roo]*
overcoat o sobretudo *[sohbrih-t**oo**doo]*
overcooked esturrado *[shtoorr**ah**doo]*
overdrive a quinta mudança *[k**ee**nta mood**a**nsa]*
overexposed *(phot)* sobreexposta *[soh-brishp**o**shta]*

overheat: it's overheating (*car*) está a aquecer demais [*shtah ahkessehr dimah-ish*]

overland por terra [*poor tairra*]

overlook: overlooking the sea virado para o mar [*veerahdoo para oo*]

overnight (*travel*) de noite [*dih noh-it*]

oversleep: I overslept acordei tarde [*akoor-day tahrd*]

overtake ultrapassar [*ooltrapassahr*]

overweight (*person*) obeso [*ohbehzoo*]

owe: how much do I owe you? quanto lhe devo? [*kwantoo l-yih dehvoo*]

own: my own ... o meu próprio ... [*oo meh-oo propr-yoo*]; **are you on your own?** está sozinho? [*shtah sawzeen-yoo*]; **I'm on my own here** estou sozinho aqui [*shtoh*]

owner o dono [*dohnoo*]

oyster uma ostra [*oshtra*]

P

pack: a pack of cigarettes um maço de cigarros [*mahsoo dih*]; **I'll go and pack** vou fazer a mala [*voh fazehr a mahla*]

package um embrulho [*embrool-yoo*]

package holiday as férias em excursão organizada [*fair-yaz aing shkoorsowng ohrganeezahda*]

package tour uma excursão organizada [*shkoorsowng ohrganeezahda*]

packed lunch um almoço embalado [*ahlmohsoo embalahdoo*]

packed out: the place was packed out estava a abarrotar [*shtahvah abarrootahr*]

packet (*parcel*) a encomenda [*aing-koomenda*]; **a packet of cigarettes** um maço de cigarros [*mahsoo dih*]

paddle o remo [*rehmoo*]

padlock o cadeado [*kad-yahdoo*]

page (*of book*) a página [*pasнeena*]; **could you page him?** pode chamá-lo? [*pod shamahloo*]

pain uma dor [*dohr*]; **I have a pain here** tenho aqui uma dor [*taing-nyoo akee*]

painful doloroso [*dooloorohzoo*]

painkillers os analgésicos [*anahlsнezee-koosh*]

paint a tinta [*teenta*]; **I'm going to do some painting** vou pintar um bocado [*voh peentahr oong bookahdoo*]

paintbrush o pincel [*peensel*]

painting uma pintura [*peentoora*]

pair: a pair of ... um par de ...

pajamas um pijama [*peesнama*]

Pakistan o Paquistão [*pakeeshtowng*]

Pakistani paquistanês [*pakeeshtanehsh*]

pal o companheiro [*kompan-yay-roo*]

palace o palácio [*palahs-yoo*]

pale pálido [*pahleedoo*]; **pale blue** azul claro [*klahroo*]

palm tree uma palmeira [*pahlmay-ra*]

palpitations as palpitações [*pahlpee-tassoingsh*]

pancake um crepe [*krep*]

panic: don't panic não entre em pânico [*nowng entr-aing paneekoo*]

panties as cuecas [*kwekash*]

pants (*trousers*) as calças [*kahlsash*]; (*underpants*) umas cuecas [*oomash kwe-kash*]

panty girdle uma cinta calça [*seenta kahlssa*]

pantyhose uns collants [*oonsh kollansh*]

paper o papel [*pa-pel*]; (*newspaper*) o jornal [*sнoornahl*]; **a piece of paper** um bocado de papel [*bookahdoo dih*]

paper handkerchiefs lenços de papel [*lensoosh dih pa-pel*]

paraffin o petróleo [*pitrol-yoo*]

paragliding o planar em pára-quedas [*planahr aing pahra-kedash*]

parallel: parallel to ... paralelo a ... [*paralehloo*]

parasol (*over table*) o chapéu de sol [*sha-pe-oo dih sol*]

parcel um embrulho [*embrool-yoo*]

pardon (me)? (*didn't understand*) desculpe? [*dishk**oo**lp*]

parents: my parents os meus pais [*oosh meh-oosh p**ah**-ish*]

parents-in-law os sogros [*s**o**groosh*]

park o parque [*park*]; **where can I park?** onde posso estacionar? [*ond p**o**ssoo shtas-yoon**ah**r*]; **there's nowhere to park** não há sítio para estacionar [*nowng ah s**ee**t-yoo*]

parka um anoraque [*anoor**ah**k*]

parking lights as luzes de presença [*l**oo**zish dih priz**e**nsa*]

parking lot o estacionamento [*shtas-yoonam**e**ntoo*]

parking place: there's a parking place! um lugar vazio! [*loog**ah**r vaz**ee**-oo*]

part uma parte [*pahrt*]

partner o companheiro [*kompan-y**ay**roo*]

party (*group*) o grupo [*gr**oo**poo*]; (*celebration*) uma festa [*f**e**shta*]; **let's have a party** vamos fazer uma festa [*v**a**moosh faz**e**hr*]

pass (*mountain*) um desfiladeiro [*dishfeelad**ay**-roo*]; (*overtake*) ultrapassar [*ooltrapass**ah**r*]; **he passed out** desmaiou [*disнma-y**oh**]; **he made a pass at me** atirou-se a mim [*ateer**oh**-sih a meeng*]

passable (*road*) transitável [*tranzeet**ah**vel*]

passenger um passageiro [*passasн**ay**roo*]

passport o passaporte [*passap**o**rt*]

past: in the past no passado [*noo pass**ah**doo*]; **just past the bank** logo a seguir ao banco [*l**o**goo a sig-**ee**r*] *see* **time** *page 118*

pastry a massa folhada [*m**ah**ssa fool-y**ah**da*]; (*cake*) um bolo [*b**oh**loo*]

patch: could you put a patch on this? podia pôr um remendo nisto? [*pood**ee**-a pohr oong rim**e**ndoo n**ee**shtoo*]

pâté (*food*) o paté [*pat**eh**]

path um caminho [*kam**ee**n-yoo*]

patient: be patient tenha paciência [*t**a**ing-nya pass-y**e**nsa*]

patio o pátio [*p**ah**t-yoo*]

pattern (*on cloth etc*) o desenho [*diz**eh**n-yoo*]; **a dress pattern** um molde de um vestido [*mold doong visht**ee**doo*]

paunch a barriga [*barr**ee**ga*]

pavement (*sidewalk*) o passeio [*pass**ay**oo*]

pay pagar; **can I pay, please?** por favor, queria pagar [*kir**ee**-a*]; **it's already paid for** já está pago [*sнah shtah p**ah**goo*]; **I'll pay for this** eu pago isto [*eh-oo p**ah**goo **ee**shtoo*]

pay phone uma cabine telefónica [*kab**ee**n tilif**o**neeka*]

peace and quiet paz e sossego [*pahz ee soos**eh**goo*]

peach um pêssego [*p**eh**ssigoo*]

peanuts os amendoins [*amend-w**ee**ngsh*]

pear uma pêra [*p**eh**ra*]

pearl a pérola [*p**ai**roola*]

peas as ervilhas [*eerv**ee**l-yash*]

peculiar (*taste etc*) estranho [*shtr**a**n-yoo*]

pedal o pedal [*pid**ah**l*]

pedalo uma gaivota [*gah-iv**o**ta*]

pedestrian um peão [*p-y**ow**ng*]

pedestrian crossing uma passadeira para peões [*passad**ay**-ra para p-y**o**ingsh*]

pedestrian precinct uma zona para peões [*p-y**o**ingsh*]

pee: I need to go for a pee preciso de fazer chichi [*pris**ee**zoo dih faz**e**hr sheesh**ee**]

peeping Tom o bisbilhoteiro [*bisнbeel-yoot**ay**-roo*]

peg (*for washing*) a mola; (*for tent*) a cavilha [*kav**ee**l-ya*]

pen uma caneta [*kan**e**hta*]; **do you have a pen?** tem uma caneta? [*taing*]

pencil um lápis [*l**ah**psh*]

pen friend um correspondente [*koorrishpond**e**nt*]; **shall we be penfriends?** quer corresponder-se comigo? [*kair koorrishpond**e**hr-sih koom**ee**goo*]

penicillin a penicilina [*pinisee**lee**na*]

penknife um canivete [*kanee**ve**ht*]

pen pal um correspondente [*koorrishpond**e**nt*]

pensioner um reformado [*rifoorm**ah**doo*]

people a gente [*sнent*]; **lots of people** muita gente [*mw**ee**ngta*]; **Portuguese people** os portugueses [*poortoog**eh**zish*]

pepper (*spice*) a pimenta [*peem**e**nta*]; **green pepper** o pimento verde [*peem**e**ntoo vehrd*]; **red pepper** o pimento encarnado [*enkarn**ah**doo*]

peppermint (*sweet*) a hortelã-pimenta [*ohrtil**a**ng peem**e**nta*]

per: per night por noite [*poor n**o**h-it*]; **how much per hour?** quanto é por hora?

[kwantoo e poor]
per cent por cento *[poor sentoo]*
perfect perfeito *[pirfay-too]*
perfume o perfume *[pirfoom]*
perhaps talvez *[tahlvehsh]*
period *(of time)* o período *[piree-oodoo]*; *(woman's)* o período
perm uma permanente *[pirmanent]*
permit uma licença *[leesensa]*
person uma pessoa *[pissoh-a]*
pessimistic pessimista *[pisseemeeshta]*
petrol a gasolina *[gazooleena]*
petrol can uma lata de gasolina *[gazooleena]*
petrol station uma bomba de gasolina *[bom-ba dih gazooleena]*
petrol tank o depósito de gasolina *[dipozeetoo dih gazooleena]*
pharmacy a farmácia *[farmahs-ya]*
phone *see* **telephone**
photogenic fotogénico *[footoosHeneekoo]*
photograph uma fotografia *[footoografee-a]*; **would you take a photograph of us?** quer tirar-nos uma fotografia? *[kair teerahr-nooz]*
photographer o fotógrafo *[footografoo]*
phrase: a useful phrase uma expressão útil *[shprissowng ooteel]*
phrasebook um livro de expressões *[leevroo dishprissoingsh]*
pianist o pianista *[p-yaneeshta]*
piano um piano *[p-yanoo]*
pickpocket um carteirista *[kartayreeshta]*
pick up: when can I pick them up? quando posso vir buscá-los? *[kwandoo possoo veer booshkah-loosh]*; **will you come and pick me up?** vem buscar-me? *[vaing booshkahr-mih]*
picnic o piquenique *[peekineek]*
picture *(drawing, painting)* pintura *[peentoora]*; *(photograph)* fotografia *[footoografee-a]*
pie *(meat)* um pastel *[pashtel]*; *(fruit)* uma torta *[torta]*
piece um pedaço *[pidahsoo]*; **a piece of ...** um bocado de ... *[bookahdoo dih]*
pig um porco *[pohrkoo]*
pigeon um pombo *[pomboo]*
piles *(med)* as hemorroidas *[eemoorroydash]*
pile-up um acidente múltiplo *[asseedent*

moolteeploo]
pill uma pílula *[peeloola]*; **I'm on the pill** estou a tomar a pílula *[shtoh a toomahr a peeloola]*
pillarbox o marco postal *[mahrkoo pooshtahl]*
pillow uma almofada *[ahlmoofahda]*
pillow case a fronha da almofada *[frohn-ya dahlmoofahda]*
pin um alfinete *[ahlfeeneht]*
pineapple o ananás *[ananahsh]*
pineapple juice um sumo de ananás *[soomoo d-yananahsh]*
pink rosa *[roza]*
pint *see page 121*
pipe o cano *[kanoo]*; *(smoking)* o cachimbo *[kasheemboo]*
pipe cleaner um desentupidor de cachimbo *[dizaingtoopeedohr dih kasheemboo]*
pipe tobacco o tabaco de cachimbo *[tabahkoo dih kasheemboo]*
pity: it's a pity é uma pena *[pehna]*
pizza uma pizza
place um lugar *[loogahr]*; **is this place taken?** este lugar está ocupado? *[ehsht loogahr shtah ohkoopahdoo]*; **would you keep my place for me?** guarda-me o lugar? *[gwahrdam-yoo]*; **at my place** em minha casa *[aing meen-ya kahza]*
place mat um individual *[eendeeveedwahl]*
plain *(food)* simples *[seemplish]*; *(not patterned)* liso *[leezoo]*
plane um avião *[av-yowng]*
plant uma planta
plaster cast um molde de gesso *[mold dih sHessoo]*
plastic plástico *[plahshteekoo]*
plastic bag o saco de plástico *[sahkoo dih plahshteekoo]*
plate um prato *[prahtoo]*
platform o cais *[kah-ish]*; **which platform, please?** qual é o cais, por favor? *[kwahl]*
play jogar *[sHoogahr]*; *(in theatre)* a peça de teatro *[pessa dih t-yahtroo]*
playboy o playboy
playground o pátio de recreio *[paht-yoo dih rikray-oo]*
pleasant agradável *[agradahvel]*
please: could you please ...? por favor, pode ...? *[poor favohr pod]*; **yes please**

sim por favor *[seeng]*

plenty: plenty of ... muito ... *[mweeng-too]*; **that's plenty, thanks** chega, obrigado *[shehga]*

pleurisy a pleurisia *[pleh-ooreezee-a]*

pliers um alicate *[aleekaht]*

plonk o vinho *[veen-yoo]*

plug (*elec*) uma tomada *[toomahda]*; (*car*) uma vela; (*bathroom*) a tampa do ralo *[doo rahloo]*

plughole o ralo *[rahloo]*

plum uma ameixa *[amay-sha]*

plumber o canalizador *[kanaleezadohr]*

plus mais *[mah-ish]*

p.m. da tarde *[tahrd]*

pneumonia a pneumonia *[pneh-oomoonee-a]*

poached egg um ovo escalfado *[ohvoo shkahlfahdoo]*

pocket o bolso *[oo bohlsoo]*; **in my pocket** no meu bolso *[noo meh-oo]*

pocketbook (*woman's*) uma mala

pocketknife um canivete *[kaneeveht]*

point: could you point to it? pode indicar-mo? *[pod eendeekahr-moo]*; **four point six** quatro vírgula seis *[kwahtroo veergoola saysh]*; **there's no point** não vale a pena *[nowng vahl a pehna]*

points (*car*) os platinados *[plateenah-doosh]*

poisonous venenoso *[vininohzoo]*

police a polícia *[poolees-ya]*; **call the police!** chamem a polícia! *[shamaing]*

policeman um polícia *[oong poolees-ya]*

police station o Posto da Polícia *[pohshtoo da poolees-ya]*

polish a graxa *[grahsha]*; **will you polish my shoes?** pode engraxar-me os sapatos? *[pod engrashahrm-yoosh sapahtoosh]*

polite bem-educado *[baing eedookahdoo]*

politician o político *[pooleeteekoo]*

politics a política *[pooleeteeka]*

polluted contaminado *[kontamee-nahdoo]*

pond o lago *[lahgoo]*

pony o ponei

pool (*swimming*) uma piscina *[peesh-seena]*; (*game*) o bilhar americano *[beel-yahr amireekanoo]*

pool table a mesa de bilhar *[mehza dih beel-yahr]*

poor (*not rich*) pobre *[pohbrih]*; (*quality etc*)

mau *[mow]*; **poor old Alberto!** coitado do Alberto! *[kohytahdo doo]*

pope o Papa

pop music a música pop *[moozeeka]*

pop singer o cantor pop *[kantohr]*

popular popular *[poopoolahr]*

population a população *[poopoola-sowng]*

pork a carne de porco *[kahrn dih pohrkoo]*

port (*for boats*) o porto *[pohrtoo]*; (*drink*) o vinho do Porto *[veen-yoo doo]*

porter (*hotel*) um porteiro *[poortay-roo]*; (*for luggage*) um carregador *[karri-gadohr]*

portrait um retrato *[ritrahtoo]*

Portugal Portugal *[poortoogahl]*

Portuguese português *[poortoogehsh]*; **the Portuguese** os portugueses *[poor-toogehzish]*

Portuguese woman uma portuguesa *[poortoogehza]*

poser (*phoney person*) um pretencioso *[pri-tens-yohzoo]*

posh chique *[sheek]*

possibility a possibilidade *[pooseebee-leedahd]*

possible possível *[pooseevel]*; **is it possible to ...?** é possível ...?; **as ... as possible** tão ... quanto possível *[towng ... kwantoo]*

post (*mail*) o correio *[koorray-oo]*; **could you post this for me?** podia-me pôr isto no correio? *[poodee-amih pohr eeshtoo noo]*

postbox a caixa do correio *[kah-isha doo koorray-oo]*

postcard um postal *[pooshtahl]*

poster o cartaz *[kartahsh]*

poste restante a posta restante *[poshta rishtant]*

post office o correio *[koorray-oo]*

pot o pote *[pot]*; **a pot of tea** um bule de chá *[bool dih shah]*; **pots and pans** tachos e panelas *[tahshooz ee pan-elash]*

potato a batata *[batahta]*

potato chips as batatas palha *[batahtash pahl-ya]*

potato salad a salada de batatas *[salahda dih batahtash]*

pottery (*place*) uma olaria *[ohlaree-a]*

pound (*money, weight*) a libra *[leebra]* see page 120

pour: it's pouring down chove a potes [shov a potsh]

powder (for face) o pó [paw]

powdered milk o leite em pó [layt aing paw]

power cut um corte de energia [kort deenirsнee-a]

power point uma tomada [toomahda]

power station (nuclear, elec) a central

practise, practice: I need to practise preciso de praticar [priseezoo dih prateekahr]

pram o carrinho de bébé [karreen-yoo dih beb-e]

prawn cocktail um cocktail de gambas [dih gambash]

prawns as gambas [gambash]

prefer: I prefer white wine prefiro vinho branco [prifeeroo]

preferably: preferably not tomorrow de preferência, não amanhã [dih prifirens-ya, nowng]

pregnant grávida [grahveeda]

prescription uma receita [rissay-ta]

present: at present actualmente [ahtwahlment]; **here's a present for you** tem aqui um presente [taing akee oong prizent]

president o presidente [prizeedent]

press: could you press these? pode passar-me estas? [pod passahr m-yeshtash]

pretty bonito [booneetoo]; **it's pretty expensive** é muito caro [mweengtoo kahroo]

price o preço [prehsoo]

prickly heat a urticária [oorteekahr-ya]

priest um padre [pahdrih]

prime minister o primeiro ministro [preemay-roo mineeshtroo]

print (picture) a gravura [gravoora]

printed matter os impressos [eempressoosh]

priority (in driving) a prioridade [pryooreedahd]

prison a cadeia [kaday-a]

private privado [preevahdoo]; **private bath** un banho privativo [ban-yoo preevateevoo]

prize o prémio [prem-yoo]

probably provavelmente [proovahvelment]

problem um problema [prooblehma]; I

have a problem tenho um problema [taing-nyoo]; **no problem** tudo bem [toodoo baing]

product um produto [proodootoo]

program(me) o programa [proograma]

promise: I promise prometo [proomehtoo]; **is that a promise?** fica prometido? [feeka proomiteedoo]

pronounce: how do you pronounce this word? como é que se diz esta palavra? [kohm-we kih sih deez eshta palahvra]

properly: it's not repaired properly não está bem arranjado [nowng shtah baing arransнahdoo]

prostitute uma prostituta [prooshteetoota]

protect proteger [prootisнehr]

protection factor o factor de protecção [fahtohr dih prootessowng]

protein remover (for contact lenses) o removedor de proteínas [rimoovidohr dih proo-te-eenash]

Protestant protestante [prootishtant]

proud orgulhoso [ohrgool-yohzoo]

prunes as ameixas passadas [amay-shash passahdash]

public o público [poobleekoo]

public convenience uma casa de banho pública [kahza dih ban-yoo poobleeka]

public holiday o feriado [fir-yahdoo]

pudding (dessert) a sobremesa [sohbrimehza]

pull puxar [pooshahr]; **he pulled out without indicating** ele atirou-se para a minha frente sem indicar [ehl ateeroh-sih parah meen-ya frent saing eendeekahr]

pullover o pullover

pump a bomba de ar [bom-ba d-yahr]

punctual pontual [pontwahl]

puncture um furo [fooroo]

pure (gold, silk etc) puro [pooroo]

purple roxo [rohshoo]

purse uma bolsa [bohlsa]; (handbag) uma mala de senhora [mahla dih sin-yohra]

push empurrar [empoorrahr]; **don't push in!** (into queue) não empurre! [nowng empoorr]

push-chair um carrinho de bébé [karreen-yoo dih beb-e]

put: where did you put ...? onde meteu ...? [ond miteh-oo]; **where can I put ...?** onde posso colocar ...? [possoo kooloo-

kahr]; **could you put the lights on?**
podia acender as luzes? *[poodee-a
assendehr ash loozish]*; **will you put the
light out?** apaga a luz? *[apahgah loosh]*;
you've put the price up subiu o preço

[soobee-oo prehsoo]; **could you put us
up for the night?** pode dar-nos acomo-
dação para uma noite? *[pod dahr-nooz
akoomoodasowng]*
pyjamas um pijama *[peesнama]*

quality a qualidade *[kwaleedahd]*; **poor
quality** má qualidade; **good quality** boa
qualidade *[boh-a]*
quarantine a quarentena *[kwarentehna]*
quart *see page 121*
quarter a quarta parte *[kwahrta pahrt]*; **a
quarter of an hour** um quarto de hora
[oong kwahrtoo d-yora] see page 118
quay o cais *[kah-ish]*
quayside: on the quayside no cais *[noo
kah-ish]*
question uma pergunta *[pirgoonta]*;
that's quite out of the question está
totalmente fora de questão *[shtah tootal-
ment fora dih kwishtowng]*
queue uma bicha *[beesha]*; **there was a**

big queue estava uma bicha grande
[shtahva]
quick rápido *[rahpeedoo]*; **that was
quick!** que rápido que foi! *[kih rahpee-
doo kih fohy]*; **which is the quickest
way?** qual é o caminho mais rápido?
[kwahl e oo kameen-yoo mah-ish]
quickly depressa
quiet (*place*) sossegado *[soosigahdoo]*; **be
quiet** cale-se! *[kahl-sih]*
quinine o quinino *[keeneenoo]*
quite: quite a lot bastante *[bashtant]*; **it's
quite different** é muito diferente
[mweengtoo]; **I'm not quite sure** não
estou muito certo *[nowng shtoh
mweengtoo sehrtoo]*

R

rabbit um coelho *[kwehl-yoo]*
rabies a raiva *[rah-iva]*
race uma corrida *[koorreeda]*; **I'll race
you there** desafio-te a uma corrida até ali
[dizafee-oo-tih ... a-te alee]
racket (*tennis etc*) uma raqueta *[rakehta]*
radiator um radiador *[rad-yadohr]*
radio um rádio *[rahd-yoo]*; **on the radio**
na rádio
rag (*cleaning*) um esfregão *[shfrigowng]*
rail: by rail por caminho de ferro *[poor
kameen-yoo dih fairroo]*

railroad, railway o caminho de ferro *[ka-
meen-yoo dih fairroo]*
railroad crossing a passagem de nível
[passah-sнaing dih neevel]
rain a chuva *[shoova]*; **in the rain** à chuva
[ah]; **it's raining** está a chover *[shtah
shoovehr]*
rain boots as botas de borracha *[botash
dih boorrahsha]*
raincoat um impermeável *[eempirm-
yahvel]*
rape a violação *[v-yoolassowng]*

rare raro *[rah-roo]*; *(steak)* em sangue *[aing sang-gih]*

rash *(on skin)* uma erupção *[eroopsowng]*

raspberries as framboesas *[frambwehzash]*

rat uma ratazana

rate *(for changing money)* o câmbio *[kamb-yoo]*; **what's the rate for the pound?** qual é o câmbio da libra? *[kwahl]*; **what are your rates?** *(car hire etc)* quais são os vossos preços? *[kwah-ish sowng osh vossosh prehsoosh]*

rather: it's rather late é um bocado tarde *[bookahdoo tahrd]*; **I'd rather have fish** prefiro peixe *[prifeeroo]*

raw cru/crua *[kroo/kroo-a]*

razor uma máquina de barbear *[mahkeena dih barb-yahr]*; *(electric)* uma máquina de barbear eléctrica *[eeletreeka]*

razor blades as lâminas para barbear *[lahmeenash]*

reach: within easy reach a curta distância *[koorta dishtans-ya]*

read ler *[lehr]*; **I can't read it** não consigo ler isso *[nowng konseegoo]*

ready: when will it be ready? quando está pronto? *[kwandoo shtah prontoo]*; **I'll go and get ready** vou-me arranjar *[vohm-yarransнahr]*; **I'm not ready yet** ainda não estou pronto *[a-eenda nowng shtoh prontoo]*

real verdadeiro *[virdaday-roo]*

really realmente *[r-yahlment]*; **I really must go** tenho mesmo que ir *[taing-nyoo mehsнmoo keer]*; **is it really necessary?** é mesmo necessário? *[e mehsнmoo nisisahr-yoo]*

realtor um agente imobiliário *[asнent eemoobeel-yahr-yoo]*

rear: at the rear atrás *[atrahsh]*

rear wheels as rodas de trás *[rodash dih trahsh]*

rearview mirror o espelho retrovisor *[shpehl-yoo ritrooveezohr]*

reason: the reason is that … a razão é que … *[razowng e kih]*

reasonable razoável *[razwahvel]*

receipt um recibo *[riseeboo]*

recently há pouco *[ah pohkoo]*

reception a recepção *[ris-essowng]*

reception desk o balcão da recepção *[bahlkowng da ris-essowng]*

receptionist o recepcionista *[ris-ess-yooneeshta]*

recipe uma receita *[risayta]*; **can you give me the recipe for this?** podia dar-me a receita disto? *[poodee-a dahrm-ya]*

recognize reconhecer *[rikoon-yisehr]*; **I didn't recognize it** não o reconheci *[nowng oo rikoon-yisee]*

recommend: could you recommend …? podia recomendar …? *[poodee-a rikoomendahr]*

record *(music)* um disco *[deeshkoo]*

record player um gira-discos *[sнeera-deeshkoosh]*

red vermelho *[virmehlyoo]*

reduction *(in price)* um desconto *[dishkontoo]*

red wine o vinho tinto *[veen-yoo teentoo]*

refreshing refrescante *[rifrishkant]*

refrigerator um frigorífico *[freegooreefeekoo]*

refund: do I get a refund? posso ser reembolsado? *[posoo sehr ree-aing-bohlsahdoo]*

region a região *[risн-yowng]*

registered: by registered mail por correio registado *[poor koorray-oo risнeeshtahdoo]*

registration number *(of car)* a matrícula *[matreekoola]*

relative: my relative o meu parente *[parent]*

relaxing: it's very relaxing é muito relaxante *[mweengtoo rihlashant]*

reliable *(person, car)* digno de confiança *[deegnoo dih konf-yansa]*

religion a religião *[rileesн-yowng]*

remains *(of old city etc)* as ruínas *[rweenash]*

remember: I don't remember não me lembro *[nowng mih lembroo]*; **do you remember?** lembra-se? *[lembra-sih]*

remote *(village etc)* distante *[dishtant]*

rent *(for room etc)* o aluguer *[aloogair]*; **I'd like to rent a bike/car** gostava de alugar uma bicicleta/um carro *[gooshtahva d-yaloogahr]*

rental car um carro de aluguer *[kahrroo d-yaloogair]*

repair uma reparação *[riparassowng]*; **can you repair this?** pode reparar isto? *[pod riparahr eeshtoo]*

repeat repetir *[ripiteer]*; **would you repeat that?** podia repetir aquilo? *[poodee-*

a ... akeeloo]
representative (of company) o repre-
sentante [riprizentant]
request um pedido [pideedoo]; **I have
one request** tenho um pedido [taing-
nyoo oong]
rescue salvar [sahlvahr]
reservation uma reserva [rizairva]; **I
have a reservation** tenho uma reserva
[taing-nyoo]
reserve reservar [rizirvahr]; **I reserved a
room in the name of ...** reservei um
quarto no nome de ... [rizirvay oong
kwahrtoo noo nom dih]; **can I reserve a
table for tonight?** posso reservar uma
mesa para hoje à noite? [possoo rizirvahr
ooma mehza para ohsнahr noh-it]
rest: I need a rest preciso dum descanso
[priseezoo doong dishkansoo]; **the rest
of the group** o resto do grupo [reshtoo]
restaurant um restaurante [rishtow-rant]
rest room a toilette [twalett]
retired: I'm retired estou reformado
[shtoh rifoormahdoo]
return: a return to Lisbon um bilhete de
ida e volta a Lisboa [beel-yeht deeda ee
volta]; **I'll return it tomorrow** eu de-
volvo-o amanhã [divohlvoo ahman-
yang]
returnable (deposit) restituível [rishteet-
weevel]
reverse charge call uma chamada paga
no destinatário [shamahda pahga noo
dishteenatahr-yoo]
reverse gear a marcha atrás [mahrshah-
trahsh]
revolting revoltante [rivohltant]
rheumatism o reumatismo [reh-
oomateesнmoo]
rib uma costela [kooshtela]; **a cracked rib**
uma costela partida [parteeda]
ribbon (for hair) uma fita [feeta]
rice arroz [arrohsh]
rich (person) rico [reekoo]; **it's too rich**
(food) é muito forte [mweengtoo fort]
ride: can you give me a ride into town?
pode dar-me uma boleia até à cidade?
[pod dahrm-yooma boolay-a a-te ah
seedahd]; **thanks for the ride** obrigado
pela boleia [ohbreegahdoo pehla]
ridiculous: that's ridiculous isso é ridículo [reekeekooloo]
right (correct) certo [sehrtoo]; (not left) di-

reito [deeray-too]; **you're right** tem razão [taing razowng]; **you were right**
tinha razão [teen-ya]; **that's right** está
certo [shtah]; **that can't be right** não
pode estar certo [nowng pod shtahr];
right! (ok) está bem [baing]; **is this the
right road for ...?** esta é a estrada certa
para ...? [eshta e a shtrahda sehrta]; **on
the right** à direita [ah deeray-ta]; **turn
right** vire à direita [veer]; **not right now**
agora não [nowng]
righthand drive com volante à direita
[kong voolant ah deeray-ta]
ring (on finger) um anel [a-nel]; (on cooker)
uma placa [plahka]; **I'll ring you** eu
telefono-lhe [eh-oo tilifonool-yih]
ring road uma circular [seerkoolahr]
ripe maduro [madooroo]
rip-off: it's a rip-off isso é um roubo
[eesoo e oong rohboo]; **rip-off prices**
preços exorbitantes [prehsooz eezoorbee-
tantish]
risky arriscado [arreeshkahdoo]; **it's too
risky** é arriscado demais [dimah-ish]
river um rio [ree-oo]; **by the river** à beira
do rio [ah bay-ra]
road a estrada [shtrahda]; **is this the
road to ...?** é esta a estrada para ...? [e
eshta]; **further down the road** mais à
frente [mah-iz ah frent]
road accident um acidente de viação
[aseedent dih v-yassowng]
road hog um louco ao volante [lohkoo ow
voolant]
road map um mapa das estradas [daz
shtrahdash]
roadside: by the roadside à beira da
estrada [ah bay-ra da shtrahda]
roadsign o sinal [seenahl]
roadwork(s) obras na estrada [obrash na
shtrahda]
roast beef a carne assada [kahrn assahda]
rob: I've been robbed roubaram-me
[rohbahrowng-mih]
robe (housecoat) um roupão [rohpowng]
rock (stone) uma rocha [rosha]; **on the
rocks** (with ice) com gelo [kong sнehloo]
rocky (coast) rochoso [rooshohzoo]
roll (bread) uma carcaça [karkahsa]
Roman Catholic católico [katoleekoo]
romance o romance [roomans]
Rome: when in Rome ... conforme o
toque, assim a dança [konform oo tok

asseeng a dansa]
roof o telhado [til-yahdoo]; **on the roof**
no telhado [noo]
roof rack (on car) um porta-bagagens na
capota [pohrta bagah-sнaingsh na]
room um quarto [kwahrtoo]; **do you
have a room?** tem um quarto? [taing]; **a
room for two people** um quarto para
duas pessoas [pissoh-ash]; **a room for
three nights** um quarto para três noites
[noh-itsh]; **a room with bathroom** um
quarto com casa de banho; **in my room**
no meu quarto [noo meh-oo]; **there's no
room** não há espaço [nowng ah
shpahsoo]
room service o seviço de quartos [sirvee-
soo dih kwahrtoosh]
rope uma corda
rose uma rosa [roza]
rosé (wine) rosé [roozeh]
rotary uma rotunda [rootoonda]
rough (sea, crossing) tempestuoso [tem-
pishtwohzoo]; **the engine sounds a
bit rough** o motor parece um bocado
desafinado [mootohr paress oong bookahdoo dizafeenahdoo]; **I've been
sleeping rough** tenho dormido ao ar
livre [taing-nyoo doormeedoo ow ahr le-
evrih]
roughly (approximately) approxima-
damente [aproosseemahdament]
roulette a roleta [rooleta]
round redondo [ridondoo]; **it's my
round** é a minha rodada [meen-ya roo-
dahda]
roundabout uma rotunda [rootoonda]

round-trip: a round-trip ticket to ... um
bilhete de ida e volta para ... [beel-yeht
deeda ee volta]
route o trajecto [trajeh-too]; **what's the
best route?** qual é o melhor trajecto?
[kwahl é oo mil-yor]
rowboat, rowing boat um barco a remos
[bahrkoo a rehmoosh]
rubber a borracha [boorrahsha]
rubber band uma fita elástica [feeta
eelahshteeka]
rubbish (waste) lixo [leeshoo]; (poor quality
items) o refugo [rifoogoo]; **rubbish!** que
disparate! [kih deeshparaht]
rucksack uma mochila [moosheela]
rude grosseiro [groosay-roo]; **he was very
rude** ele foi muito grosseiro [fohy
mweengtoo]
rug um rapete [tapeht]
ruins as ruínas [rweenash]
rum rum [roong]
rum and coke uma cuba livre [kooba
leevrih]
run (person) correr [koorrehr]; **I go
running** corro [kohrroo]; **quick, run!**
corra, depressa! [kohrra diprehsa]; **how
often do the buses run?** de quanto em
quanto tempo há autocarros? [dih
kwantoo aing kwantoo tempoo ah owtoo-
kahrroosh]; **he's been run over** foi atropelado [fohy atroopilahdoo]; **I've run
out of gas/petrol** já não tenho gasolina
[sнah nowng taing-nyoo gazooleena]
rupture (med) uma ruptura [rooptoora]
Russia a Rússia [roos-ya]
rust a ferrugem [firroosнaing]

S

saccharine a sacarina [sakareena]
sad triste [treesht]
saddle uma sela
safe seguro [sigooroo]; **will it be safe
here?** posso deixá-lo aqui? [posoo day-
shahloo akee]; **is it safe to drink?** pode-
se beber? [pod-sih bibehr]; **is it a safe**

beach for swimming? é uma praia se-
gura para nadar? [ooma pry-a sigoora
para nadahr]; **could you put this in
your safe?** podia pôr isto no seu cofre?
[podee-a pohr eeshtoo noo seh-oo kofrih]
safety pin um alfinete de segurança
[alfeeneht dih sigooransa]

sail uma vela; **can we go sailing?** podemos ir fazer vela? *[poodehmooz eer fazehr]*
sailboard a prancha à vela *[pranshah vela]*
sailboarding: I like sailboarding gosto de andar de prancha à vela *[goshtoo d-yandahr dih pranshah vela]*
sailor um marinheiro *[mareen-yay-roo]*
salad uma salada
salad cream o molho de salada *[mohl-yoo]*
salad dressing o têmpero da salada *[tempehroo]*
sale: is it for sale? está à venda? *[shtah ah venda]*; **it's not for sale** não está à venda *[nowng]*
sales clerk um vendedor *[vendidohr]*
salmon o salmão *[sahlmowng]*
salt o sal
salty: it's too salty tem demasiado sal *[taing dimaz-yahdoo]*
same mesmo *[mehsнmoo]*; **one the same as this** um igual a este *[eegwahl a ehsht]*; **the same again, please** o mesmo, por favor; **have a good day — same to you** um bom dia para si — igualmente *[eegwahlment]*; **it's all the same to me** tanto faz *[tantoo fahsh]*; **thanks all the same** obrigado de qualquer modo *[oh-breegahdoo dih kwahlkair modoo]*
sand a areia *[aray-a]*
sandal: a pair of sandals umas sandálias *[oomash sandahl-yash]*
sandwich uma sandes *[sandsh]*; **a chicken sandwich** uma sandes de galinha *[galeen-ya]*
sandy *(beach)* arenoso *[arinohzoo]*
sanitary napkin/towel toalhas higiénicas *[twahlyaz eesн-yeneekash]*
sarcastic sarcástico *[sarkahshteekoo]*
sardines umas sardinhas *[sardeen-yash]*
satisfactory satisfatório *[sateeshfatoryoo]*; **this is not satisfactory** isto não é satisfatório *[eeshtoo nowng e]*
Saturday sábado *[sahbadoo]*
sauce o molho *[mohl-yoo]*
saucepan uma caçarola *[kassarola]*
saucer um pires *[peersh]*
sauna uma sauna *[sowna]*
sausage uma salsicha *[sahlseesha]*
saute potatoes as batatas salteadas *[batahtash sahlt-yahdash]*

save *(life)* salvar
savo(u)ry saboroso *[saboorohzoo]*
say: how do you say ... in Portuguese? como se diz ... em português? *[kohmoo sih deez aing poortoogehsh]*; **what did you say?** que disse? *[kih dees]*; **what did he say?** o que é que ele disse? *[oo k-ye kehl]*; **I wouldn't say no** não diria que não *[nowng diree-a kih nowng]*
scald: he's scalded himself queimou-se *[kay-mohsih]*
scarf un lenço de pescoço *[lensoo dih pishkohsoo]*; *(head)* um lenço de cabeça *[kabehsa]*
scarlet escarlate *[shkarlaht]*
scenery a paisagem *[pye-zahsнaing]*
scent *(perfume)* o aroma
schedule o programa *[proograma]*
scheduled flight um voo regular *[voh-oo rigoolahr]*
school uma escola *[shkola]*; *(university)* uma universidade *[ooneevirseedahd]*; **I'm still at school** ainda ando a estudar *[a-eenda andoo a shtoodahr]*
science a ciência *[s-yensa]*
scissors: a pair of scissors uma tesoura *[tizohra]*
scooter uma motoreta *[mootooretta]*
scorching: it's really scorching está mesmo quente *[shtah mehsнmoo kent]*
score: what's the score? qual é o resultado? *[kwahl e oo rizooltahdoo]*
scotch (whisky) um whisky *[weeshkee]*
Scotch tape *(tm)* a fita cola *[feeta]*
Scotland a Escócia *[shkos-ya]*
Scottish escocês *[shkoosehsh]*
scrambled eggs ovos mexidos *[ovoosh misheedoosh]*
scratch um arranhão *[arran-yowng]*; **it's only a scratch** é só um arranhão *[saw]*
scream gritar *[greetahr]*
screw um parafuso *[parafoozoo]*
screwdriver uma chave de fendas *[shahv dih fendash]*
scrubbing brush uma escova de esfregar *[shkohva dishfrigahr]*
scruffy desmazelado *[disнmazilahdoo]*
scuba diving mergulhar com garrafa *[mirgool-yahr kong garrahfa]*
sea o mar; **by the sea** à beira-mar *[ah bay-ra]*
sea air o ar do mar
seafood os mariscos *[mareeshkoosh]*

seafood restaurant um restaurante de mariscos *[rishtowrant dih mareeshkoosh]*

seafront: on the seafront de frente para o mar *[dih frent]*

seagull uma gaivota *[gah-ivota]*

search procurar *[prookoorahr]*; **I searched everywhere** procurei por todo o lado *[prookooray poor tohdoo lahdoo]*

search party uma expedição de socorro *[shpideesowng dih sookohrroo]*

seashell uma concha do mar *[konsha]*

seasick: I feel seasick estou enjoado *[shtoh ensнwahdoo]*; **I get seasick** enjoo sempre *[ensноh-oo semprih]*

seaside: by the seaside à beira do mar *[ah bay-ra]*; **let's go to the seaside** vamos para a praia *[vamoosh prah pry-a]*

season a época *[epooka]*; **in the high season** na estação alta *[na shtassowng ahlta]*; **in the low season** na estação baixa *[bah-isha]*

seasoning o condimento *[kondeementoo]*

seat um assento *[assentoo]*; **is this anyone's seat?** este lugar está ocupado? *[esht loogahr shtah ohkoopahdoo]*

seat belt o cinto de segurança *[seentoo dih sigooransa]*; **do you have to wear a seatbelt?** tem que se usar cinto de segurança? *[taing kih s-yoozahr]*

sea urchin um ouriço-do-mar *[ohreesoo]*

seaweed a alga

secluded retirado *[riteerahdoo]*

second um segundo *[sigoondoo]*; **just a second!** espera um momento! *[shpaira oong moomentoo]*; **can I have a second helping?** pode servir-me mais por favor? *[pod sirveer-mih mah-ish]*

second class (*travel*) de segunda classe *[dih sigoonda klahs]*

second-hand em segunda mão *[aing sigoonda mowng]*

secret secreto *[sikrehtoo]*

security check um controlo de segurança *[kontroloo dih sigooransa]*

sedative um sedativo *[sidateevoo]*

see ver *[vehr]*; **I didn't see it** não vi *[nowng vee]*; **have you seen my husband?** viu o meu marido? *[vee-oo]*; **I saw him this morning** vi-o esta manhã *[vee-oo]*; **can I see the manager?** posso falar com o gerente? *[possoo falahr kong]*; **see you tonight!** até logo à noite!

[a-te logoo ah noh-it]; **can I see?** posso ver?; **oh, I see** já percebo *[sнah pirsehboo]*; **will you see to it?** cuida disso? *[kweeda deesoo]*

seldom raras vezes *[rahrasн vehzish]*

self-catering apartment um aparthotel *[apartohtel]*

self-service o self-service

sell vender *[vendehr]*; **do you sell ...?** vende ...? *[vend]*; **will you sell it to me?** vende-me isso? *[vendimih eesoo]*

sellotape (*tm*) a fita cola *[feeta]*

send mandar *[mandahr]*; **I want to send this to England** quero mandar isto para Inglaterra *[kairoo]*; **I'll have to send this food back** tenho que mandar esta comida de volta *[taing-nyoo kih mandahr eshta koomeeda dih volta]*

senior: Mr Jones senior Senhor Jones pai *[sin-yohr ... py]*

senior citizen um cidadão de terceira idade *[seedadowng dih tirsay-ra eedahd]*

sensational sensacional *[sensas-yoonahl]*

sense: I have no sense of direction não tenho sentido de orientação *[nowng taing-nyoo senteedoo d-yohr-yentassowng]*; **it doesn't make sense** não faz sentido *[nowng fahsh senteedoo]*

sensible sensato *[sensahtoo]*

sensitive sensível *[senseevel]*

sentimental sentimental *[senteementahl]*

separate separado *[siparahdoo]*; **can we have separate bills?** pode fazer-nos contas separadas? *[pod fazehr-noosh kontash siparahdash]*

separated: I'm separated estou separado *[shtoh siparahdoo]*

separately separadamente *[siparahdament]*

September Setembro *[sitembroo]*

septic séptico *[septeekoo]*

serious sério *[sair-yoo]*; **I'm serious** estou a falar a sério *[shtoh a falahr a]*; **you can't be serious!** não está a falar a sério! *[nowng shtah]*; **is it serious, doctor?** é grave, Sr. doutor? *[e grahv sin-yohr dohtohr]*

seriously: seriously ill gravemente doente *[grahviment dwent]*

service: the service was excellent o serviço foi óptimo *[oo sirveesoo fohy oteemoo]*; **could we have some service, please!** podia-nos alguém atender por favor! [*poodee-anooz ahlgaing atendehr*]; **(church) service** o serviço religioso [*sirveesoo rileesн-yohzoo*]; **the car needs a service** o carro precisa duma revisão [*kahrroo priseeza dooma riveezowng*]

service charge a taxa de serviço [*tahsha dih sirveesoo*]

service station uma estação de serviço [*shtassowng dih sirveesoo*]

serviette um guardanapo [*gwahrdanahpoo*]

set: it's time we were setting off é altura de nós partirmos [*ahltoora dih nosh parteermoosh*]

set menu a ementa fixa [*eementa feeksa*]

settle up: can I settle up now? posso pagar agora? [*posoo pagahr*]

several vários [*vahr-yoosh*]

sew: could you sew this back on? podia coser isto outra vez? [*poodee-a koozehr eeshtoo ohtra vehsh*]

sex (*activity*) o sexo

sexist um sexista [*sekseeshta*]

sexy sexy

shade: in the shade à sombra [*ah*]

shadow a sombra

shake: to shake hands apertar a mão [*apirtahr a mowng*]

shallow pouco profundo [*pohkoo proofoondoo*]

shame: what a shame! que pena! [*kih pehna*]

shampoo um champô [*shampoh*]; **can I have a shampoo and set?** podia fazer champô e mise? [*poodee-a fazehr shampoh ee meez*]

shandy uma cerveja com limonada [*sirvehsнah kong leemoonahda*]

share partilhar [*perteel-yahr*]; **let's share the cost** vamos partilhar o custo [*vamoosh parteel-yahr oo kooshtoo*]

shark um tubarão [*toobarowng*]

sharp (*knife etc*) afiado [*af-yahdoo*]; (*taste, pain*) agudo [*agoodoo*]

shattered: I'm shattered (*very tired*) estou estafado [*shtoh shtafahdoo*]

shave: I need a shave preciso de me barbear [*priseezoo dih mih barb-yahr*]; **can you give me a shave?** pode fazer-me a barba? [*pod fazehrm-ya bahrba*]

shaver uma máquina de barbear [*mahkeena dih barb-yahr*]

shaving brush uma escova de barbear [*shkohva dih barb-yahr*]

shaving foam a espuma para a barba [*shpooma prah bahrba*]

shaving point a tomada para a máquina de barbear [*toomahda prah mahkeena dih barb-yahr*]

shaving soap um sabonete para a barba [*sabooneht prah bahrba*]

shawl um chale [*shahl*]

she ela; **is she staying here?** ela fica aqui? [*feekahkee*]; **is she a friend of yours?** ela é sua amiga? [*soo-a ameega*]; **she left yesterday** ela partiu ontem [*partee-oo ontaing*]; **she's not English** ela não é inglesa [... *nowng* ...] *see page 112*

sheep uma ovelha [*ohvehl-ya*]

sheet um lençol [*lensol*]

shelf uma prateleira [*pratilay-ra*]

shell (*seashell*) uma concha [*konsha*]

shellfish os mariscos [*mareeshkoosh*]

sherry o vinho de Xerêz [*veen-yoo dih shirehsh*]

shingles (*med*) as herpes [*airpish*]

ship um barco [*bahrkoo*]; **by ship** de barco

shirt uma camisa [*kameeza*]; **a clean shirt** uma camisa lavada [*lavahda*]

shit merda [*mairda*]

shock (*surprise*) um choque [*shock*]; **I got an electric shock from the ...** apanhei um choque eléctrico de ... [*apan-yay oong shock eeletreekoo*]

shock-absorber o amortecedor [*amoortisidohr*]

shocking chocante [*shookant*]

shoelaces os atacadores [*atakadohrish*]

shoe polish a graxa para sapatos [*grahsha para sapahtoosh*]

shoes os sapatos [*sapahtoosh*]; **a pair of shoes** um par de sapatos

shop uma loja [*losнa*]

shopping: I'm going shopping vou às compras [*voh ahsh komprash*]

shop window uma montra

shore (*of sea, lake*) a margem [*mahr-sнaing*]

short (*person*) baixo [*bah-ishoo*]; (*time*) curto [*koortoo*]; **it's only a short distance** é uma distância curta [*dishtans-ya*]

short-change: you've short-changed me deu-me troco a menos [*deh-oomih trohkoo a mehnoosh*]

short circuit um curto-circuito *[koortoo seerkweetoo]*
shortcut um atalho *[atahl-yoo]*
shorts os calções *[kahlsoingsh]*; (*underwear*) as cuecas *[kwekash]*
should: what should I do? que devo fazer? *[kih dehvoo fazehr]*; **he shouldn't be long** ele não deve demorar *[nowng dev dimoorahr]*; **you should have told me** devia ter-me dito *[divee-a tehrmih deetoo]*
shoulder o ombro *[ombroo]*
shoulder blade uma omoplata *[ohmooplahta]*
shout gritar *[greetahr]*
show: could you show me? podia mostrar-me? *[poodee-a mooshtrahrmih]*; **does it show?** vê-se? *[vehss]*; **we'd like to go to a show** gostávamos de ir a um espectáculo *[gooshtahvamoosh deer a oong shpetahkooloo]*
shower (*in bathroom*) o duche *[doosh]*; **with shower** com duche *[kong]*
shower cap a touca de duche *[tohka dih doosh]*
show-off: don't be a show-off não dê espectáculo *[nowng deh shpitahkooloo]*
shrimps os camarões *[kamaroingsh]*
shrine um santuário *[santwahr-yoo]*
shrink: it's shrunk está encolhido *[shtah enkool-yeedoo]*
shut fechar *[fishahr]*; **when do you shut?** a que horas fecha? *[a k-yorash fehsha]*; **when do they shut?** quando é que eles fecham? *[kwandoo e k-yehlsh fehshowng]*; **it was shut** estava fechado *[shtahva fishahdoo]*; **I've shut myself out** a porta está fechada e a chave dentro *[shtah fishahda e a shahv dentroo]*; **shut up!** cale-se! *[kahlisih]*
shutter (*phot*) o obturador *[ohbtooradohr]*; (*on window*) um postigo *[pooshteegoo]*
shutter release um disparador *[dishparadohr]*
shy tímido *[teemeedoo]*
sick doente *[dwent]*; **I think I'm going to be sick** acho que vou vomitar *[ahshoo kih voh voomeetahr]*
side o lado *[lahdoo]*; (*in game*) a equipa *[eekeepa]*; **at the side of the road** ao lado da estrada *[ow lahdoo da shtrahda]*; **the other side of town** o outro lado da

cidade *[ohtroo lahdoo da seedahd]*
side lights (*car*) as luzes de presença *[ash loozish dih prizensa]*
side salad uma salada a acompanhar *[akompan-yahr]*
side street uma rua secundária *[roo-a sikoondahr-ya]*
sidewalk um passeio *[passay-oo]*
sidewalk cafe um café esplanada *[ka-fe shplanahda]*
siesta a sesta *[sehsta]*
sight: the sights of ... os centros de interesse de ... *[oosh sentroosh deentrehs dih]*
sightseeing: sightseeing tour um circuito turístico *[seerkweetoo tooreeshteekoo]*; **we're going sightseeing** vamos ver os lugares de interesse *[vamoosh vehr oosh loogahrish deentrehs]*
sign (*roadsign*) o sinal *[seenahl]*; (*notice*) o letreiro *[litray-roo]*; **where do I sign?** onde assino? *[ond asseenoo]*
signal: he didn't give a signal ele não deu um sinal *[nowng deh-oo oong seenahl]*
signature a assinatura *[asseenatoora]*
signpost um poste indicador *[posht eendeekadohr]*
silence silêncio *[seelens-yoo]*
silencer a panela de escape *[dishkahp]*
silk a seda *[sehda]*
silly tolo *[tohloo]*; **that's silly** isso é tolice *[eesoo e toolees]*
silver a prata
silver foil a folha de prata *[fohl-ya]*
similar semelhante *[simil-yant]*
simple simples *[seemplish]*
since: since yesterday desde ontem *[dehsʜd-yontaing]*; **since we got here** desde que cá chegámos *[dehsʜd kih kah shigahmoosh]*
sincere sincero *[seensehroo]*
sing cantar
singer um cantor *[kantohr]*
single: a single room um quarto individual *[kwahrtoo eendiveed-wahl]*; **a single to ...** uma ida para ... *[eeda]*; **I'm single** sou solteiro *[soh sohltay-roo]*
sink (*kitchen*) o lava-louça *[lahva-lohysa]*; **it sank** afundou-se *[afoondoh-sih]*
sir senhor *[sin-yohr]*; **excuse me, sir** desculpe *[dishkoolp]*
sirloin um bife de lombo *[beef dih*

lomboo]
sister: my sister a minha irmã *[meen-ya eermang]*
sister-in-law: my sister-in-law a minha cunhada *[meen-ya koon-yahda]*
sit: may I sit here? posso sentar-me aqui? *[possoo sentahr-mih akee]*; **is anyone sitting here?** está alguém sentado aqui? *[shtah ahlgaing sentahdoo akee]*
site *(campsite etc)* um parque *[pahrk]*
sitting: the second sitting for lunch o segundo turno para o almoço *[sigoondoo toornoo para oo ahlmohsoo]*
situation a situação *[seetwassowng]*
size o tamanho *[taman-yoo]*
sketch o esboço *[sнbohsoo]*
skid: I skidded o carro derrapou *[kahrroo dihrrapoh]*
skin a pele *[pel]*
skin-diving mergulhar *[mirgɔ͞ɔl-yahr]*; **I'm going skin-diving** eu vou mergulhar *[eh-oo voh]*
skinny magricela *[magreesela]*
skirt uma saia *[sah-ya]*
skull a caveira *[kahvay-ra]*
sky o céu *[seh-oo]*
sleep: I can't sleep não posso dormir *[nowng possoo doormeer]*; **did you sleep well?** dormiu bem? *[doormee-oo baing]*; **I need a good sleep** preciso de dormir bem *[priseezoo dih]*
sleeper *(rail)* a carruagem-cama *[karrwah-sнaing kama]*
sleeping bag um saco de dormir *[sahkoo dih doormeer]*
sleeping car a carruagem-cama *[karrwah-sнaing kama]*
sleeping pill um comprimido para dormir *[kompreemeedoo para doormeer]*
sleepy: I'm feeling sleepy eu estou com sono *[shtoh kong sohnoo]*
sleeve a manga *[mang-ga]*
slice *(bread, meat)* uma fatia *[fatee-a]*
slide *(phot)* um diapositivo *[dee-apoozi-teevoo]*
slim magro *[mahgroo]*; **I'm slimming** estou de dieta *[shtoh dih d-yeнta]*
slip *(under dress)* a combinação *[kombee-nassowng]*; **I slipped** *(on pavement etc)* eu escorreguei *[eh-oo shkoorigay]*
slipped disc um disco deslocado *[deesh-koo disнlookahdoo]*

slippery escorregadio *[shkoorrigadee-oo]*
slow lento *[lentoo]*; **slow down** abrandar *[abrandahr]*
slowly devagar *[divagahr]*; **could you say it slowly?** pode dizer devagar? *[pod deezehr]*
small pequeno *[pikehnoo]*
small change os trocos *[trokoosh]*
smallpox a varíola *[varee-oola]*
smart *(clothes)* elegante *[eeligant]*
smashing formidável *[foormeedahvel]*
smell: there's a funny smell há um cheiro desagradável *[ah oong shay-roo dizagradahvel]*; **what a lovely smell** que bem que cheira *[kih baing kih shay-ra]*; **it smells** cheira mal
smile sorrir *[soorreer]*
smoke o fumo *[foomoo]*; **do you smoke?** fuma? *[fooma]*; **do you mind if I smoke?** importa-se que fume? *[eemporta-sih kih foomih]*; **I don't smoke** eu não fumo *[eh-oo nowng]*
smooth *(surface, sea)* liso *[leezoo]*
smoothy um galã *[galang]*
snack: I'd just like a snack eu só quero uma refeição ligeira *[eh-oo saw kairoo ooma rifay-sowng lisнay-ra]*
snackbar um snackbar
snails os caracóis *[karakoysh]*
snake uma cobra
sneakers os sapatos de treino *[sapahtoosh dih tray-noo]*
snob um pedante *[pidant]*
snorkel o tubo de respiração *[tooboo dih rishpeerasowng]*
snow a neve *[nev]*
so: it's so hot está tanto calor *[shtah tantoo kalohr]*; **it was so beautiful!** foi tão belo! *[fohy towng beloo]*; **not so fast** mais devagar *[mah-ish divagahr]*; **thank you so much** muitíssimo obrigado *[mweengteeseemoo]*; **it wasn't — it was so!** não foi — foi sim! *[fohy seeng]*; **so am I, so do I** eu também *[eh-oo tambaing]*; **how was it? — so-so** como era? — assim, assim *[asseeng]*
soaked: I'm soaked estou todo molhado *[shtoh toнdoo mool-yahdoo]*
soaking solution a loção para lentes de contacto *[loosowng para lentsh dih kontahktoo]*
soap o sabonete *[sabooneht]*
soap-powder um detergente *[ditirsнent]*

sober sóbrio [sobr-yoo]
soccer o futebol [footibol]
sock uma peúga [p-yooga]
socket (elec) uma tomada [toomahda]
soda (water) a soda
sofa o sofá [soofah]
soft mole [mol]
soft drink bebida não alcoólica [bibeeda nowng ahlkwoleeka]
soft lenses umas lentes gelatinosas [lentsh shilateenozash]
soldier o soldado [sohldahdoo]
sole (of shoe) a sola; **could you put new soles on these?** pode pôr-lhes solas novas? [pod pohrl-yish solash novash]
solid sólido [soleedoo]
some: may I have some water? pode trazer-me água por favor? [pod trazehrmih]; **do you have some matches?** tem fósforos? [taing]; **that's some drink!** mas que grande bebida! [mash kih grand bibeeda]; **some of them** alguns [ahlgoongsh]; **can I have some of those/some of that?** pode-me dar alguns/um bocado? [ahlgoongsh/oong bookahdoo]
somebody, someone alguém [ahlgaing]
something alguma coisa [ahlgooma kohiza]; **something to drink** alguma coisa para beber [para bibehr]
sometime: sometime this afternoon durante esta tarde [doorant eshta tahrd]
sometimes às vezes [ahsh vehzish]
somewhere nalguma parte [nahlgooma pahrt]
son: my son o meu filho [meh-oo feelyoo]
song uma canção [kansowng]
son-in-law: my son-in-law o meu genro [meh-oo shenroo]
soon em breve [aing brev]; **I'll be back soon** estarei de volta em breve [shtaray dih volta]; **as soon as you can** o mais depressa que você puder [oo mah-ish dipressa kih vosseh poodair]
sore: it's sore dói-me [doy-mih]
sore throat uma dor de garganta [dohr dih garganta]
sorry: (I'm) sorry desculpe [dishkoolp]; **sorry?** (pardon) como? [kohmoo]
sort: what sort of ...? que tipo de ...? [kih teepoo dih]; **a different sort of ...** um tipo diferente de ... [deefirent]; **will you sort**

it out? pode resolvê-lo? [pod rezohlvehloo]
soup uma sopa
sour (taste, apple) azedo [azehdoo]
south o sul; **to the south** a sul
South Africa a África do Sul [afreeka doo sool]
South African sul-africano [sool-afreekanoo]
southeast o sudeste [soodehsht]; **to the southeast** a sudeste
southwest o sudoeste [soodwesht]; **to the southwest** a sudoeste
souvenir uma lembrança [lembransa]
spa as termas [tairmash]
space heater o aquecedor [a-kessidohr]
spade uma enxada [enshahda]
Spain a Espanha [shpan-ya]
Spaniard um espanhol [shpan-yol]
Spanish espanhol [shpan-yol]; **a Spanish woman** uma espanhola [shpan-yola]; **the Spanish** os espanhóis [shpan-yoish]
spanner a chave de porcas [shahv dih porkash]
spare part uma peça sobresselente [pessa sohbrisilent]
spare tyre o pneu sobresselente [pneh-oo sohbrisilent]
spark(ing) plug uma vela
speak: do you speak English? fala inglês? [fahla eenglehsh]; **I don't speak ...** não falo ... [nowng fahloo]; **can I speak to ...?** posso falar com ...? [possoo falahr kong]; **speaking** (telephone) é o próprio [e oo propr-yoo]
special especial [shpis-yahl]; **nothing special** nada de especial [nahda dih]
specialist um especialista [shpisyaleeshta]
special(i)ty (in restaurant) uma especialidade [shpis-yaleedahd]; **the special(i)ty of the house** a especialidade da casa [da kahza]
spectacles os óculos [okooloosh]
speed a velocidade [viloosseedahd]; **he was speeding** excedia o limite de velocidade [eesh-sidee-a limeet]
speedboat um barco a motor [bahrkoo a mootohr]
speed limit o limite de velocidade [limeet da viloosseedahd]
speedometer o conta-quilómetros [konta-keelomitroosh]

spell: how do you spell it? como é que se soletra? *[kohmoo e kih sih sooletra]*

spend (*money*) gastar *[gashtahr]*; **I've spent all my money** gastei o meu dinheiro todo *[gashtay oo meh-oo deenyay-roo tohdoo]*

spice uma especiaria *[shpis-yaree-a]*

spicy: it's very spicy está muito condimentado *[shtah mweengtoo kondeementahdoo]*

spider uma aranha *[aran-ya]*

spin-dryer o secador de roupa *[sikadohr dih rohpa]*

splendid esplêndido *[shplendeedoo]*

splint (*for broken limb*) uma tala

splinter uma falha *[fahl-ya]*

splitting: I've got a splitting headache tenho uma grande enxaqueca *[taing-nyoo ooma grand enshakehka]*

spoke (*in wheel*) um raio *[rye-oo]*

sponge uma esponja *[shponsна]*

spoon uma colher *[kool-yehr]*

sport o desporto *[dishpohrtoo]*

sport(s) jacket o blusão *[bloozowng]*

spot: will they do it on the spot? vão fazê-lo na altura? *[vowng fazeh-loo na ahltoora]*; (*on skin*) uma borbulha *[boorbool-ya]*

sprain: I've sprained my ... torci o ... *[toorsee]*

spray (*for hair*) a laca

spring (*season*) a Primavera *[preema-vehra]*; (*of car, seat etc*) a mola

square (*in town*) uma praça *[prahsa]*; **ten square metres** dez metros quadrados *[metroosh kwadrahdoosh]*

squash (*sport*) o squash *[shkwahsh]*

stain (*on clothes*) uma nódoa *[nodwa]*

stairs a escada *[shkahda]*

stale (*bread*) duro *[dooroo]*

stall: the engine keeps stalling o motor está sempre a falhar *[oo mootohr shtah sempra fal-yahr]*

stalls a plateia *[platay-a]*

stamp um selo *[seloo]*; **a stamp for England please** um selo para Inglaterra por favor

stand: I can't stand ... (*olives etc*) detesto ... *[diteshtoo]*

standard normal *[normahl]*

standby um standby

star uma estrela *[shtrehla]*

start o começo *[koomehsoo]*; (*verb*) co-

meçar *[koomisahr]*; **when does the film start?** quando é que começa o filme? *[kwandoo e kih koomessa]*; **the car won't start** o carro não pega *[oo kahrroo nowng pega]*

starter (*car*) o motor de arranque *[mootohr darrank]*; (*food*) a entrada *[aign-trahda]*

starving: I'm starving estou morto de fome *[shtoh mohrtoo dih fom]*

state (*in country*) o estado *[shtahdoo]*; **the States** (*USA*) os Estados Unidos *[shtahdooz ooneedoosh]*

station a estação *[shtassowng]*

statue uma est´tua *[shtaht-wa]*

stay: we enjoyed our stay gostámos imenso da nossa estadia *[gooshtahmooz eemensoo da nossa shtadee-a]*; **where are you staying?** onde está hospedado? *[ond shtah ohshpidahdoo]*; **I'm staying at ...** estou hospedado em ... *[shtoh ohshpidahdoo aing]*; **I'd like to stay another week** gostaria de ficar por mais uma semana *[gooshtaree-a dih feekahr poor mah-iz ooma simana]*; **I'm staying in tonight** eu não saio esta noite *[eh-oo nowng sah-yoo eshta noh-it]*

steak um bife *[beef]*

steal: my bag has been stolen roubaram-me a mala *[rohbahrowng m-ya mahla]*

steep (*hill*) íngreme *[eengrim]*

steering (*car*) a direcção *[deeressowng]*

steering wheel o volante *[voolant]*

step (*stair*) um degrau *[digrow]*

stereo estereofónico *[shtir-yoofoneekoo]*

sterling libras esterlinas *[leebraz ishtir-leenash]*

stew um guisado *[g-eezahdoo]*

steward (*on plane*) o comissário de bordo *[koomeesahr-yoo dih bohrdoo]*

stewardess a hospedeira *[ohshpiday-ra]*

sticking plaster um adesivo *[adizeevoo]*

sticky pegajoso *[pigasн-ohzoo]*

sticky tape a fita adesiva *[feeta adizeeva]*

still: I'm still waiting continuo à espera *[konteenoo-oo ah shpaira]*; **will you still be open?** estará aberto ainda? *[shtar-ahbairtoo a-eenda]*; **it's still not right** ainda não está bem *[a-eenda nowng shtah baing]*; **that's still better** melhor ainda *[mil-yor a-eenda]*

sting: a bee sting uma picada de abelha *[peekahda d-yabehl-ya]*; **I've been**

stung fui picado *[fwee peekahdoo]*
stink um mau cheiro *[mah-oo shay-roo]*
stockings as meias collants *[may-ash kollansh]*
stolen: my wallet's been stolen roubaram-me a carteira *[rohbahrowng-mih]*
stomach o estômago *[shtohmagoo]*; **do you have something for an upset stomach?** tem alguma coisa para as dores de estômago? *[taing ahlgooma koh-iza para ash dohrish dishtohmagoo]*
stomach-ache uma dor de estômago *[dohr dishtohmagoo]*
stone (*rock*) uma pedra *see page 120*
stop (*bus stop*) uma paragem *[parah-shaing]*; **which is the stop for ...?** qual é a paragem para ...? *[kwahl e]*; **please stop here** (*to taxi driver*) pare aqui, por favor *[pahr akee]*; **do you stop near ...?** pára perto de ...? *[pahra pairtoo dih]*; **stop doing that!** pare com isso! *[pahr kong eesoo]*
stopover uma paragem *[parah-shaing]*
store uma loja *[losha]*
storey o piso *[peezoo]*
storm uma tempestade *[tempishtahd]*
story uma história *[eeshtor-ya]*
stove o fogão *[foogowng]*
straight (*road etc*) recto *[rektoo]*; **it's straight ahead** é sempre em frente *[sempraing frent]*; **straight away** imediatamente *[eemid-yatament]*; **a straight whisky** um whisky puro *[pooroo]*
straighten: can you straighten things out? você pode resolver o assunto? *[vosseh pod rizohlvehr oo assoontoo]*
strange (*odd*) esquisito *[shkeezeetoo]*; (*unknown*) desconhecido *[dishkoon-yiseedoo]*
stranger um estranho *[shtran-yoo]*; **I'm a stranger here** sou de fora *[soh dih fora]*
strap (*on watch, suitcase*) a correia *[koorray-a]*; (*on dress*) a alça *[ahlssa]*
strawberries os morangos *[moorangoosh]*
streak: could you put streaks in? (*in hair*) pode fazer madeixas? *[pod fazehr maday-shash]*
stream a corrente *[koorrent]*
street a rua *[roo-a]*; **on the street** na rua
street café um café esplanada *[ka-fe*

shplanahda]*
streetcar o carro eléctrico *[eeletreekoo]*
streetmap um mapa da cidade *[seedahd]*
strep throat uma garganta inflamada
strike: they're on strike estão em greve *[shtowng aing grev]*
string o cordel *[koordel]*
striped às riscas *[ahsh reeshkash]*
striptease o striptease
stroke: he's had a stroke teve uma trombose *[tehv ooma trombohzih]*
stroll: let's go for a stroll vamos dar um passeio a pé *[vamoosh dahr oong passay-oo]*
stroller um carrinho de bébé *[karreenyoo dih beb-e]*
strong forte *[fort]*
stroppy antipático *[anteepahteekoo]*
stuck: the key's stuck a chave emperrou *[empirroh]*
student um estudante *[shtoodant]*
stupid estúpido *[shtoopeedoo]*
sty (*in eye*) um terçolho *[tirsohl-yoo]*
subtitles as legendas *[lishendash]*
suburb os arredores *[arridohrish]*
subway o metropolitano *[mitroopooleetanoo]*
successful: was it successful? foi bem sucedido? *[fohy baing soosideedoo]*
suddenly subitamente *[soobeetament]*
sue: I intend to sue eu faco tenção de processar *[fahsoo tensowng dih proosisahr]*
suede a camurça *[kamoorsa]*
sugar o açúcar *[assookahr]*
suggest: what do you suggest? o que é que sugere? *[oo k-ye kih soosshair]*
suit um fato *[fahtoo]*; **it doesn't suit me** (*colour etc*) não me fica bem *[nowng mih feeka baing]*; **it suits you** fica-lhe bem *[feekal-yih baing]*; **that suits me fine** para mim está bem *[para meeng shtah baing]*
suitable adequado *[adikwahdoo]*
suitcase uma mala
sulk: he's sulking ele está amuado *[amwahdoo]*
sultry (*weather*) abafado *[abafahdoo]*
summer o Verão *[virowng]*; **in the summer** no Verão
sun o sol; **in the sun** ao sol *[ow]*; **out of the sun** à sombra *[ah]*; **I've had too much sun** estive ao sol tempo demais *[shteev*

ow sol tempoo dimah-ish]
sunbathe tomar banhos de sol *[toomahr ban-yoosh]*
sun block a loção écran total *[loosowng ehkrang tootahl]*
sunburn uma queimadura de sol *[kaymadoora]*
sunburnt queimado de sol *[kay-mahdoo]*
Sunday domingo *[doomeengoo]*
sunglasses os óculos de sol *[okooloosh]*
sun lounger *(recliner)* uma cadeira reclinável *[kaday-ra rikleenahvel]*
sunny: if it's sunny se estiver sol *[sishteevair]*
sunrise o nascer do sol *[nash-sehr]*
sun roof *(in car)* o tejadilho para sol *[tisнadeel-yoo para sol]*
sunset o pôr do sol *[pohr]*
sunshade *(over table)* o chapéu de sol *[shap-e-oo]*
sunshine a luz do sol *[loosh]*
sunstroke uma insolação *[eensoolasowng]*
suntan um bronzeado *[bronz-yahdoo]*
suntan lotion/oil a loção/óleo de bronzear *[loosowng/ohleeoo dih bronz-yahr]*
suntanned bronzeado *[bronz-yahdoo]*
sun worshipper um fanático do sol *[fanahteekoo]*
super óptimo *[oteemoo]*
superb soberbo *[soobairboo]*
supermarket um supermercado *[soopirmirkahdoo]*
supper o jantar *[sнantahr]*
supplement um suplemento *[sooplimentoo]*
suppose: I suppose so penso que sim *[pensoo kih seeng]*
suppository um supositório *[soopoozeetor-yoo]*
sure: I'm sure tenho a certeza *[taingnyoo a sirtehza]*; **are you sure?** tem a certeza? *[taing a sirtehza]*; **he's sure** ele tem a certeza; **sure!** claro! *[klahroo]*
surf o surf
surfboard uma prancha de surf *[pransha]*

surfing: to go surfing fazer surf *[fazehr]*
surname o apelido *[apileedoo]*
surprise uma surpresa *[soorprehza]*
surprising: that's not surprising não me surpreende *[nowng mih soorpr-yend]*
suspension *(on car)* a suspensão *[sooshpensowng]*
swallow engolir *[aing-gooleer]*
swearword uma asneira *[asнnay-ra]*
sweat suar *[swahr]*; **covered in sweat** todo suado *[tohdoo swahdoo]*
sweater a camisola *[kameezola]*
Sweden a Suécia *[swess-ya]*
sweet *(taste)* doce *[dohs]*; *(dessert)* a sobremesa *[sohbrimehza]*
sweets os rebuçados *[riboosahdoosh]*
swelling um inchaço *[eenshahsoo]*
sweltering abrasador *[abrazadohr]*
swerve: I had to swerve tive de guinar para o lado *[teev dih g-eenahr pro lahdoo]*
swim: I'm going for a swim vou tomar banho *[voh toomahr ban-yoo]*; **do you want to go for a swim?** quer ir tomar banho? *[kair eer]*; **I can't swim** eu não sei nadar *[nowng say nadahr]*
swimming: I like swimming eu gosto de nadar *[eh-oo goshtoo dih nadahr]*
swimming costume um fato de banho *[fahtoo dih ban-yoo]*
swimming pool a piscina *[peesh-seena]*
swimming trunks os calções de banho *[kalsoingsh dih ban-yoo]*
switch o interruptor *[eentirooptohr]*; **could you switch it on?** *(lamp)* pode acendê-la? *[pod asendeh-la]*; *(appliance)* pode ligá-lo? *[leegah-loo]*; **could you switch it off?** *(lamp)* pode apagá-la?; *(appliance)* pode desligá-lo? *[disнleegah-loo]*
Switzerland a Suíça *[sweesa]*
swollen inchado *[eenshahdoo]*
swollen glands glândulas inchadas *[glandoolaz eenshahdash]*
synagogue uma sinagoga *[seenagoga]*
synthetic sintético *[seenteteekoo]*

table   69   teetotal

T

table uma mesa *[mehza]*; **a table for two** uma mesa para dois *[para doh-ish]*; **at our usual table** na nossa mesa habitual *[mehza abeetwahl]*

tablecloth a toalha de mesa *[twahl-ya dih mehza]*

table tennis o ténis de mesa *[teneesh dih mehza]*

table wine o vinho de mesa *[veen-yoo dih mehza]*

tactful de tacto *[dih tahktoo]*

tailback uma fila de carros *[feela dih kahrroosh]*

tailor um alfaiate *[ahlfay-aht]*

take tomar *[toomahr]*; **will you take this to room 12?** pode levar isto ao quarto 12? *[pod livahr eeshtoo ow kwahrtoo]*; **will you take me to Hotel ...?** pode levar-me ao hotel ...?; **do you take credit cards?** aceita cartões de crédito? *[asay-ta kartoingsh dih kredeetoo]*; **ok, I'll take it** está bem, levo-o *[shtah baing, levoo]*; **how long does it take?** quanto tempo leva? *[kwantoo tempoo leva]*; **it took 2 hours** levou duas horas *[livoh]*; **is this seat taken?** este lugar está ocupado? *[ehsht loogahr shtah ohkoopahdoo]*; **I can't take too much sun** não posso apanhar muito sol *[nowng possoo apan-yahr mweengtoo sol]*; **to take away** (*food*) para levar *[para livahr]*; **will you take this back, it's broken?** aceita isto de volta, está partido? *[assayta eeshtoo dih volta, shtah parteeda]*; **could you take it in at the side?** (*dress*) pode apertá-lo do lado? *[pod apirtah-loo doo lahdoo]*; **when does the plane take off?** a que horas parte o avião? *[a k-yorash pahrt oo av-yowng]*; **can you take a little off the top?** pode cortar um pouco em cima? *[pod koortahr oong pohkoo aing seema]*

talcum powder o pó de talco *[paw dih tahlkoo]*

talk falar

tall alto *[ahltoo]*

tampax (*tm*) os tampões tampax *[tampoingsh]*

tan um bronzeado *[bronz-yahdoo]*; **I want to get a good tan** quero ficar com um bom bronzeado *[kairoo feekahr kong oong bong bronz-yahdoo]*

tank (*of car*) o depósito *[dipozeetoo]*

tap a torneira *[toornay-ra]*

tape (*for cassette*) a fita *[feeta]*; (*sticky*) a fita adesiva *[adizeeva]*

tape measure o metro *[metroo]*

tape recorder um gravador *[gravadohr]*

taste o sabor *[sabohr]*; **can I taste it?** posso provar? *[posoo proovahr]*; **it has a peculiar taste** tem um sabor estranho *[taing oong sabohr shtran-yoo]*; **it tastes very nice** sabe muito bem *[sahb mweengtoo baing]*; **it tastes revolting** sabe muito mal *[mahl]*

taxi um táxi; **will you get me a taxi?** pode chamar-me um táxi? *[pod shamahr-mih]*

taxi-driver o pracista *[praseeshta]*

taxi rank uma praça de táxis *[prahsa]*

tea (*drink*) chá *[shah]*; **tea for two please** chá para dois por favor; **could I have a cup of tea?** queria um chá *[kiree-a]*

teabag uma carteira de chá *[kartay-ra dih shah]*

teach: could you teach me? pode ensinar-me? *[pod aing-seenahr-mih]*; **could you teach me Portuguese?** pode ensinar-me português? *[pod aing-seenahr-mih poortoogehsh]*

teacher o professor *[proofisohr]*

team a equipa *[eekeepa]*

teapot um bule *[bool]*

tea towel um pano de cozinha *[panoo dih koozeen-ya]*

teenager um adolescente *[adoolish-sent]*

teetotal abstémio *[abshtem-yoo]*

telegram um telegrama [tiligrama]; **I want to send a telegram** quero enviar um telegrama [kairoo env-yahr]

telephone o telefone [tilifon]; **can I make a telephone call?** posso usar o telefone? [possoo oozahr]; **could you talk to him for me on the telephone?** pode falar com ele por mim ao telefone? [pod falahr kong ehl poor meeng ow]

telephone box a cabine telefónica [kabeen tilifoneeka]

telephone directory a lista telefónica [leeshta tilifoneeka]

telephone number o número de telefone [noomiroo dih tilifon]; **what's your telephone number?** qual é o seu número de telefone? [kwahl e oo seh-oo]

telephoto lens a teleobjectiva [tilyobsнeteeva]

television a televisão [tiliveezowng]; **I'd like to watch television** gostava de ver televisão [gooshtahva dih vehr]; **is the match on television?** vão dar o jogo na televisão? [vowng dahr oo sнohgoo na]

tell: **could you tell him ...?** pode dizer-lhe ...? [pod deezehrl-yih]; **I can't tell the difference** não vejo diferença [nowng vehsнoo deefirensa]

temperature (weather etc) a temperatura [tempiratoora]; **he has a temperature** tem febre [taing febrih]

temporary temporário [tempoorahr-yoo]

tenant o inquilino [eenkeeleenoo]

tennis o ténis [teneesh]

tennis ball uma bola de ténis [teneesh]

tennis court o campo de ténis [kampoo dih teneesh]; **can we use the tennis court?** podemos usar o campo de ténis? [poodehmooz oozahr]

tennis racket uma raquete de ténis [rakett dih teneesh]

tent uma tenda

term (school) o período escolar [pireeoodoo shkoolahr]

terminus o terminal [tirmeenahl]

terrace o terraço [tirrahsoo]; **on the terrace** no terraço [noo]

terrible terrível [tirreevel]

terrific esplêndido [shplendeedoo]

testicle o testículo [tishteekooloo]

than do que [doo kih]; **smaller than** mais pequeno do que [mah-ish pikehnoo]

thanks, thank you obrigado [ohbree-gahdoo]; (said by woman) obrigada; **thank you very much** muito obrigado [mweengtoo]; **thank you for everything** obrigado por tudo [poor toodoo]; **no thanks** não obrigado [nowng]

that: **that woman** essa mulher [moolyair]; **that man** esse homen [ehsyomaing]; **that one** esse/essa; **I hope that ...** espero que ... [shpairoo kih]; **that's perfect** perfeito [pirfaytoo]; **that's very strange** isso é muito estranho [eesoo e mweengtoo shtran-yoo]; **that's not ...** isso não e ... [eessou nowng e]; **that's it** (that's right) certo [sehrtoo]; **is it that expensive?** é assim tão caro? [e asseeng towng kahroo]

the (singular) o, a [oo]; (plural) os, as [oosh, ash] see page 108

theater, theatre o teatro [t-yahtroo]

their: **their bags** as malas deles (delas) [dehlsh, delash] see page 110

theirs deles (delas) see page 113

them: **I saw them** vi-os (vi-as) [vee-oosh, —ash]; **for them** para eles (elas) [para ehlsh, elash] see page 112

then então [entowng]

there ali [alee]; **over there** ali adiante [ad-yant]; **up there** ali acima [aseema]; **there is/are ...** há ... [ah]; **is there ...?** há ...?; **are there ...?** há ...?; **there you are** (giving something) tome lá [tom lah]

thermal spring uma fonte termal [font tirmahl]

thermometer o termómetro [tirmomitroo]

thermos flask um termo [tairmoo]

thermostat (in car) o termostato [tirmooshtahtoo]

these estes, estas [ehshtish, eshtash]; **can I have these?** pode dar-me estes? [pod dahr-mih ehshtish]

they eles, elas [ehlsh, elash]; **are they ready?** estão prontos? [shtowng prontoosh]; **are they coming?** eles vêm? [ehlsh vaing-aing] see page 112

thick espesso [shpehsoo]; (stupid) estúpido [shtoopeedoo]

thief um ladrão [ladrowng]

thigh a coxa [kohsha]

thin (material) fino [feenoo]; (person) magro [mahgroo]

thing uma coisa [koh-iza]; **have you seen my things?** viu as minhas coisas? [vee-oo

ash *meen-yash]*; **first thing in the morning** logo de manhã *[logoo dih man-yang]*
think pensar; **what do you think?** o que acha? *[oo k-yahsha]*; **I think so** acho que sim *[ahshoo kih seeng]*; **I don't think so** acho que não *[ahshoo kih nowng]*; **I'll think about it** vou pensar *[voh pensahr]*
third class *(travel)* terceira classe *[tirsay-ra klahs]*
third party *(insurance)* contra terceiros *[tirsay-roosh]*
thirsty: I'm thirsty tenho sede *[taing-nyoo sehd]*
this: this hotel este hotel *[ehsht ohtel]*; **this street** esta rua *[eshta roo-a]*; **this one** este/esta; **this is my wife** esta é a minha mulher *[meen-ya mool-yair]*; **this is my favo(u)rite cafe** este é o meu café favorito *[ehsht e oo]*; **is this yours?** isto é seu? *[eeshtoo e seh-oo]*; **this is ...** *(on phone)* daqui ... *[dakee]*
those esses, essas *[ehsish, essash]*; **not these, those** estes não, esses
thread o fio *[fee-oo]*
throat a garganta
throat lozenges as pastilhas para as dores de garganta *[pashteel-yash prahsh dohrish dih]*
throttle o acelerador *[asiliradohr]*
through através de *[atravesh dih]*; **does it go through Paris?** passa em Paris? *[aing]*; **Monday through Friday** de segunda a sexta-feira inclusive *[dih ... eenkloozeev-e]*; **straight through the city centre** através do centro da cidade *[sentroo da seedahd]*; **through train** um combóio directo *[komboy-oo deeretoo]*
throw atirar *[ateerahr]*; **don't throw it away** não o deite fora *[nowng oo daytih]*; **I'm going to throw up** vou vomitar *[voh voomeetahr]*
thumb o polegar *[poolgahr]*
thumbtack um pionês *[p-yoonehsh]*
thunder um trovão *[troovowng]*
thunderstorm a trovoada *[troovwahda]*
Thursday quinta-feira *[keenta fay-ra]*
ticket um bilhete *[beel-yeht]*; *(cloakroom, checkroom)* a senha *[sen-ya]*
ticket office a bilheteira *[beel-yitay-ra]*
tide: at low tide com a maré baixa *[kong a ma-re bah-isha]*; **at high tide** com a

maré alta *[ahlta]*
tie *(necktie)* uma gravata
tight *(clothes)* apertado *[apirtahdoo]*; **the waist is too tight** está demasiado apertado na cintura *[shtah dimaz-yahdoo]*
tights uns collants *[kolansh]*
time tempo *[tempoo]*; **what's the time?** que horas são? *[k-yorash sowng]*; **at what time do you close?** a que horas fecha? *[a k-yorash fehsha]*; **there's not much time** não há tempo a perder *[nowng ah tempoo a pirdehr]*; **for the time being** por enquanto *[poor enkwantoo]*; **from time to time** de vez em quando *[dih vehz aing kwandoo]*; **right on time** mesmo a tempo *[mehsнmoo]*; **this time** esta vez *[eshta vehsh]*; **last time** a última vez *[a oolteema]*; **next time** a próxima vez *[prosseema]*; **four times** quatro vezes *[kwahtroo vehzish]*; **have a good time!** divirta-se! *[deevehrta-sih] see page 118*
timetable o horário *[oo orahr-yoo]*
tin *(can)* uma lata
tinfoil o papel de alumínio *[pa-pel d-aloomeen-yoo]*
tin-opener um abre-latas *[ahbrilahtash]*
tint *(hair)* pintar o cabelo *[peentahr oo kabehloo]*
tiny minúsculo *[meenooshkooloo]*
tip uma gorjeta *[goor-sнehta]*; **does that include the tip?** isso inclui a gorjeta? *[eesoo eenklooy]*
tire um pneu *[p-neh-oo]*
tired cansado *[kansahdoo]*; **I'm tired** estou cansado *[shtoh]*
tiring cansativo *[kansateevoo]*
tissues os lenços de papel *[lensoosh dih pa-pel]*
to: to Lisbon/England para Lisboa/Inglaterra; **to the airport** para o aeroporto; **here's to you!** *(toast)* à sua saúde! *[ah soo-a sa-ood] see page 118*
toast uma torrada *[toorah-da]*; *(drinking)* um brinde *[breend]*
tobacco o tabaco *[tabahkoo]*
tobacconist, tobacco store uma tabacaria *[tabakaree-a]*
today hoje *[ohsн]*; **today week** de hoje a uma semana *[d-yohsнa ooma simana]*
toe um dedo do pé *[dehdoo doo pe]*
toffee um caramelo *[karamehloo]*
together junto *[sнoontoo]*; **we're together** viemos juntos *[v-yemoosh*

sнoontoosh]; **can we pay together?** podemos pagar junto? [poodehmoosh pagahr]

toilet o quarto de banho [kwahrtoo dih ban-yoo]; **where's the toilet?** onde é o quarto de banho? [ond-ye]; **I have to go to the toilet** tenho de ir ao quarto de banho [taing-nyoo deer ow]; **she's in the toilet** ela está no quarto de banho [ela shtah]

toilet paper papel higiénico [pa-pel eesн-yeneekoo]

toilet water a água de toilette [ahgwa dih twahlet]

toll a portagem [poortah-sнaing]; **motorway toll** a portagem de auto-estrada [d-yowtooshtrahda]

tomato um tomate [toomaht]

tomato juice um sumo de tomate [soomoo dih toomaht]

tomato ketchup o ketchup

tomorrow amanhã [ahman-yang]; **tomorrow morning** amanhã de manhã [dih man-yang]; **tomorrow afternoon** amanhã à tarde [ah tahrd]; **tomorrow evening** amanhã à noite [ah noh-it]; **the day after tomorrow** depois de amanhã [dipoh-ish d-yahman-yang]; **see you tomorrow** até amanhã [a-te]

ton tonelada [toonilahda] see page 120

toner o tónico [toneekoo]

tongue a língua [leeng-gwa]

tonic (water) a água tónica [ahgwa toneeka]

tonight esta noite [eshta noh-it]; **not tonight** esta noite não [nowng]

tonsillitis a amigdalite [ameegdaleet]

tonsils as amígdalas [az ameegdalash]

too demasiado [dimaz-yahdoo]; (also) também [tambaing]; **too much** demais [dimah-ish]; **me too** eu também [eh-oo tambaing]; **I'm not feeling too good** não estou a sentir-me muito bem [nowng shtoh a seenteer-mih nweengtoo baing]

tooth um dente [dent]

toothache uma dor de dentes [dohr dih dentsh]

toothbrush uma escova de dentes [shkohva dih dentsh]

toothpaste a pasta de dentes [pahshta dih dentsh]

top: on top of ... em cima de ... [aing seema dih]; **on top of the car** em cima do carro; **on the top floor** no último andar [noo oolteemoo andahr]; **at the top** no alto [noo ahltoo]; **at the top of the hill** na cima do monte [na seema doo mont]; **top quality** de alta qualidade [d-yahlta kwaleedahd]; **bikini top** a parte de cima do bikini [pahrt dih seema]

topless monokini; **topless beach** uma praia de monokinis

torch uma lanterna [lantairna]

total o total [tootahl]

touch tocar [tookahr]; **let's keep in touch** vamos manter-nos em contacto [vamoosh mantehr-nooz aing kontahktoo]

tough (meat) dura [doora]; **tough luck!** azar! [azahr]

tour (outdoors) uma excursão [shkoorsowng]; (indoors) uma visita guiada [vizeeta g-ee-ahda]; **is there a tour of ...?** há alguma excursão/visita guiada a ...? [ahlgooma]

tour guide o guia turístico [g-ee-a tooreeshteekoo]

tourist um turista [tooreeshta]

tourist office o turismo [tooreesнmoo]

touristy: somewhere not so touristy um sítio não tão turístico [seet-yoo nowng towng tooreeshteekoo]

tour operator o operador turístico [ohpiradohr tooreeshteekoo]

tow: can you give me a tow? pode rebocar o meu carro? [pod ribookahr oo meh-oo kahrroo]

toward(s) para; **towards Lisbon** para Lisboa

towel uma toalha [twahl-ya]

town uma cidade [seedahd]; (smaller) uma vila [veela]; **in town** na cidade; **which bus goes into town?** qual é o autocarro que passa na cidade? [kwahl e oo owtookahrroo kih pahssa na seedahd]; **we're staying just out of town** estamos hospedados à saída da cidade [shtamooz ohshpidahdooz ah sa-eeda]

town hall a câmara municipal [mooneeseepahl]

tow rope o cabo de reboque [kahboo dih ribok]

toy um brinquedo [breenkehdoo]

track suit um fato de treino [fahtoo dih tray-noo]

traditional tradicional [tradeesyoonahl]; **a traditional Portuguese**

meal uma refeição tradicional portuguesa [riʃay-**sowng** tradees-yoon**ah**l poortoog**eh**za]

traffic o trânsito [tr**a**nzeetoo]

traffic circle uma rotunda [root**oo**nda]

traffic cop um polícia de trânsito [poolees-ya dih tr**a**nzeetoo]

traffic jam um engarrafamento [ainggarrafam**e**ntoo]

traffic light(s) os semáforos [simahʃooroosh]

trailer (for carrying tent etc) um atrelado [atril**ah**doo]; (caravan) uma caravana

train o combóio [komb**o**y-oo]; **when's the next train to ...?** a que horas é o próximo combóio para ...? [a k-y**o**raz e oo pros**ee**moo]; **by train** de combóio [dih]

trainers (shoes) uns sapatos de treino [sap**ah**toosh dih tr**a**y-noo]

train station a estação de combóio [shta**sowng** dih komb**o**y-oo]

tram o eléctrico [eel**e**treekoo]

tramp (person) um vagabundo [vagab**oo**ndoo]

tranquillizers os tranquilizantes [trankweele**e**z**a**ntsh]

transatlantic transatlântico

transformer um transformador [transhfoormad**oh**r]

transistor (radio) uma rádio transistor [r**a**hd-yoo tranzeesht**oh**r]

transit desk o balcão de trânsito [bahlk**owng** dih tr**a**nzeetoo]

translate traduzir [tradooz**eer**]; **could you translate that?** pode traduzir isto? [pod]

translation a tradução [tradoos**owng**]

transmission (of car) a transmissão [transhmeess**owng**]

travel viajar [v-yas**n**ahr]; **we're travel(l)ing around** estamos a viajar por aí [sht**a**mooz a v-yas**n**ahr poor a-**ee**]

travel agency a agência de viagens [as**n**ens-ya dih v-y**a**h-s**n**aingsh]

travel(l)er um viajante [v-yas**n**ant]

traveller's cheque, traveler's check um travel-cheque [shek]

tray uma trav**e**ssa

tree uma árvore [**ah**rvoorih]

tremendous bestial [bisht-y**ah**l]

trendy à m**o**da [ah]

tricky difícil [dif**ee**seel]

trim: just a trim please só aparar por

fav**o**r [saw]

trip uma excursão [shkoor-**sowng**]; **I'd like to go on a trip to ...** eu gostava de ir numa viagem a ... [goosht**a**hva deer n**oo**ma v-y**a**h-s**n**aing]; **have a good trip** boa viagem [b**oh**-a v-y**a**h-s**n**aing]

tripod um tripé [tree-p**e**]

tropical tropical [troopeek**ah**l]

trouble problemas [pr**oo**bl**eh**mash]; **I'm having trouble with ...** tenho tido problemas com ... [t**a**ing-nyoo t**ee**doo]; **sorry to trouble you** desculpe incomodá-lo [dishk**oo**lp eenkoomood**ah**-loo]

trousers as calças [k**ah**lsash]

trouser suit um conjunto de calças e casaco [kons**n**oontoo dih k**ah**lsash ee kaz**ah**koo]

trout uma truta [tr**oo**ta]

truck um camião [kam-y**owng**]

truck driver um camionista [kam-yoon**ee**shta]

true verdadeiro [virdad**a**y-roo]; **that's not true** nao é verdade [nowng e vird**ah**d]

trunk o porta-bagagens [—bag**ah**-s**n**aingsh]

trunks (swimming) os calções de banho [k**ah**ls**o**ingsh dih ban-yoo]

truth a verdade [vird**ah**d]; **it's the truth** isto é a verdade [**ee**shtoo e]

try tentar; **please try** tente, por fav**o**r [tent]; **I've never tried it** (food) nunca provei [n**oo**nka proov**ay**]; (sport etc) nunca experimentei [shpireement**ay**]; **can I have a try?** posso provar/experimentar? [p**o**soo]; **may I try it on?** posso prová-lo? [p**o**ssoo proov**ah**-loo]

T-shirt uma T-shirt

tube (inner tube) a câmara de ar [d-yahr]

Tuesday terça-feira [t**eh**rsa f**a**y-ra]

tuition: I'd like tuition eu queria explicações [**eh**-oo kir**ee**-a shpleekas**o**ingsh]

tulip uma tulipa [tool**ee**pa]

tuna fish o atum [at**oo**ng]

tune uma música [m**oo**zeeka]

tunnel um túnel [t**oo**nel]

Turkey a Turquia [toork**ee**-a]

turn: it's my turn next eu sou a seguir [**eh**-oo soh a sig-**eer**]; **turn left** volte à esquerda [volt ah shk**eh**rda]; **where do we turn off?** onde é que viramos? [ondye kih veer**a**moosh]; **can you turn the air-conditioning on?** pode ligar o ar condicionado? [pod leeg**ah**r]; **can you**

turn the air-conditioning off? pode desligar o ar condicionado? *[pod disнleegaнr]*; **he didn't turn up** ele não apareceu *[ehl nowng apariseн-oo]*

turning (*in road*) uma curva *[koo*rva]

TV TV *[teh-veh]*

tweezers uma pinça *[peensa]*

twice duas vezes *[doo-ash veнzish]*; **twice as much** o dobro *[oo doнbroo]*

twin beds umas camas separadas *[ka-mash siparaнdash]*

twins os gémeos *[sнem-yoosh]*

twist: I've twisted my ankle torci o meu tornozelo *[toorsee]*

type o tipo *[teepoo]*; **a different type of** ... um tipo diferente de ... *[deefirent dih]*

typewriter uma máquina de escrever *[maнkeena dih shkriveнr]*

typhoid o tifo *[teefoo]*

typical típico *[teepeekoo]*

tyre um pneu *[p-neн-oo]*

U

ugly feio *[fay-oo]*

ulcer uma úlcera *[oolsira]*

Ulster o Ulster *[oolstair]*

umbrella um guarda-chuva *[gwaнrda-shoova]*

uncle: my uncle o meu tio *[oo meн-oo tee-oo]*

uncomfortable desconfortável *[dishkonfoortaнvel]*

unconscious inconsciente *[eenkonsh-syent]*

under debaixo de *[dibaн-ishoo]*

underdone (*food*) mal passado *[passaн-doo]*

underground (*rail*) o metro *[metroo]*

underpants as cuecas *[kwekash]*

undershirt a camisola interior *[kamee-zola eentir-yoнr]*

understand: I don't understand não percebo *[nowng perseнboo]*; **I understand** já percebi *[sнah pirsibee]*; **do you understand?** está a compre-ender? *[shtah a kompree-endeнr]*

underwear a roupa interior *[rohpa eentir-yoнr]*

undo (*clothes*) desapertar *[dizapirtaнr]*

uneatable: it's uneatable não se pode comer *[nowng sih pod koomeнr]*

unemployed desempregado *[dizaing-prigaнdoo]*

unfair: that's unfair não é justo *[nowng é sнooshtoo]*

unfortunately infelizmente *[eenfi-leesнment]*

unfriendly antipático *[anteepaнteekoo]*

unhappy infeliz *[eenfileesh]*

unhealthy (*food, climate, lifestyle*) pouco saudável *[pohkoo sowdaнvel]*

United States os Estados Unidos *[shtaн-dooz ooneedoosh]*; **in the United States** nos Estados Unidos

university a universidade *[ooneevir-seedaнd]*

unlimited mileage (*on hire car*) quilome-tragem ilimitada *[keeloomitraн-sнaing ilimeetaнda]*

unlock abrir *[abreнr]*; **the door was unlocked** a fechadura estava aberta *[a fishadoora shtahv ahbaнirta]*

unpack desfazer as malas *[dishfazeнr ash maнlash]*

unpleasant desagradável *[dizagra-daнvel]*

untie desatar *[dizataнr]*

until até a *[a-te]*; **until we meet again** até à vista *[a-te ah veeshta]*; **not until Wednesday** não antes de quarta-feira *[nowng antish]*

unusual pouco vulgar *[pohkoo voolgaнr]*

up: further up the road mais acima *[maн-iz aseema]*; **up there** lá em cima *[lah aing seema]*; **he's not up yet** ele ainda não está levantado *[a-eenda nowng shtah livantaн-doo]*; **what's up?** o que a conteceu? *[oo kih akontisseh-oo]*

upmarket (*restaurant, bar*) sofisticado *[soofeeshteekahdoo]*

upset stomach um desarranjo intestinal *[dizarranshoo eentishteenahl]*

upside down de pernas para o ar *[dih pairnash pro ahr]*

upstairs lá em cima *[aing seema]*

urgent urgente *[oor-shent]*; **it's really very urgent** é muito urgente *[mweengtoo]*

urinary tract infection uma infecção urinária *[eenfeksowng ooreenahr-ya]*

us nos *[noosh]*; **with us** connosco *[konoshkoo]*; **for us** para nós *[para nosh]*;

please help us ajude-nos, por favor *[ashoodinoosh] see page 112*

use: may I use ...? posso usar ...? *[possoo oozahr]*

used: I used to swim a lot eu costumava nadar muito *[eh-oo kooshtoomahva]*; **when I get used to the heat** quando eu me habitar ao calor *[kwandoo m-yabeetahr]*

useful útil *[ooteel]*

usual usual *[ooz-wahl]*; **as usual** como de costume *[kohmoo dih kooshtoom]*

usually geralmente *[shirahlment]*

U-turn inversão de marcha *[eenvir-sowng dih mahrsha]*

V

vacancy: do you have any vacancies? tem quartos livres? *[taing kwahrtoosh leevrish]*

vacation as férias *[fair-yash]*; **we're here on vacation** estamos aqui em férias *[shtamooz akee aing]*

vaccination a vacinação *[vasseena-sowng]*

vacuum cleaner um aspirador *[ash-peeradohr]*

vacuum flask um termo *[tairmoo]*

vagina a vagina *[vasheena]*

valid válido *[vahleedoo]*; **how long is it valid for?** é válido para quanto tempo? *[kwantoo tempoo]*

valley um vale *[vahl]*

valuable valioso *[val-yohzoo]*; **can I leave my valuables here?** posso deixar aqui os meus artigos de valor? *[possoo day-shahr akee oosh meh-ooz arteegoosh dih valohr]*

value o valor *[valohr]*

van um furgão *[foorgowng]*

vanilla baunilha *[bowneel-ya]*; **vanilla ice cream** um gelado de baunilha *[shilahdoo]*

varicose veins as varizes *[vareezish]*

variety show um espectáculo de varie-

dades *[shpetahkooloo dih var-yidahdish]*

vary: it varies varia *[varee-a]*

vase uma jarra *[shahrra]*

vaudeville um espectáculo de revista *[shpetahkooloo dih riveeshta]*

VD uma doença venérea *[dwensa vinair-ya]*

veal a vitela *[veetela]*

vegetables os legumes *[ligoomsh]*

vegetarian vegetariano *[vishitar-yanoo]*; **I'm a vegetarian** sou vegetariano *[soh]*

velvet o veludo *[viloodoo]*

vending machine uma máquina de venda *[mahkeena dih venda]*

ventilator o exaustor *[eezowshtohr]*

verruca uma verruga *[virrooga]*

very muito *[mweengtoo]*; **just a very little Portuguese** apenas um pouco de português *[apehnash oong pohkoo dih]*; **just a very little for me** apenas muito pouco para mim *[meeng]*; **I like it very much** gosto muito disso *[goshtoo mwe-engtoo deesoo]*

vest (*undershirt*) uma camisola interior *[kameezola eentir-yohr]*; (*waistcoat*) um colete *[kooleht]*

via via *[vee-a]*

video um video *[veed-**eh**-oo]*
view a vista *[**vee**shta]*; **what a superb view!** que bela vista! *[kih]*
viewfinder o visor *[veez**ohr**]*
villa uma vivenda *[veev**enda**]*
village uma aldeia *[ahld**ay**-a]*
vine uma videira *[veed**ay**-ra]*
vinegar vinagre *[veen**ah**grih]*
vine-growing area uma região de vinhos *[rish-**yow**ng dih v**een**-yoosh]*
vineyard uma vinha *[v**een**-ya]*
vintage (*noun*) a colheita *[kool-y**ay**-ta]*; (*adjective*) velho *[v**ehl**-yo]*; **vintage wine** um vinho velho *[v**een**-yoo]*

visa um visto *[v**ee**shtoo]*
visibility a visibilidade *[vizibeeleed**ahd**]*
visit visitar *[vizeet**ahr**]*; **I'd like to visit ...** eu gostaria de visitar ... *[**eh**-oo gooshtahr**ee**-a dih]*; **come and visit us** venha visitar-nos *[v**eh**n-ya vizeet**ahr**-noosh]*
vital: it's vital that ... é vital que ... *[e veet**ahl** kih]*
vitamins as vitaminas *[veetam**ee**nash]*
vodka um vodka
voice a voz *[vosh]*
voltage a voltagem *[v**oh**ltah-shaing]*
vomit vomitar *[voomeet**ahr**]*

W

wafer (*biscuit*) uma bolacha *[bool**ah**sha]*; (*ice cream*) um gelado com bolacha *[shil**ah**doo]*
waist a cintura *[seent**oo**ra]*
waistcoat um colete *[kool**eht**]*
wait esperar *[shpir**ahr**]*; **wait for me** espere por mim *[shpair poor meeng]*; **don't wait for me** não espere por mim *[nowng]*; **it was worth waiting for** valeu a pena esperar *[val**eh**-oo a p**eh**na]*; **I'll wait till my wife comes** vou esperar que a minha mulher chegue *[voh shpir**ahr** k-ya m**een**-ya mool-y**air** shehg]*; **I'll wait a little longer** vou esperar mais um pouco *[m**ah**-iz oong p**oh**koo]*; **can you do it while I wait?** você pode fazer isso enquanto eu espero? *[voss**eh** pod faz**ehr** **ee**ssoo enkw**an**too **eh**-oo shp**ai**roo]*
waiter o empregado *[emprig**ah**doo]*; **waiter!** se faz favor! *[sih fahsh fav**ohr**]*
waiting room a sala de espera *[dishp**ai**ra]*
waitress a empregada *[emprig**ah**da]*; **waitress!** se faz favor! *[sih fahsh fav**ohr**]*
wake: will you wake me up at 6.30? pode acordar-me às seis e meia? *[pod akoord**ahr**-mih]*
Wales o País de Gales *[pa-**ee**sh dih g**ah**lish]*

walk: let's walk there vamos caminhar até ali *[v**a**moosh kameen-y**ahr** a-te al**ee**]*; **is it possible to walk there?** pode-se ir a pé até ali? *[p**o**d-sih eer a pe a-te al**ee**]*; **I'll walk back** eu volto para trás a pé *[v**o**ltoo para trahsh a pe]*; **is it a long walk?** é muito longe a pé? *[mw**ee**ngtoo lonsh]*; **it's only a short walk** é perto a pé *[p**ai**rtoo]*; **I'm going out for a walk** vou sair para um passeio a pé *[voh sa-**ee**r para oong pass**ay**-oo]*; **let's take a walk around town** vamos caminhar pela vila *[v**a**moosh kameen-y**ahr** p**eh**la v**ee**la]*
walking: I want to do some walking quero andar a pé um pouco *[k**ai**roo and**ah**r a pe oong p**oh**koo]*
walking boots as botas *[b**o**tash]*
walking stick uma bengala
walkman (*tm*) um walkman
wall (*inside*) a parede *[par**ehd**]*; (*outside*) o muro *[m**oo**roo]*
wallet uma carteira *[kart**ay**-ra]*
wander: I like just wandering around gosto de andar a ver *[g**o**shtoo d-yand**ahr** a vehr]*
want: I want a ... queria um ... *[k**ee**re-a]*; **I don't want any ...** não quero ... *[nowng k**ai**roo]*; **I want to go home** quero ir para casa *[k**ai**roo eer para k**ah**za]*; **but I want**

to mas eu quero *[maz **eh**-oo]*; **I don't want to** não quero; **he wants to ...** ele quer ... *[kair]*; **what do you want?** o que deseja? *[oo kih diz**eh**-sнa]*

war a guerra *[g**ai**rra]*

ward (*in hospital*) a enfermaria *[aingfirmar**ee**-a]*

warm quente *[kent]*; **it's so warm today** hoje está tão quente *[ohsнshtah towng]*; **I'm so warm** tenho tanto calor *[taingnyoo t**a**ntoo kal**oh**r]*

warning um aviso *[av**ee**zoo]*

was: it was ... era; estava *[sht**a**hva] see pages 115, 117*

wash lavar; **I need a wash** preciso de me lavar *[pris**ee**zoo dih mih]*; **can you wash the car?** pode lavar o carro? *[pod lav**a**hr]*; **can you wash these?** pode lavar isto? *[pod lav**a**hr eeshtoo]*; **it'll wash off** (*stain etc*) há-de desaparecer lavando *[ah dih dizaparis**eh**r lav**a**ndoo]*

washcloth uma toalha da cara *[tw**a**hl-ya da k**a**hra]*

washer (*for bolt etc*) uma bucha *[b**oo**sha]*

washhand basin um lavatório *[lavator-yoo]*

washing (*clothes*) a roupa para lavar *[r**oh**pa]*; **where can I hang my washing?** onde posso pendurar a minha roupa para lavar? *[ond p**o**ssoo pendoorahr a m**ee**n-ya]*; **can you do my washing for me?** pode lavar a roupa para mim? *[pod lav**a**hr a r**oh**pa para meeng]*

washing machine uma máquina de lavar *[m**a**hkeena dih lav**a**hr]*

washing powder o detergente *[ditirsнent]*

washing-up: I'll do the washing-up eu lavo a louça *[**eh**-oo l**a**hvoo a l**oh**-isa]*

washing-up liquid o líquido de lavar a louça *[l**ee**keedoo dih lav**a**hr a l**oh**-isa]*

wasp uma vespa *[v**e**shpa]*

wasteful: that's wasteful é um desperdício *[dishpird**ee**s-yoo]*

wastepaper basket um cesto de papéis *[s**e**hshtoo dih pa-p**a**ysh]*

watch (*wrist-*) um relógio (de pulso) *[ril**o**sн-yoo dih p**oo**lsoo]*; **will you watch my things for me?** pode tomar conta das minhas coisas? *[pod toom**a**hr k**o**nta dash m**ee**n-yash koh-izash]*; **I'll just watch** eu fico a ver *[**eh**-oo f**ee**koo a vehr]*; **watch**

out! cuidado! *[kweed**a**hdoo]*

watch strap a correia de relógio *[korr**a**y-a dih ril**o**sн-yoo]*

water a água *[**a**hgwa]*; **may I have some water?** pode trazer-me água? *[pod traz**eh**r-mih]*

watercolour (*painting*) a aguarela

waterproof impermeável *[eempirm-y**a**hvel]*

waterski: I'd like to learn to waterski eu gostava de aprender a fazer esqui aquático *[**eh**-oo goosht**a**hva d-yaprend**eh**r a faz**eh**r shkee akw**a**hteekoo]*

waterskiing o esqui aquático *[shkee akw**a**hteekoo]*

water sports os desportos aquáticos *[dishp**o**rtooz akw**a**hteekoosh]*

water wings umas bóias para braços *[b**o**yash para br**a**hsoosh]*

wave (*sea*) uma onda

way: which way is it? qual é o caminho? *[kw**a**hl e oo kam**ee**n-yoo]*; **it's this way** é por aqui *[poor ak**ee**]*; **it's that way** é por ali *[poor al**ee**]*; **could you tell me the way to ...?** pode indicar-me o caminho para ...? *[pod eendeek**a**hrm-yoo kam**ee**n-yoo]*; **is it on the way to Lisbon?** fica no caminho para Lisboa? *[f**ee**ka noo kam**ee**n-yoo]*; **you're blocking the way** (*with parked car etc*) você está a tapar o caminho *[voss**eh** shtah a tap**a**hr]*; **is it a long way to ...?** é muito longe para ...? *[mw**ee**ngtoo lonsн]*; **would you show me the way to do it?** ensina-me como se faz *[aing-s**ee**na mih k**oh**moo sih fahsh]*; **do it this way** faça assim *[f**a**hssa ass**ee**ng]*; **we want to eat the Portuguese way** queremos comer cozinha portuguesa *[kir**eh**moosh koom**eh**r kooz**ee**n-ya poortoog**eh**za]*; **no way!** de maneira nenhuma! *[dih man**a**y-ra nin-y**oo**ma]*

we nós *[nosh] see page 112*

weak (*person*) fraco *[fr**a**hkoo]*

wealthy rico *[r**ee**koo]*

weather o tempo *[t**e**mpoo]*; **what foul weather!** que tempo horrível! *[kih t**e**mpoo ohrr**ee**vel]*; **what beautiful weather!** que tempo maravilhoso! *[maraveel-y**oh**zoo]*

weather forecast a previsão do tempo *[priveez**ow**ng doo t**e**mpoo]*

wedding o casamento *[kazam**e**ntoo]*

wedding anniversary o aniversário de

casamento *[aneevirsahr-yoo dih ka-zamentoo]*

wedding ring o anel de casamento *[a-nel dih kazamentoo]*

Wednesday quarta-feira *[kwahrta fayra]*

week uma semana *[simana]*; **a week (from) today** de hoje a uma semana *[d-yohsн]*; **a week (from) tomorrow** de amanhã a uma semana *[d-yahman-yang]*; **Monday week** de segunda-feira a uma semana

weekend: at/on the weekend no fim de semana *[noo feeng dih simana]*

weight o peso *[pehzoo]*; **I want to lose weight** quero perder peso *[kairoo pirdehr]*

weight limit o limite de peso *[limeet dih pehzoo]*

weird esquisito *[shkizeetoo]*

welcome: welcome to ... bem vindo a ... *[baing veendoo a]*; **you're welcome** não tem de quê *[nowng taing dih keh]*

well: I don't feel well não me sinto bem *[nowng mih seentoo baing]*; **I haven't been very well** não tenho passado muito bem *[nowng taing-nyoo pasahdoo mweengtoo baing]*; **she's not well** ela não está bem *[nowng shtah baing]*; **how are you? — very well, thanks** como está? — muito bem, obrigado *[mwe-engtoo baing]*; **you speak English very well** fala inglês muito bem *[fahla eenglehsh]*; **me as well** eu também *[eh-oo tambaing]*; **well done!** muito bem!; **well, ...** bem ...; **well well!** ah sim! *[seeng]*

well-done *(steak)* bem passado *[baing pasahdoo]*

wellingtons botas de borracha *[botash dih boorahsha]*

Welsh galês *[galehsh]*

were *see pages 115, 117*

west o oeste *[weshtt]*; **to the west** a oeste

West Indian antilhano *[anteel-yanoo]*

West Indies as Antilhas *[anteel-yash]*

wet molhado *[mool-yahdoo]*; **it's all wet** está todo molhado *[shtah tohdoo]*; **it's been wet all week** tem chovido toda a semana *[taing shooveedoo tohdah simana]*

wet suit um fato isotérmico *[fahtoo eezootairmeekoo]*

what? o quê? *[oo keh]*; **what's that?** o que é isso? *[oo k-ye eessoo]*; **what are you drinking?** (= *can I get you one*) o que bebe? *[oo kih beb]*; **I don't know what to do** não sei o que fazer *[nowng say oo kih fazehr]*; **what a view!** mas que vista! *[mash kih veeshta]*

wheel uma roda

wheelchair uma cadeira de rodas *[kadayra dih rodash]*

when? quando? *[kwandoo]*; **when we get back** quando nós voltarmos *[kwandoo nosh vohltahrmoosh]*

where? onde? *[ond]*; **where is ...?** onde é ...? *[ond-ye]*; **I don't know where he is** não sei onde ele está *[nowng say ond ehl shtah]*; **that's where I left it** foi aqui que o deixei *[fohy akee k-yoo day-shay]*

which: which bus? qual autocarro? *[kwahl owtookahrroo]*; **which one?** qual deles? *[kwahl dehlish]*; **which is yours?** qual é o seu? *[kwahl e oo seh-oo]*; **I forget which it was** esqueci-me qual deles foi *[shkessee-mih kwahl dehlish fohy]*; **the one which ...** aquele que ... *[akehl kih]*

while: while I'm here enquanto estou aqui *[enkwantoo shtoh akee]*

whipped cream umas natas batidas *[nahtash bateedash]*

whisky o whisky *[weeshkee]*

whisper sussurrar *[soosoorrahr]*

white branco *[brankoo]*

white wine o vinho branco *[veen-yoo brankoo]*

Whitsun Pentecostes *[pentikoshtish]*

who? quem? *[kaing]*; **who was that?** quem era?; **the man who ...** o homem que ... *[kih]*

whole: the whole week toda a semana *[tohdah simana]*; **two whole days** dois dias inteiros *[doh-ish dee-az eentay-roosh]*; **the whole lot** tudo isto *[toodoo eeshtoo]*

whooping cough a tosse convulsa *[toss konvoolsa]*

whose: whose is this? de quem é isto? *[dih kaing e eeshtoo]*

why? porquê? *[poorkeh]*; **why not?** porque não? *[poorkih nowng]*; **that's why it's not working** é por causa disso que não funciona *[e poor kowza deesoo kih nowng foons-yona]*

wide largo *[lahrgoo]*

wide-angle lens uma lente grande angular *[lent grand angoolahr]*
widow a viúva *[v-yoova]*
widower o viúvo *[v-yoovoo]*
wife: my wife a minha mulher *[meen-ya mool-yair]*
wig uma peruca *[pirooka]*
will: will you ...? pode ...? *[pod] see page 116*
win ganhar *[gan-yahr]*; **who won?** quem ganhou? *[kaing gan-yoh]*
wind o vento *[ventoo]*
windmill um moínho de vento *[mween-yoo dih ventoo]*
window a janela *[sнanela]* *(of shop)* a montra; **near the window** ao pé da janela *[ow pe]*; **in the window** *(of shop)* na montra
window seat um lugar ao pé de janela *[loogahr ow pe da sнanela]*
windscreen, windshield o pára-brisas *[pahra-breezash]*
windscreen wipers, windshield wipers os limpa-vidros *[leempa-veedroosh]*
windsurf: I'd like to windsurf eu gostava de fazer windsurf *[gooshtahva dih fazehr]*
windsurfing o windsurf
windy: it's windy está vento *[shtah ventoo]*
wine o vinho *[veen-yoo]*; **can we have some more wine?** pode trazer mais vinho? *[pod trazehr mah-ish]*
wine glass um copo de vinho *[kopoo dih veen-yoo]*
wine list uma lista dos vinhos *[leeshta doosh veen-yoosh]*
wine-tasting a prova de vinhos *[dih veen-yoosh]*
wing *(of bird, plane)* a asa *[ahza]*; *(of car)* o painel lateral *[pah-inel latirahl]*
wing mirror o espelho lateral *[shpehl-yoo latirahl]*
winter o inverno *[eenvairnoo]*; **in the winter** no inverno *[noo]*
winter holiday as férias de inverno *[fairyash deenvairnoo]*
wire o arame *[aram]*; *(elec)* um fio *[fee-oo]*
wireless o rádio *[rahd-yoo]*
wiring *(in house)* os fios eléctricos *[fee-ooz eeletreekoosh]*
wish: wishing you were here quem dera

que aqui estivessem *[kaing daira k-yakee shteevesaing]*; **best wishes** com os melhores cumprimentos *[kong oosh milyorish koompreementoosh]*
with com *[kong]*
without sem *[saing]*
witness uma testemunha *[tishtimoonya]*; **will you be a witness for me?** quer ser minha testemunha? *[kair sehr meenya]*
witty *(person)* espirituoso *[shpireetwohzoo]*
wobble: it wobbles *(wheel etc)* está a oscilar *[shtah ohsh-seelahr]*
woman uma mulher *[mool-yair]*; **women** as mulheres *[mool-yairish]*
wonderful maravilhoso *[maraveelyohzoo]*
won't: it won't start não pega *[nowng pega] see page 116*
wood *(material)* a madeira *[maday-ra]*
woods *(forest)* um bosque *[boshk]*
wool a lã *[lang]*
word uma palavra *[palahvra]*; **what does that word mean?** o que significa essa palavra? *[oo kih seegneefeeka]*; **you have my word** dou-lhe a minha palavra *[dohl-yih a meen-ya]*
work trabalhar *[trabal-yahr]*; **how does it work?** como funciona? *[kohmoo foonsyona]*; **it's not working** não funciona *[nowng]*; **I work in an office** eu trabalho num escritório *[trabahl-yoo]*; **do you have any work for me?** tem trabalho para mim? *[taing trabahl-yoo para meeng]*; **when do you finish work?** quando é que sai do trabalho? *[kwandoo e kih sahy doo]*
world o mundo *[moondoo]*
worn-out *(person)* estragado *[shtragahdoo]*; *(clothes, shoes)* gasto *[gahshtoo]*
worry: I'm worried about her estou preocupado com ela *[shtoh pr-yookoopahdoo]*; **don't worry** não se preocupe *[nowng sih pree-ookoop]*
worse: it's worse está pior *[shtah p-yor]*; **it's getting worse** está a piorar *[p-yoorahr]*
worst o pior *[oo p-yor]*
worth: it s not worth 500 não vale quinhentos *[nowng vahl keen-yentoosh]*; **it's worth more than that** vale mais do que isso *[vahl mah-ish doo keesoo]*; **is it**

worth a visit? vale a pena uma visita? *[vahl a pehna]*

would: would you give this to …? pode dar isto a …? *[pod dahr eeshtoo]*; **what would you do?** o que faria você? *[oo kih faree-a vosseh]*

wrap: could you wrap it up? pode embrulhá-lo? *[pod embrool-yah-loo]*

wrapping um embrulho *[embrool-yoo]*

wrapping paper o papel de embrulho *[pa-pel dembrool-yoo]*

wrench *(tool)* uma chave inglesa *[shahv eenglehza]*

wrist o pulso *[poolsoo]*

write escrever *[shkrivehr]*; **could you write it down?** pode escrever isso? *[pod shkrivehr eesoo]*; **how do you write it?** como é que escreve isso? *[kohmoo e kishkrev]*; **I'll write to you** vou escrever-te *[voh shkrivehr-tih]*; **I wrote to you last month** eu escrevi-te o mês passado *[shkriveetih]*

write-off *(car)*: **it's a write-off** é para a sucata *[sookahta]*

writer um escritor *[shkreetohr]*

writing paper o papel de carta *[pa-pel dih kahrta]*

wrong: you're wrong está enganado *[shtah enganahdoo]*; **the bill's wrong** a conta está enganada; **sorry, wrong number** desculpe, enganou-se no número *[dishkoolp, enganoh-sih noo noomiroo]*; **I'm on the wrong train** vou no combóio errado *[voh noo komboy-oo eerrahdoo]*; **I went to the wrong room** fui ao quarto errado *[fwee ow kwahrtoo]*; **that's the wrong key** não é essa chave *[nowng e essa shahv]*; **there's something wrong with …** passa-se qualquer coisa com … *[pahssa-sih kwahl-kair koh-iza kong]*; **what's wrong?** o que se passa? *[oo kih sih pahssa]*; **what's wrong with it?** qual é o problema? *[kwahl e oo prooblehma]*

X-ray raio X *[rah-yoo sheesh]*

yacht um iate *[yaht]*

yacht club o clube naval *[kloob na-vahl]*

yard: in the yard no quintal *[noo keentahl] see page 119*

year um ano *[anoo]*

yellow amarelo *[amareloo]*

yellow pages as páginas amarelas *[pahsheenaz]*

yes sim *[seeng]*

yesterday ontem *[ontaing]*; **yesterday morning** ontem de manhã *[dih man-yang]*; **yesterday afternoon** ontem à tarde *[ah tahrd]*; **the day before yesterday** anteontem *[ant-yontaing]*

yet: has it arrived yet? já chegou? *[sнah shigoh]*; **not yet** ainda não *[a-eenda nowng]*

yobbo um vândalo *[vandaloo]*

yog(h)urt um iogurte *[yoogoort]*

you você *[vosseh]*; *(more formal, to a man)* o senhor *[oo sin-yohr]*; *(more formal, to a woman)* a senhora/a *[sin-yohra]*; *(familiar form)* tu *[too] see pages 112, 113*

young jovem *[sнovaing]*

young people os jovens *[sнovaingsh]*

your: is this your camera? esta máquina é de você? *[eshta mahkeena e dih vosseh] see page 110*

yours de você *[dih vosseh] see page 113*

youth hostel o albergue de juventude *[ahlbairg dih sнooventood]*

youth hostelling: we're youth hostelling estamos a ficar em albergues de juventude *[shtamooz a feekahr aing ahlbairgish dih sнooventood]*

Yugoslavia Yugoslavia *[yoogooslahvee-a]*

Z

zero zero [*zairoo*]

zip, zipper um fecho de correr [*fehshoo dih koorrehr*]; **could you put a new zip on?** pode pôr um fecho de correr novo?

[*pod pohr ... nohvoo*]

zoo o jardim zoológico [*sнardeeng zwolosнeekoo*]

zoom lens uma lente zoom [*lent*]

Portuguese – English

A

a abrir brevemente open soon
aberto open
aberto até as 19 horas open until 7 p.m.
aberto das ... às ... horas open from ... to ... o'clock
abóbora [aboboora] pumpkin
abrande slow down
a/c (ao cuidado) c/o
acenda os médios switch on dipped headlights
acenda os mínimos switch on your parking lights
açorda de alho [asohrda d-yahl-yoo] thick bread soup with garlic
açorda de marisco [asohrda dih mareeshkoo] thick bread soup with shellfish
açorda de miolos [asohrda dih m-yoloosh] thick bread soup with brains
A.C.P. (Automóvel Clube de Portugal) Portuguese motoring organization
acrílico acrylic
açúcar [asookar] sugar
adeus [adeh-oosh] goodbye
adeusinho [adehoozeen-yoo] cheerio
aeroporto airport
agência de viagens travel agency
agitar bem antes de usar shake well before using
agriões [agr-yoingsh] watercress
água water
água mineral [ahgwa meenirahl] mineral water
água potável drinking water
água quente warm water
água tépida lukewarm water
aguardente [agwahrdent] brandy
aguardentes bagaceiras [agwahrdentish bagasayrash] grape brandies
aguardentes velhas [agwahrdentish vehl-yash] matured brandies
aipo [eye-poo] celery
al. (alameda) avenue
alarme alarm

albergue de juventude youth hostel
alcachofras [ahlkashofrash] artichokes
Alemanha Germany
alface [ahlfahss] lettuce
alfaiate tailor
alfândega customs
algodão cotton
alheira [al-yay-ra] garlic sausage
alho [ahl-yoo] garlic
alho francês [ahl-yoo fransehsh] leek
almoço [ahlmohsoo] lunch
almóndegas [ahlmondigash] meat balls
alperces [ahlpairsish] apricots
altura máxima maximum headroom
alugam-se quartos rooms to let/rent
aluga-se for hire, for rent
aluguer de automóveis car rental
ameijoas [amaysнw-ash] clams
ameijoas à Bulhão Pato [amaysн-waza bool-yowng pahtoo] clams with coriander, onion and garlic
ameijoas na cataplana [amaysн-wash na kataplana] clams in a sweet tomato sauce served in a large dish
ameixas [amay-shash] plums
ameixas de Elvas [amay-shash d-yelvash] dried plums from Elvas
ameixas secas [amay-shash sehkas] prunes
amêndoa amarga [amendwa amahrga] bitter almond liqueur
amêndoas [amendw-ash] almonds
amendoins [amendweengsh] peanuts
americano American
à moda de ... [ah moda dih] in the ... style
ampolas bebíveis ampoules (for medicine)
analgésico painkiller
ananás [ananahsh] pineapple
anchovas [anshovash] anchovies
andares flats, apartments
anho à moda do Minho [an-yoo ah moda doo meen-yoo] roast lamb served

with roast potatoes
aniz *[aneesh]* aniseed
anonas *[anonash]* custard apples (tropical fruit)
ao preço de custo cost price
aparelhagem de som audio equipment
apart. (apartamento) apartment
apelido surname, family name
aperitivo *[apireeteevoo]* aperitif
apertar o cinto de segurança fasten your seat belt
aquecimento heating
ar condicionado air conditioning
Árabes the Arabs
armazém warehouse; big store
aroma natural/artificial natural/artificial fragrance
arq. (arquitecto) architect
arraial local fair with fireworks, dances and songs
arranjos repairs
arroz árabe *[arroz ahrab]* fried rice served with dried nuts and fruits
arroz à valenciana *[arroz ah valensyana]* rice served with chicken, pork and seafood
arroz branco *[arrohsh brankoo]* plain rice
arroz de cabidela *[arrohsh dih kabeedela]* rice with bird's blood
arroz de frango *[arrohsh dih frangoo]* chicken with rice
arroz de funcho *[arrohsh dih foonshoo]* fennel rice
arroz de marisco *[arrohsh dih mareeshkoo]* rice served with shellfish
arroz de pato *[arrohsh dih pahtoo]* duck with rice
arroz de polvo *[arrohsh dih pohlvoo]* rice with octopus

arroz doce *[arrohsh dohs]* sweet rice dessert
artesanato handicrafts
artigos de luxo luxury goods
artigos de bébé baby goods
artigos de campismo camping equipment
artigos de casa household goods
artigos de desporto sports goods
artigos de viagem travel goods
artigos regionais regional goods
ascensor lift, elevator
aspirina aspirin
até já *[a-te sнah]* see you in a moment
até logo *[a-te logoo]* see you later
atenção please note, caution, warning
atenção, portas automáticas warning: automatic doors
atrasado delayed
atravesse go, walk
atum *[atoong]* tuna
atum assado *[atoong assahdoo]* baked tuna
autocarro bus, coach
autoestrada motorway, highway
av. (avenida) avenue
avance go, walk
avariado out of order
avarias breakdown service
avelãs *[avilangsh]* hazelnuts
à venda aquí on sale here
aviários aviaries
aviso warning; notice
azeitonas *[azay-tonash]* olives
azeitonas recheadas *[azay-tonash rishyahdash]* stuffed olives
azeitonas com pimentos *[azaytonash kong peementoosh]* olives stuffed with pimento
azulejaria tile maker's workshop

B

bacalhau assado *[bakal-yahoo assahdoo]* roast cod
bacalhau à brás *[bakal-yahoo ah brahsh]*

cod with egg and fried potatoes
bacalhau à Gomes de Sá *[bakal-yahoo ah gomsh dih sah]* cod fried with onions,

boiled eggs, boiled potatoes and black olives

bacalhau à Zé do Pipo *[bakal-yahoo a ze doo peepoo]* cod in an egg sauce

bacalhau com natas *[bakal-yahoo kong nahtash]* cod with cream

bacalhau dourado *[bakal-yahoo dohrahdoo]* cod baked in the oven

bacalhau grelhado *[bakal-yahoo grilyahdoo]* grilled cod

bacalhau nas brasas *[bakal-yahoo nash brahzash]* barbecued cod

bagagem de mão hand baggage

Bairrada wine growing area famous for fruity red wines

balcão counter (*in store*)

balcão de informações information desk

banana flambée *[banana flambeh]* banana flambé

banco bank

banco de poupança savings bank

bar botequim coffee house

barbeiro barber shop

barcos de aluguer boats for hire/to rent

barros earthenware

bata (à porta) knock

batata assada *[batahtah-sahda]* baked potato

batata murro *[batahta moorroo]* small baked potato

batata palha *[batahta pahl-ya]* thinly cut French fries

batatas *[batahtash]* potatoes

batatas cozidas *[batahtash koozeedash]* boiled potatoes

batatas fritas *[batahtash freetash]* French fries

batido de leite *[bateedoo dih layt]* milk shake

baunilha *[bowneel-ya]* vanilla

bavaroise *[bavarwahz]* dessert made from egg whites and cream

bebida drink

beco sem saída cul de sac, dead end

Bélgica Belgium

bem passado *[baing passahdoo]* well done

bem-vindo *[baing veendoo]* welcome

bengaleiro cloakroom, checkroom

berbigão *[birbeegowng]* mussel-like shellfish

berinjelas *[bireensʜelash]* aubergines, eggplants

besugos *[bizoogoosh]* sea bream

beterraba *[bitirrahba]* beetroot

biblioteca library

bica *[beeka]* small black coffee like espresso

bifanas *[beefanash]* pork slice in a roll

bife *[beef]* steak

bife à cortador *[beef a koortadohr]* thick tender steak

bife de alcatra *[beef d-yahlkahtra]* rump steak

bife de atum *[beef d-yatoong]* tuna steak

bife de javali *[beef dih sʜavalee]* wild boar steak

bife de pojadouro *[beef dih poosʜadohroo]* top round steak

bife de vaca (com ovo a cavalo) *[beef dih vahka (kong ohvoo a kavahloo)]* steak (with an egg on top)

bife grelhado *[beef gril-yahdoo]* grilled steak

bife tártaro *[beef tahrtaroo]* steak tartare

bifes de cebolada *[beefsh dih siboolahda]* steak with onions

bifinhos de porco *[beefeen-yoosh dih pohrkoo]* small slices of pork

bifinhos nas brasas *[beefeen-yoosh nash brahzash]* small slices of barbecued beef

bilheteira ticket office

bilhetes tickets

blusas blouses

boa noite *[boh-a noh-it]* good night

boa tarde *[boh-a tahrd]* good afternoon, good evening

boite disco

bola de carne *[bola dih karn]* meat ball

bolachas *[boolahshas]* biscuits

bolo rei *[bohloo ray]* ring-shaped cake eaten at Christmas time

bolo de chocolate *[bohloo dih shookoolaht]* chocolate cake

bolo de nozes *[bohloo dih nozish]* walnut cake

bolo inglês *[bohloo eenglehsh]* sponge cake containing dried fruit

bolos *[bohloosh]* cakes

bolos e bolachas *[bohlooz ee boolahshash]* cakes and biscuits

bom dia *[bong dee-a]* good morning

bombeiros fire brigade

boudin *[boodeeng]* black pudding, blood sausage

brinquedos toys
brioche *[br-yosh]* round bun

broas *[broh-ash]* corn cakes
bugigangas bric-à-brac

C

cabeça de pescada cozida *[kabehssa dih pishkahda koozeeda]* boiled head of hake
cabedais leather goods
cabeleireiro hairdresser
cabine telefónica telephone booth
cabrão! *[kabrowng]* bastard!
cabrito *[kabreetoo]* kid
cabrona! bastard!
cachola frita *[kashola freeta]* fried pig's heart and liver
cachorros *[kashorroosh]* hot dogs
café *[ka-fe]* coffee
café com leite *[ka-fe kong layt]* white coffee, coffee with milk
café com pingo *[ka-fe kong peeng-goo]* espresso coffee with brandy
café duplo *[ka-fe dooploo]* two espressos in the same cup
café glacé *[ka-fe glasseh]* iced coffee
cais platform, track, quay
caixa cash point
caixa fechada till closed
caixa de primeiros socorros first aid box
caldeirada *[kahlday-rahda]* fish stew
caldo *[kahldoo]* broth
caldo de aves *[kahldoo d-yahvish]* bird soup
caldo de carne *[kahldoo dih kahrn]* meat soup
caldo verde *[kahldoo vehrd]* cabbage soup
câmara municipal town hall
camarim dressing room
camarões *[kamaroingsh]* prawns
câmbio exchange
camioneta coach, bus, light truck
camisaria shop/store selling shirts
camisas shirts
camisolas sweaters

campo de golf golf course
Canal da Mancha the English Channel
canapés *[kanapesh]* canapes
cancelado cancelled
canela *[ka-nela]* cinnamon
canja de galinha *[kansha dih galeen-ya]* chicken soup
cão de guarda guard dog
capelista haberdasher
capilé *[kapeele]* drink made with water, sugar and syrup
caracóis *[karakoish]* snails
carago! *[karahgoo]* oh hell!
caranguejos *[karangayshoosh]* crabs
carapaus de escabeche *[karapowsh d-yishkabesh]* marinated mackerel
carapaus fritos *[karapowsh freetoosh]* fried mackerel
carapinhada de café *[karapeen-yahda dih ka-fe]* coffee drink with crushed ice
carapinhada de chocolate *[karapeen-yahda dih shookoolat]* chocolate drink with crushed ice
carapinhada de groselha *[karapeen-yahda dih groozehl-ya]* blackcurrant drink with crushed ice
carapinhada de morango *[karapeen-yahda dih moorangoo]* strawberry drink with crushed ice
carga máxima maximum load
caril *[kareel]* curry
carioca *[kar-yoka]* small weak black coffee
carne de porco com ameijoas *[kahrn dih pohrkoo kong amayshw-ash]* pork with clams
carne de vaca assada *[kahrn dih vahka assahda]* roast beef
carne de vaca guisada *[kahrn dih vahka g-eezahda]* stewed meat
carne estufada *[kahrn ishtoofahda]*

stewed meat
carneiro *[karnayroo]* mutton
carneiro assado *[karnayroo assahdoo]* roast mutton
carnes *[kahrnish]* meats
carnes frias *[kahrnish free-ash]* selection of cold meat, cold cuts
carros de aluguer car hire/rental
carruagem coach (*of a train*), car
carruagem restaurante restaurant car, dining car
carta verde green card
cartão bancário cheque/check card
cartão de crédito credit card
cartas letters
casa de banho toilet, restroom
casa de fados restaurant where fados are sung
casa de jantar dining room
casa de saúde nursing home
casas de banho toilets, restrooms
casta the kind of grape used in a particular wine
castanhas *[kastan-yash]* chestnuts
castelo castle
categoria category
cautela take care
cavalheiro gentleman
cavalheiros gentlemen, men's room
cave basement
cemitério cemetery
centro comercial shopping centre/center
centro da cidade city centre/center
centro de enfermagem clinic
centro de informação turistica tourist information office
centro de turismo tourist information
cerâmicas ceramics
cerejas *[siray-shash]* cherries
cerveja *[sirvay-sha]* beer
cerveja branca *[sirvay-sha branka]* lager
cerveja de pressão *[sirvay-sha dih prissowng]* draught beer
cerveja preta *[sirvay-sha prehta]* bitter (*beer*)
cervejaria *[sirvay-sharee-a]* snack bar
chá com mel *[shah kong mel]* tea with honey
chá de Lucialima *[shah dih loos-yaleema]* herb tea
chá de limão *[shah dih leemowng]* lemon tea
chá de mentol *[shah dih mentol]* mint tea

chá de tília *[shah dih teel-ya]* linden blossom tea
chamada internacional international call
chamada interurbana long distance call
chamada local local call
champanhe champagne
chanfana de porco *[shanfana dih pohrkoo]* pork casserole
chantilly *[shantee-yee]* whipped cream
chapelaria hat shop/store
charcutaria delicatessen
charlottes *[sharlotsh]* biscuits/cookies with fruit and cream
charutos cigars
chegadas arrivals
cheques cheques, checks
chocolate glacé *[shookoolaht glasseh]* iced chocolate
chocolate quente *[shookoolaht kent]* hot chocolate
chocos *[shohkoosh]* cuttle fish
chouriço *[shohreessoo]* spiced sausage
choux choux pastry
churros *[shoorrosh]* long tube-like fritters
Cia. (companhia) company
cidade town centre/center
cidra *[seedra]* cider
cigarros cigarettes
cimbalino *[seembaleenoo]* small black coffee
cinema cinema, movie theater
cintas corsets
cintos belts
civet lebre *[seevet lebrih]* jugged hare
clarete *[klareht]* claret
clínica médica medical clinic
clínica veterinária veterinary clinic
cobertores blankets
cocktail de camarão *[koktel dih kamarowng]* prawn cocktail
cod. postal (código postal) post code, zip code
codorniz *[koodoorneesh]* quail
codornizes fritas *[koodoorneezish freetash]* fried quail
coelho de escabeche *[kwehl-yoo dih shkabesh]* marinated rabbit
coelho de fricassé *[kwehl-yoo dih freekasseh]* rabbit fricassee
coelho frito *[kwehl-yoo freetoo]* fried rabbit
coêntros *[kwentroosh]* coriander

cogumelos *[koogoomehloosh]* mushrooms
cogumelos com alho *[koogoomehloosh kong al-yoo]* mushrooms with garlic
colégio school
collants tights, pantyhose
com certeza *[kong sirtehza]* of course
com licença *[kong leessensa]* excuse me
combóio train
combóio rápido express train
comissão commission
completo full
compota *[kohmpota]* stewed fruit
compra purchase
comprimidos tablets
condições terms
conduza com cuidado drive carefully
confeitaria sweet shop, candy store
conhaque *[koon-yak]* cognac
conquilhas *[kongkeel-yash]* baby clams
conservar afastado da luz solar directa store away from direct sunlight
conservar no frio store in a cold place
consulado consulate
consultório dentário dental surgery
consumir dentro de ... dias to be consumed within ... days
conta account
conto (de réis) one thousand escudos
contra ... against ...
contra-indicações contra-indications
controlo de passaportes passport control
convento convent
coração *[koorassowng]* heart
corações de alcachofra *[koorassoingsh d-yahlkashofra]* artichoke hearts
correio post office
correio aéreo air mail
cortiças cork goods
cortinados curtains
corvina *[koorveena]* large sea fish
cosméticos make-up, cosmetics
costeletas *[kooshtilehtash]* chops
costeletas de carneiro *[kooshtilehtash dih karnayroo]* lamb chops
costeletas de porco *[kooshtilehtash dih pohrkoo]* pork chops
costeletas fritas *[kooshtilehtash freetash]* fried chops
costeletas grelhadas *[kooshtilehtash gril-yahdash]* grilled chops
courgettes com creme no forno

[koorsHetsh kong krem noo fohrnoo] baked courgettes/zucchinis served with cream
courgettes fritas *[koorsHetsh freetash]* fried courgettes/zucchinis
couve branca com vinagre *[kohv branka kong veenahgrih]* white cabbage with vinegar
couve roxa *[kohv rohsha]* red cabbage
couve-flor *[kohv flohr]* cauliflower
couve-flor com molho branco no forno *[kohv flohr kong mohl-yoo brankoo noo fohrnoo]* cauliflower cheese
couve-flor com natas *[kohv flohr kong nahtash]* cauliflower with cream
couvert cover charge
couves de bruxelas *[kohvsh dih brooss-elash]* brussels sprouts
couves de bruxelas com natas *[kohvsh dih broosselash kong nahtash]* brussels sprouts with cream
couves de bruxelas salteadas *[kohvsh dih broosselash sahlt-yahdash]* brussels sprouts in butter sauce
couves guisadas com salsichas *[kohvsh g-eezahdash kong sahlseeshas]* stewed cabbage and sausage
cozido à portuguesa *[koozeedoo ah poortoogehza]* Portuguese stew (*contains chicken, sausage etc*)
C.P. (Caminhos de ferro Portugueses) Portuguese Railways/Railroad
crédito credit
creme de cogumelos *[krem dih koogoomeloosh]* cream of mushroom soup
creme de marisco *[krem dih mareeshkoo]* cream of shellfish soup
crepe de camarão *[krep dih kamarowng]* prawn crepe
crepe de carne *[krep dih kahrn]* meat crepe
crepe de cogumelos *[krep dih koogoomeloosh]* mushroom crepe
crepe de espinafres *[krep dih shpeenahfrish]* spinach crepe
crepe de legumes *[krep dih ligoomsh]* vegetable crepe
crepe de pescada *[krep dih pishkahda]* hake crepe
crianças children crossing
Cruz Vermelha Red Cross
cuecas pants
cuidado take care

cuidado com o cão beware of the dog
curva perigosa dangerous bend

cutelaria cutlery, flatware
c/v (cave) basement

D

d. (direito) right
damas ladies, ladies' restroom
Dão wine growing region: mostly dry reds matured in casks before bottling
dar prioridade give way
de luxo de luxe
dê prioridade give way, yield
décimo (10o) andar (*UK*) tenth floor; (*USA*) eleventh floor
depósito de bagagem left luggage, baggage checkroom
depósitos deposits
desconto de ... ... discount
desculpe [*dishkoolp*] sorry
desfolhada party which is held at threshing time
desgarradas spontaneous songs
desinfectante disinfectant
desligue o motor switch off your engine
destino destination
desvio diversion
devagar slow
diária cost per day
diáriamente daily

dias de semana weekdays
diluir num pouco de água dissolve in a little water
dinheiro money
direito right
direitos duty
discos records
discoteca record shop/store; disco
divisas foreign currency
dobrada [*doobrahda*] tripe with chick peas
doce [*dohss*] sweet (*of wine*)
doce [*dohss*] jam; any sweet dish
doce de amêndoa [*dohss d-yamendwa*] almond spread
doce de ovos [*dohss d-yovoosh*] custard-like dessert made with eggs and sugar
doces regionais regional desserts
domingos e dias feriados Sundays and holidays
dourada [*dohrahda*] dory (*sea fish*)
drogaria drugstore
dto. (direito) right
duche(s) shower(s)

E

e. (esquerdo) left
éclair de chantilly whipped cream eclair
éclairs de café [*ka-fe*] coffee eclairs
éclairs de chocolate [*shookoolaht*] chocolate eclairs
écran screen
é favor fechar a porta please close the

door
efervescente [*eefirvish-sent*] sparkling
eirozes [*ayrozish*] eels
eléctrico tram, streetcar
electro-domésticos electrical appliances
elevador lift, elevator
embaixada embassy

embalagem económica economy pack
embalagem familiar family pack
ementa menu
emergências casualty, emergencies
empada *[empahda]* pie
empadão de carne *[empadowng dih kahrn]* large meat pie
empadão de peixe *[empadowng dih paysh]* large fish pie
empregada de quarto chambermaid, maid
empurrar push
E.N. (Estrada Nacional) national highway
encerrado closed
encharcada *[ensharkahda]* dessert made of almonds and eggs
end. tel. (endereço telegráfico) telegraphic address
enfermaria ward
enguias *[eng-ee-ash]* eels
enguias fritas *[eng-ee-ash freetash]* fried eels
ensopado de borrego *[ensoopahdoo dih boorehgoo]* lamb stew
ensopado de enguias *[ensoopahdoo dih eng-ee-ash]* eel stew
entrada way in, entrance; starter
entrada livre admission free
entradas *[entrahdash]* starters
entrecosto *[entrikoshtoo]* entrecote
entrecosto com ameijoas *[entrikoshtoo kong amaysʜw-ash]* entrecote with clams
entrecosto frito *[entrikoshtoo freetoo]* fried entrecote
entrega ao domicílio delivery service
ermida hermitage
ervanário herbalist
ervilhas *[irveel-yash]* peas
ervilhas de manteiga *[irveel-yash dih mantayga]* peas in butter sauce
ervilhas reboçadas *[irveel-yash riboosahdash]* peas in butter sauce with bacon
esc. (escudo) escudo, Portuguese unit of currency
escadas stairs
escadas rolantes escalator
escalope *[shkalop]* escalope
escalope ao Madeira *[shkalop ow madayra]* escalope with Madeira wine
escalope de carneiro *[shkalop dih karnayroo]* mutton escalope
escalope de porco *[shkalop dih pohr-*

koo] pork escalope
escalope panado *[shkalop panahdoo]* breaded escalope
Escócia Scotland
escola school
Espanha Spain
espargos *[shpahrgoosh]* asparagus
esparguete à bolonhesa *[shpargett ah booloon-yehza]* spaghetti bolognese
esparregado *[shparrigahdoo]* puréed spinach
espectáculo show
espelhos mirrors
espere wait
espere pelo sinal wait for the tone
espetada de leitão *[shpitahda dih laytowng]* sucking pig kebab
espetada de rins *[shpitahda dih reengsh]* kidney kebab
espetada de vitela *[shpitahda dih veetela]* veal kebab
espetada mista *[shpitahda meeshta]* mixed kebab
espinafres gratinados *[shpeenahfrish grateenahdoosh]* spinach au gratin
espinafres salteados *[shpeenahfrish sahlt-yahdoosh]* spinach with butter sauce
esplanada terrace cafe
espumante *[shpoomant]* sparkling wine
esq. (esquerdo) left
esquadra da polícia police station
estação alta high season
estação baixa low season
estação de caminho de ferro railway/railroad station
estação de camionetas bus/coach station
estação de serviço service station
estacionamento privado private parking
estacionamento proibido no parking
estacionamento reservado aos hóspedes private car park/parking lot: guests only
estádio stadium
estância timber yard
estrada principal main road
estrangulamento traffic jam
estreia first showing
E.U.A. (Estados Unidos da América) USA
Ex.mo. Sr. (Excelentíssimo Senhor)

Dear Sir
excursões excursions

expresso espresso coffee
extintor fire extinguisher

F

F (fria) cold
fabricado em ... made in ...
factura invoice
fadista fado singer
fado traditional Portuguese song
faiança pottery
faisão *[fayzowng]* pheasant
farmácia chemist, pharmacist
farmácias de serviço emergency chemists/pharmacies
farófias *[farof-yash]* whipped egg white with vanilla and cinnamon
farturas *[fartoorash]* long tube-like fritters
fatias recheadas *[fatee-ash rish-yahdash]* slices of bread with fried mince/ground beef
favas *[fahvash]* broad beans
favor não incomodar please do not disturb
fazem-se chaves keys cut here
faz favor excuse me
febras de porco *[febrash dih pohrkoo]* thin slices of pork
fechado closed
fechado até ... closed until ...
fechado para férias closed for holidays/vacations
fechado para balanço closed for stocktaking
feijões verdes *[faysHoingsh vehrdsh]* French beans
feijoada *[faysH-wahda]* bean stew
feira popular fairground
feiras das vilas local village fairs
feito à mão handmade
ferra cattle branding party
ferragens ironware
festas dos santos populares feast days of saints
fiambre caramelizado *[f-yambrih kara-*

mileezahdoo] ham coated in caramel
fibras naturais natural fibres
fígado *[feegadoo]* liver
figos *[feegoosh]* figs
figos moscatel *[feegoosh mooshkatel]* muscatel figs
figos secos *[feegoosh sehkoosh]* dried figs
filete *[feeleht]* fillet
filete de bife com foie gras *[feeleht dih beef kong fwa gra]* beef fillet steak with foie gras
filho da puta! *[feel-yoo da poota]* son-of-a-bitch!
filhozes *[feel-yozish]* sugared buns
fim de autoestrada end of motorway/highway
fim de estação end of season
florista florist
folhetos leaflets
fondue de carne *[fongdoo dih kahrn]* meat fondue
fondue de chocolate *[fongdoo dih shoo-koolaht]* chocolate fondue
fondue de queijo *[fongdoo dih kay-sHoo]* cheese fondue
forcados a group of men who wrestle with the bull during a bullfight
fotocópias photocopies
fotografia photographic goods
frágil fragile
França France
frango *[frangoo]* chicken
frango assado *[frangoo assahdoo]* roast chicken
frango na púcara *[frangoo na pookara]* chicken casserole done with Port and almonds
frango no churrasco *[frangoo noo shoo-rahshkoo]* barbecued chicken
frango no espeto *[frangoo noo shpeh-too]* spit roast chicken

frio cold
frito de ... (fruta) *[freetoo dih]* (fruit) fritter
fronteira frontier
fruta *[froota]* fruit

fruta da época *[froota da epooka]* seasonal fruit
frutaria fruit shop/store
fumadores smokers
funcho *[foonshoo]* fennel

G

gado cattle
gado bravo unfenced cattle
galantine de coelho *[galanteen dih kwehl-yoo]* cold rabbit roll
galantine de galinha *[galanteen dih galeen-ya]* cold chicken roll
galantine de vegetais *[galanteen dih vishitah-ish]* cold vegetable roll
galão *[galowng]* large milky coffee
galeria de arte art gallery
Gales Wales
galinha de África *[galeen-ya d-yahfreeka]* guinea fowl
galinha de fricassé *[galeen-ya dih freekasseh]* chicken fricassee
gambas *[gambash]* prawns
gambas grelhadas *[gambash grilyahdash]* grilled prawns
garagem garage
garantia guarantee
garoto *[garohtoo]* small brown coffee
garrafa *[garrahfa]* bottle
garrafeira special old red wine set aside by the producer in years of exceptional quality
gasóleo diesel
gasolina-normal 2 star petrol, regular
gasolina-super 4 star petrol, premium

gaspacho *[gaspashoo]* chilled vegetable soup
G.B. (Grã Bretanha) Great Britain
gelado *[shilahdoo]* ice cream
gelado de baunilha *[shilahdoo dih bowneel-ya]* vanilla ice cream
gelado de frutas *[shilahdoo dih frootash]* fruit ice cream
gelataria ice cream parlo(u)r
geleia *[shilay-a]* preserve
gelo *[shehloo]* ice
ginja *[sheensha]* cherry
ginginha *[sheensheen-ya]* cherry-based liqueur
G.N.R (Guarda Nacional Republicana) branch of the Portuguese police
Golfo da Biscáia Bay of Biscay
gotas drops
Gov. (Governo) government
grão *[growng]* chickpeas
grátis free
gravatas ties, neckties
groselha *[groozehl-ya]* blackcurrant
Guarda Fiscal customs police
guerra civil civil war
guia turístico tourist guide
guichet window (*in a bank, post office etc*)
guisado *[g-eezahdoo]* stew

H

hamburguer *[amboorgir]* hamburger
hamburguer com batatas fritas *[amboorgir kong batahtash freetash]* hamburger and chips/French fries
hamburguer com ovo *[amboorgir kong ohvoo]* hamburger with an egg
hamburguer no pão *[amboorgir no powng]* hamburger roll

há vagas vacancies, rooms free
H.C. (Hospital Civil) hospital
homens gentlemen, men's room
hora de chegada time of arrival
hora de partida time of departure
horários timetables, schedules
hortaliças *[ohrtaleesash]* green vegetables

I

igreja church
indicações instructions for use
indicativo dialling code, area code
inflamável inflammable
Inglaterra England
ingredientes ingredients
início de autoestrada start of motorway/highway
Inquisição the Inquisition
interdito a menores de ... anos no admission to those under ... years of age
introduza a moeda na ranhura insert coin in slot
inválidos invalids
iogurte *[yoogoort]* yoghurt
iscas fritas com batatas *[eeshkash freetash kong batahtas]* fried liver and French fries
italiana *[eetal-yana]* half of one espresso coffee

J

jardim zoológico zoo
jardineira *[shardeenay-ra]* vegetable stew

joalharia jewel(l)er
jóias jewels

K

kg. (kilograma) kilogram

L

l. (largo) square

lagosta *[lagoshta]* lobster

lagosta à Americana *[lagoshta ah amireekana]* lobster with tomato and onions

lagosta thermidor *[lagoshta tirmeedohr]* lobster thermidor

lagostins *[lagooshteengsh]* crayfish

lampreia à moda do Minho *[lampray-a ah moda doo meen-yoo]* whole lamprey in a thick sauce

lampreia de ovos *[lampray-a d-yovoosh]* dessert made of eggs and sugar served in the form of a lamprey

lanche *[lansh]* afternoon tea

laranjas *[laransHash]* oranges

largo square

lasanha *[lasan-ya]* lasagne

lavabos toilets, restrooms

lavagem a seco dry cleaning

lavagem automática automatic car wash

lavandaria laundry

lavar à mão hand wash

lavar na máquina machine wash

legumes *[ligoomsh]* vegetables

leitão da Bairrada *[lay-towng da bahirrahda]* sucking pig from Bairrada

leitaria dairy

leite *[leh-it]* milk

leite creme *[leh-it krem]* light custard with cinnamon

lembranças souvenirs

levante o auscultador lift the receiver

libras esterlinas pounds sterling

liceu secondary school, high school

licor de medronho *[leekohr dih midrohn-yoo]* strawberry liqueur

licor de ovo *[leekohr d-yohvoo]* advokat

licor de peras *[leekohr dih pehrash]* pear liqueur

licor de sinsverga *[leekohr dih seensHuairga]* herb liqueur

licor de whisky *[leekohr dih weeshkee]* drambuie (tm)

ligação com ... connects with ...

limite de velocidade speed limit

limonada fresh lemon juice

limpar a seco dry-clean

limpeza a seco dry cleaning

língua *[leeng-gwa]* tongue

língua de porco *[leeng-gwa dih pohrkoo]* tongue of pork

língua de vaca *[leeng-gwa dih vahka]* tongue of beef

linguado à meunière *[leeng-gwahdoo ah min-yair]* sole meunière

linguado grelhado *[leeng-gwahdoo grilyahdo]* grilled sole

linguado frito *[leeng-gwahdoo freetoo]* fried sole

linguado no forno *[leeng-gwahdoo no fohrnoo]* baked sole

liquidação (total) (clearance) sale

Lisboa Lisbon

lista de preços price list

lista telefónica telephone directory
livraria bookshop, bookstore
livre vacant, free
livro de cheques cheque book, check book
livros books
lixo litter
loiça crockery
loja de antiguidades antique shop/store
loja de artesanato handicrafts shop/store
loja de desportos sports shop/store
loja de ferragens ironmonger, hardware store
loja de fotografia photography shop/store
loja de malas handbag shop/store
lomba crest of hill
lombo de porco [lomboo dih pohrkoo] loin of pork

lombo de vaca [lomboo dih vahka] sirloin
lotação esgotada all tickets sold
lugares em pé standing room
lugares reservados a cegos, inválidos, grávidas e acompanhantes de crianças com menos de 4 anos seats reserved for the blind, infirm, expectant mothers and those accompanying children under 4
lulas com natas [loolash kong nahtash] stewed squid with cream
lulas fritas [loolash freetash] fried squid
lulas guisadas [loolash g-eezahdash] stewed squid
lulas recheadas [loolash rish-yahdash] stuffed squid
luvas gloves
Lx (Lisboa) Lisbon

M

M. (Metro) underground, subway
maçã assada [massang assahda] baked apple
maçãs [massangsh] apples
macedónia de frutas [massidon-ya dih frootash] fruit cocktail
Madeira wine producing region: fortified wines, sweet and dry
mal passado [mahl passahdoo] rare
malas handbags
manteiga [mantay-ga] butter
manteiga de anchova [mantay-ga d-yanshova] anchovy butter
manteiga queimada [mantay-ga kay-mahda] butter sauce used with fish
mantenha-se à direita, caminhe pela esquerda keep to the right, walk on the left
marca registada registered trade mark
marinada [mareenahda] marinade
marisco [mareeshkoo] shellfish
marmelada [marmilahda] quince jam
marmelos [marmeloosh] quince
marmelos assados [marmelooz assah-

doosh] roast quince
marque o número desejado dial the number you require
marroquinaria leather goods store
maternidade maternity hospital
mayonnaise de alho [ma-yoonez d-yahl-yoo] garlic mayonnaise
mazagrin [mazagrang] iced coffee with lemon
medida size
meia de leite [may-a dih leh-it] glass of milk
meia desfeita [may-a dishfay-ta] cooked cod and chickpeas with olive oil and vinegar
meia pensão half board, European plan
meio seco [may-oo sehkoo] medium sweet
meias de vidro hosiery
melancia [milansee-a] watermelon
melão [milowng] melon
melão com presunto [milowng kong prizoontoo] melon with ham
meloa com vinho do Porto/Madeira

[miloh-a kong veen-yoo doo pohrtoo/ maday-ra] small melon with Port/ Madeira wine

melocoton *[milookootong]* peach melba

mercado market selling fresh fish, vegetables, fruit, meat

mercearia grocer

merda! *[mairda]* shit!

merengue *[mirang-gih]* meringue

metade do preço half price

Metropolitano/Metro underground, subway

mexilhões *[misheel-yoingsh]* mussels

migas à Alentejana *[meegaz ah alan-tisнana]* thick bread soup

mil folhas *[meel fohl-yash]* sweet flaky pastry

ministério ministry, government department

miolos *[m-yoloosh]* brains

miolos com ovos *[m-yoloosh kong ovoosh]* brains with eggs

miradouro scenic view, vantage point

míscaros *[meeshkaroosh]* mushrooms

mistura petrol and oil mixture for two stroke engines

mobílias furniture

modas para senhora ladies' fashions

moedas coins

moleja *[mooleh-sнa]* soup made with pig's blood

molho mornay *[mohl-yoo mornay]* bechamel sauce with cheese

molho mousseline *[mohl-yoo moosileen]* sauce hollandaise with cream

molho tártaro *[mohl-yoo tahrtaroo]* tartare sauce (mayonnaise with herbs, gherkins and capers)

molho à Espanhola *[mohl-yoo ah shpan-yola]* spicy onion and garlic sauce

molho ao Madeira *[mohl-yoo ow maday-ra]* Madeira wine sauce

molho bearnaise *[mohl-yoo beh-arnez]* sauce made from egg yolks, lemon juice and herbs

molho béchamel *[mohl-yoo behshamel]* bechamel sauce, (white sauce made from cream, butter and flour)

molho branco *[mohl-yoo brankoo]* white sauce

molho holandês *[mohl-yoo ohlandehsh]* sauce hollandaise (served with fish)

molho veloutée *[mohl-yoo vilooteh]* white sauce with egg yolks and cream

monumento nacional national monument

morangos *[moorangoosh]* strawberries

morangos com chantilly *[moorangoosh kong shantee-yee]* strawberries and whipped cream

morena *[moorehna]* beer (mixture of lager and bitter)

moscatel *[mooshkatel]* muscatel wine

Mouros the Moors

mousse de chocolate *[moos dih shookoolaht]* chocolate mousse

mousse de fiambre *[moos dih f-yambrih]* ham soufflé

mousse de leite condensado *[moos dih leh-it kondensahdoo]* condensed milk mousse

móveis de cozinha kitchen furniture

mudar em ... change at ...

muito obrigado thank you very much

muito prazer em conhecê-lo *[mweengtoo prazehr aing koon-yiseh-loo]* very pleased to meet you

multa fine

museu museum

n. (número) number

nada a declarar nothing to declare

nadador salvador lifeguard

não aconselhável a menores de ... anos not recommended for those under ... years of age

não alcoólico *[nowng ahlkwoleekoo]* non-alcoholic
não beber do not drink
não congelar do not freeze
não contém ... does not contain ...
não engolir do not swallow
não engomar do not iron
não exceder a dose indicada do not exceed the dose indicated
não faz mal *[nowng fahsh mahl]* it's ok
não fumar no smoking
não há vagas no vacancies
não ingerir do not swallow
não mexer do not touch
não pendurar do not hang
não pisar a relva please keep off the grass
não secar na máquina do not spin dry
não torcer do not wring

napolitanas *[napooleetanash]* long, flat biscuits/cookies
Na. Sra. (Nossa Senhora) Our Lady
natas *[nahtash]* cream
nêsperas *[neshpirash]* loquats (*fruit*)
no. (número) number
Noite de Santo António festivities held on the night of 13 June
Noite de São João festivities held on the night of 24 June
Noite de São Pedro festivities held on the night of 29 June
nono (9o) andar (*UK*) ninth floor; (*USA*) tenth floor
norte north
No. Sr. (Nosso Senhor) Our Lord
notas banknotes, bills
nozes *[nozish]* walnuts

O

objectos perdidos lost property, lost and found
obras roadwork(s)
obrigado *[obreegahdoo]* thank you
oculista optician
ocupado occupied, engaged
oferta especial special offer
oitavo (8o) andar (*UK*) eighth floor; (*USA*) ninth floor
olá *[aw-lah]* hello
óleo oil
omolette *[omoolett]* omelet(te)
omolette com ervas *[omoolett kong airvash]* vegetable omelet(te)
omolette de cogumelos *[omoolett dih koogoomehloosh]* mushroom omelet(te)
omolette de fiambre *[omoolett dih f-yambrih]* ham omelet(te)
omolette de queijo *[omoolett dih káysшoo]* cheese omelet(te)
orelha de porco de vinaigrette *[orehl-*

ya dih pohrkoo de veenigrett] pig's ear in vinaigrette
orquestra orchestra
ourivesaria jewel(l)er
outras localidades other places (not Lisbon)
ovo com mayonnaise *[ohvoo kon mayoonez]* egg mayonnaise
ovo em geleia *[ohvoo aing sшilay-a]* jellied egg
ovo estrelado *[ohvoo shtrilahdoo]* fried egg
ovo quente *[ohvoo kent]* soft boiled egg
ovos mexidos *[ovoosh misheedoosh]* scrambled eggs
ovos mexidos com tomate *[ovoosh misheedoosh kong toomaht]* scrambled eggs with tomato
ovos verdes *[ovoosh vehrdish]* stuffed eggs

P

P. (Praça) square
padaria baker
pag. (página) page
pagamento payment
pagamento a pronto cash payment
páginas amarelas yellow pages
palácio palace
palco stage
pão de centeio *[powng dih sentay-oo]* rye bread
pão de ló de Alfazeirão *[powng dih law d-yahlfazay-rowng]* sweet sponge cake
pão de ló de Ovar *[powng dih law d-yohvahr]* sweet sponge cake
pão de milho *[powng dih meel-yoo]* corn bread
pão integral *[powng eentigrahl]* wholemeal bread
pão torrado *[powng toorrahdoo]* toasted bread
papéis waste paper
papelaria stationery
para todos suitable for all age groups
parabéns *[parabaingsh]* congratulations; happy birthday
paragem stop
parar stop
parar: alfândega stop: customs
páre, escute e olhe stop, look and listen
pargo *[pahrgoo]* sea-bream
pargo assado *[pahrgoo assahdoo]* roast bream
pargo cozido *[pahrgoo koozeedoo]* boiled bream
parque de campismo campsite
parque de estacionamento car park/ parking lot
parque de estacionamento subterrâneo underground car park/parking lot
parque recreativo amusement park
parrilhada *[pareel-yahda]* grilled fish
particular private
partidas departures

passagem de nível level crossing, grade crossing
passagem subterrânea underpass
passaportes passports
passe go, walk
pastéis de Tentúgal *[pashtay-sh dih tentoogahl]* custard pie with almonds and nuts
pastel *[pashtel]* cake; pie
pastelaria café (*also sells cakes*)
pastelinhos de bacalhau *[pashtileen-yoosh dih bakal-yah-oo]* fish cakes made with cod
patanisca *[pataneeshka]* salted cod fritter
patanisca de miolos *[pataneeshka dih m-yoloosh]* brain fritter
paté de aves *[pateh d-yahvish]* bird pâté
paté de coelho *[pateh dih kwehl-yoo]* rabbit pâté
paté de fígado *[pateh dih feegadoo]* liver pâté
paté de galinha *[pateh dih galeen-ya]* chicken pâté
paté de lebre *[pateh dih lebrih]* hare pâté
pato à Cantão *[pahtoo ah kantowng]* Chinese style duck
pato assado *[pahtoo assahdoo]* roast duck
pato com laranja *[pahtoo kong laransнa]* duck à l'orange
pavilhão desportivo sports pavilion
pega action of wrestling with the bull during a bull fight
peixaria fishmonger
peixe *[paysh]* fish
peixe espada *[paysh shpahda]* swordfish
peixe espada de escabeche *[paysh shpahda dishkabehsh]* marinated swordfish
peixinhos da horta *[paysheen-yoosh da orta]* French bean fritters
pele leather, suede, fur
peleiro furrier

pensão boarding house
pensão completa full board, American plan
peões pedestrians
pequeno almoço continental *[peekeh-noo ahlmohsoo konteenentahl]* continental breakfast
pera abacate *[pehra abakaht]* avocado pear
pera bela helena *[pehra bella eelehna]* pear in chocolate sauce
peras *[pehrash]* pears
percebes *[pirsebish]* kind of shellfish
perdidos e achados lost and found, lost property
perdizes fritas *[pirdeezish freetash]* fried partridge
perdizes na púcara *[pirdeezish na pookara]* casseroled partridge
perdizes de escabeche *[pirdeezish dishkabehsh]* marinated partridge
perfumaria perfume shop/store
perigo danger
perigo de morte extreme danger
perigo, parar danger: stop
perna de carneiro assada *[pairna dih karnay-roo assahda]* roast leg of lamb
perna de carneiro entremeada *[pairna dih karnay-roo entrim-yahda]* stuffed leg of lamb
perninhas de rã *[pirneen-yash dih rang]* frogs' legs
perú *[piroo]* turkey
perú assado *[piroo assahdoo]* roast turkey
perú de fricassé *[peroo dih freekasseh]* turkey fricassé
perú recheado *[piroo rish-yahdoo]* stuffed turkey
pescada cozida *[pishkahda koozeeda]* boiled hake
pescadinhas de rabo na boca *[pishkadeen-yash dih rahboo na bohka]* whiting served with their tails in their mouths
peso líquido net weight
peso neto net weight
pêssego careca *[pehssigoo kar-eka]* nectarine
pêssegos *[pehssigoosh]* peaches
pessoal staff, employees
petiscos *[piteeshkoosh]* savo(u)ries
peúgas socks

pimenta *[peementa]* pepper
pimentos *[peementoosh]* peppers (*red or green*)
pintado de fresco wet paint
piperate *[peepiraht]* pepper stew
piri-piri *[peeree-peeree]* seasoning made from chillies and olive oil
piscina swimming pool
piso escorregadio slippery road surface
piso irregular uneven road surface
plataforma platform, track
plateia stalls
P.M.P. (por mão própria) deliver by hand
polícia police
poliéster polyester
polvo *[pohlvoo]* octopus
ponche punch
ponte bridge
ponto de encontro meeting point
porcelanas china
porco *[pohrkoo]* pork
porreiro *[poorray-roo]* bloody good
porta no ... gate number ...
portagem toll
porteiro porter
Porto Oporto
posologia dose
postal post card
posto de socorros first aid centre/center
pousada state-owned hotel, often a historic building which has been restored
praça square; market selling fresh fish/vegetables/fruit/meat
praça de touros bullring
prato do dia *[prahtoo doo dee-a]* today's special
prato especial da casa *[prahtoo shpisyahl da kahza]* special(i)ty of the house
prazer em conhecê-lo *[prazehr aing koon-yiseh-loo]* pleased to meet you
precipício cliff
preço por dia price per day
preço por pessoa price per person
preço por semana price per week
preços reduzidos reduced prices
prego *[pregoo]* thin slice of steak in a roll
prendas, presentes gifts
preservativo contraceptive
pressão tyre/tire pressure
presunto *[prizoontoo]* ham
primeira classe (1a. cl.) first class
primeiro (lo) andar (*UK*) first floor;

(*USA*) second floor
primeiros socorros first aid
privado private
procissão procession
produtos para diabéticos products for diabetics
produtos alimentares foodstuffs
produtos de beleza beauty products
produtos de limpeza household cleaning goods
proibida a entrada no entry
proibida a entrada a ... no admittance to ...
proibida a entrada a cães no dogs
proibida a entrada a menores de ... anos no admittance to those under ... years of age
proibida a paragem no stopping
proibida a passagem no access
proibida a pessoas estranhas ao serviço personnel only
proibido acampar no camping
proibido estacionar no parking
proibido fumar no smoking
proibido tirar fotografias no photographs

proibido tomar banho no bathing
pronto a vestir ready to wear
propriedade privada private property
proteger do calor e humidade store away from heat and damp
próxima sessão às ... horas next showing at ... o'clock
ps. (peso) weight
P.S.P. (Polícia de Segurança Pública) branch of the Portuguese police
pudim de ovos [*poodeeng d-yovoosh*] egg pudding
pudim flã [*poodeeng flang*] type of creme caramel
pudim molotov [*poodeeng molotoff*] creme caramel with egg white
pura lã pure wool
pura lã virgem pure new wool
puré de batata [*pooreh dih batahta*] mashed potatoes
puré de castanhas [*pooreh dih kashtanyash*] chestnut purée
puxar pull
puxar (a alavanca) em caso de emergência pull (lever) in case of emergency
p.v. (preço variado) price varies

Q

qualquer medicamento deve estar fora do alcance das crianças keep all medicines out of the reach of children
quarto (4o) andar (*UK*) fourth floor; (*USA*) fifth floor
quarto para duas pessoas double room
quarto para uma pessoa single room
queda de pedras falling stones
queda de rochas falling rocks
queijo curado [*kay-shoo koorahdoo*] cured cheese
queijo da Ilha [*kay-shoo da eel-ya*] strong peppery cheese from the Azores
queijo da Serra [*kay-shoo da sairra*] cheese from the Serra da Estrela

queijo de cabra [*kay-shoo dih kahbra*] goat's cheese
queijo de ovelha [*kay-shoo d-yohvehl-ya*] sheep's cheese
queijo de Palmela [*kay-shoo dih pahlmela*] small dried cheese
queijo de Serpa [*kay-shoo dih sairpa*] small dried cheese
queijo fresco [*kay-shoo frehshkoo*] very mild goat's cheese
queijos [*kay-shoosh*] cheeses
queixas complaints
quente hot
quinto (5o) andar (*UK*) fifth floor; (*USA*) sixth floor

R

R. (Rua) street
rabanadas *[rabanahdash]* French toast
ráia *[rah-ya]* skate
raios o partam! *[rah-yooz oo pahrtowng]* damn you!
r/c (rés do chão) (*UK*) ground floor; (*USA*) first floor
R.D.P. (Radiodifusão Portuguesa) Portuguese Radio
recepção reception
recibo receipt
reclamação da bagagem baggage claim
reclamações complaints
região demarcada wine producing region subject to official controls
reg. (registado) registered
reg.to. (regulamento) regulation
Reino Unido United Kingdom
relojoaria watchmaker's shop/store
rem. (remetente) sender
remoulade *[rimoolahd]* dressing with mustard and herbs
Renascimento the Renaissance
rendas lace
requeijão *[rikay-sHowng]* curd cheese
rés do chão (*UK*) ground floor; (*USA*) first floor

reserva special old red wine set aside by the producer in years of exceptional quality
reservado reserved
reservas reservations
restaurante restaurant
retalho oddment
retrosaria haberdasher
rillettes *[reelet]* potted pork and goose meat
rins *[reengsh]* kidneys
rins ao Madeira *[reengz ow maday-ra]* kidneys served with Madeira wine
rissol *[reesol]* rissole
rissol de camarão *[reesol dih kamarowng]* prawn rissole
R.N. (Rodoviária Nacional) National bus/coach service
robalo *[roobahloo]* rock-bass
rojões *[roosHoingsh]* cubes of pork
rolo de carne *[rohloo dih kahrn]* meat loaf
roupa interior underwear
R.T.P. (Radiotelevisão Portuguesa) Portuguese Television
rua street
ruínas ruins

S

S. saint
S/ (sem) without
sabayon *[sabayong]* dessert with egg yolks and white wine
sacana! bastard!

saída exit
saída de emergência emergency exit
sal salt
sala de chá tea room
sala de convívio lounge

sala de espera waiting room
salada [salahda] salad
salada de agriões [salahda d-yagr-yoingsh] cress salad
salada de atum [salahda d-yatoong] tuna salad
salada de chicória [salahda dih shee-koree-a] chicory salad
salada de frutas [salahda dih frootash] fruit salad
salada de lagosta [salahda dih lagoshta] lobster salad
salada de ovas [salahda d-yovash] fish roe salad
salada de tomate [salahda dih toomaht] tomato salad
salada mista [salahda meeshta] mixed salad
salada russa [salahda roossa] salad with diced vegetables in mayonnaise, Russian salad
salão de beleza beauty salon
saldos sale
salmão [sahlmowng] salmon
salmão fumado [sahlmowng foomah-doo] smoked salmon
salmonetes grelhados [sahlmoonehtsh gril-yahdoosh] grilled mullet
salsicha [sahlseesha] sausage
salsichas de cocktail [sahlseeshash dih koktel] cocktail sausages
salsichas de perú [sahlseeshash dih pi-roo] turkey sausages
salsichas de porco [sahlseeshas dih pohrkoo] pork sausages
sandes de fiambre [sandish dih f-yambrih] ham sandwich
sandes de lombo [sandish dih lomboo] steak sandwich
sandes de paio [sandish dih pah-yoo] sausage sandwich
sandes de presunto [sandish dih pri-zoontoo] ham sandwich
sandes de queijo [sandish dih kay-shoo] cheese sandwich
sandes mista [sandish meeshta] mixed sandwich
santinho [santeen-yoo] bless you
santola [santola] spider crab
santola gratinada [santola grateenahda] spider crab au gratin
sapataria shoe shop/store
sapateira [sapatay-ra] spider crab

sapateiro cobbler
sardinhada party where grilled sardines are eaten
sardinhas assadas [sardeen-yaz assah-dash] roast sardines
S.A.R.L. (Sociedade Anónima de Responsabilidade Limitada) limited company
saúde [sa-ood] cheers
secção de criança children's department
seco dry
seda silk
se faz favor [sih fahsh favohr] please
seguir pela direita keep to your right
seguir pela esquerda keep to your left
segunda classe second class
segundo (2o) andar (UK) second floor; (USA) third floor
seguro de viagem travel insurance
selecção de queijos [silessowng dih kay-shoosh] selection of cheeses
selo de garantia seal of guarantee (on a wine bottle)
selos stamps
selos fiscais fiscal stamps
sem conservantes does not contain preservatives
sem corantes does not contain artificial colo(u)ring
sem corantes nem conservantes does not contain artificial colo(u)ring or preservatives
sem pensão no meals served
semáforos traffic light
senha ticket (at disco etc)
senhoras ladies
sentido único one way
serve-se ... das ... horas às ... horas ... served from ... o'clock until ... o'clock
serviço (não) incluído service (not) included
serviço expresso express service
serviço permanente 24 hour service
sétimo (7o) andar (UK) seventh floor; (USA) eighth floor
sexto (6o) andar (UK) sixth floor; (USA) seventh floor
S.f.f. (Se faz favor) please
silêncio silence
sintético synthetic
sirva-se à temperatura ambiente serve at room temperature
sirva-se fresco serve cool

sirva-se gelado serve chilled
só pode vender-se mediante receita médica available only on prescription
sobremesas [sohbrimehzash] desserts
soirée evening performance
solha [sohl-ya] flounder
solha assada no forno [sohl-ya assahda noo fohrnoo] baked flounder
solha frita [sohl-ya freeta] fried flounder
solha recheada [sohl-ya rish-yahda] stuffed flounder
sonhos [son-yoosh] doughnut-type cakes
sonífero sleeping pill
sopa juliana [sohpa sнool-yana] vegetable soup
sopa de agriões [sohpa d-yagr-yoingsh] cress soup
sopa de alho francês [sohpa d-yahl-yoo fransehsh] leek soup
sopa de camarão [sohpa dih kamarowng] prawn soup
sopa de caranguejo [sohpa dih karanggay-sнoo] crab soup
sopa de cebola gratinada [sohpa dih sibola grateenahda] onion soup au gratin
sopa de cogumelos [sohpa dih koogoomeloosh] mushroom soup
sopa de cozido [sohpa dih koozeedoo] meat soup
sopa de espargos [sohpa dihspahrgoosh] asparagus soup
sopa de grão [sohpa dih growng] chickpea soup
sopa de lagosta [sohpa dih lagoshta] lobster soup
sopa de ostras [sohpa d-yoshtrash] oyster soup
sopa de panela [sohpa dih panela] eggbased dessert
sopa de pão e coentros [sohpa dih powng ee kwentroosh] soup with bread and coriander
sopa de pedra [sohpa dih pedra] thick vegetable soup
sopa de peixe [sohpa dih paysh] fish soup
sopa de rabo de boi [sohpa dih rahboo dih boy] oxtail soup
sopa de tartaruga [sohpa dih tartarooga] turtle soup
sopa do dia [sohpa doo dee-a] soup of the day
sopa dourada [sohpa dohrahda] eggbased dessert
sopas soups [sohpash]
soporíferos sleeping pills
soufflé de camarão [soofleh dih kamarowng] prawn soufflé
soufflé de chocolate [soofleh dih shookoolaht] chocolate soufflé
soufflé de cogumelos [soofleh dih koogoomeloosh] mushroom soufflé
soufflé de espinafres [soofleh dishpeenahfrish] spinach soufflé
soufflé de peixe [soofleh dih paysh] fish soufflé
soufflé de queijo [soofleh dih kay-sнoo] cheese soufflé
soufflé gelado [soofleh sнilahdoo] ice cream soufflé
soutiens bras
Sr. (Senhor) Mr
Sra. (Senhora) Mrs
Sta. saint
Sto. saint
Suíça Switzerland
sul south
sumo de laranja [soomoo dih laransнa] orange juice
sumo de lima [soomoo dih !eema] lime juice
sumo de limão [soomoo dih leemowng] lemon juice
sumo de maçã [soomoo de massang] apple juice
sumo de tomate [soomoo de toomaht] tomato juice
supermercado supermarket
suplemento supplement
supositórios suppositories

T

tabacaria tobacconist, tobacco store
taberna pub
tabuleiros trays
talho butcher
tamanho size
tapetes carpets
tarte de amêndoa *[tart damendwa]* almond tart
tarte de cogumelos *[tart dih koogoomeloosh]* mushroom quiche
tarte de limão *[tart dih leemowng]* lemon tart
tarte de maçã *[tart dih massang]* apple tart
tecidos fabrics
tel. (telefone) telephone
telefonista operator
televisão portátil portable television
televisões televisions
terceiro (3o) andar *(UK)* third floor; *(USA)* fourth floor
termas spa
terraço terrace
têxteis textiles
tinturaria dry-cleaner
toalhas towels
todos os dias daily
tomar ... vezes ao dia to be taken ... times a day
tomar a seguir às refeições to be taken after meals
tomar antes de se deitar to be taken before going to bed
tomar em jejum take on an empty stomach

tomates recheados *[toomahtish rishyahdoosh]* stuffed tomatoes
toque (a campaínha) ring (the bell)
toranja *[tooransha]* grapefruit
torrada *[toorrahda]* toast
torre tower
torresmos *[toorrehshmoosh]* small rashers of bacon
tortilha *[toorteel-ya]* Spanish omelet(te) (with potato)
tosta *[toshta]* toasted sandwich
tosta mista *[toshta meeshta]* toasted ham and cheese sandwich
tostão a tenth of one escudo
toucinho do céu *[tohseen-yoo doo se-oo]* kind of sweetmeat
tourada bullfight
toureiro bullfighter
tóxico toxic, poisonous
transferência transfer
trânsito condicionado restricted traffic
trânsito fechado road blocked
trânsito nos dois sentidos two way traffic
trânsito proibido no thoroughfare, no entry
tribunal court
trufas de chocolate *[troofash dih shookoolaht]* chocolate truffles
truta *[troota]* trout
truta assada no forno *[troota assahda noo fohrnoo]* baked trout
truta cozida *[troota koozeeda]* boiled trout
truta frita *[troota freeta]* fried trout

U

um momento *[oong moomentoo]* hold on, just a moment
únicamente para adultos for adults only
universidade university
urgência casualty, emergencies

uso externo for external use only
uvas brancas/pretas *[oovash brankash/ prehtash]* green/black grapes
uvas moscatel *[oovash mooshkatel]* muscatel grapes

V

validação de bilhetes punch your ticket here
válido até … valid until …
vá para o caralho! *[vah para oo karahlyoo]* go to hell!
vá-se foder! *[vah-sih foodehr]* go to hell!
veado assado *[v-yahdoo assahdoo]* roast venison
vedado ao trânsito no thoroughfare
veículos longos long vehicles
veículos pesados heavy vehicles
velocidade máxima … km/h maximum speed … km/h
venda sale
vende-se for sale
vendedor de jornais newsagent, news vendor
veneno(so) poison(ous)
vergas wicker goods
vermute vermouth
V. Ex. (Vossa Excelência) you (*highly formal*)
via via, lane
via intravenosa intravenously
via nasal nasally
via oral orally
via rápida dual carriageway, divided highway
via rectal per rectum
vidraria glazier

vieiras recheadas *[v-yay-rash rishyahdash]* stuffed scallops
vinagre de estragão *[veenahgrih dishtragowng]* tarragon vinegar
vindima grape harvest
vinho branco *[veen-yoo brankoo]* white wine
vinho da casa *[veen-yoo da kahza]* house wine
vinho de aperitivo *[veen-yoo d-yapiriteevoo]* aperitif
vinho de mesa *[veen-yoo dih mehza]* table wine
vinho de Xerêz *[veen-yoo dih shirehsh]* sherry
vinho do Porto *[veen-yoo doo pohrtoo]* Port wine
vinho espumante *[veen-yoo shpoomant]* sparkling wine
vinho moscatel *[veen-yoo mooshkatel]* muscatel wine
vinho rosé *[veen-yoo roozeh]* rosé wine
vinho verde *[veen-yoo vehrd]* slightly sparkling wine made from young grapes
vire à esquerda/direita turn left/right
viscoso viscous
vistos visas
vitela *[veetela]* veal
volátil volatile
volto já *[voltoo sнah]* back in a minute

W X Z

whisky de malte *[weeshkee dih mahlt]*
malt whisky

xarope *[sharop]* syrup
xarope de groselha *[sharop dih groozehl-ya]* blackcurrant syrup

xarope de morango *[sharop dih moo-rangoo]* strawberry syrup

zona azul parking permit zone
zona de banhos swimming area under the surveillance of life guards

zona interdita no thoroughfare

NOUNS

GENDER

All nouns in Portuguese are either masculine or feminine in gender. Almost all nouns ending in **-o** are masculine and those ending in **-a**, **-ão** or **-ade** are feminine. Nouns with other endings may be either gender.

PLURALS

To form the plurals of nouns, follow the rules given below:

ending of noun

any vowel except **-ão**	add **-s**
-ão	change **-ão** to **-ões**
any consonant except **-l** or **-m**	add **-es**
-l	change **-l** to **-is**
-m	change **-m** to **-ns**

For example:

o vinho	os vinhos	the wine(s)
a estação	as estações	the station(s)
o cartaz	os cartazes	the poster(s)
o hotel	os hotéis	the hotel(s)
o homem	os homens	the man (men)

ARTICLES

THE DEFINITE ARTICLE (THE)

The form of the definite article depends on whether the noun is masculine or feminine, singular or plural:

	sing.	pl.
m.	o	os
f.	a	as

For example:

o restaurante	os restaurantes	the restaurant(s)
a loja	as lojas	the shop(s)

The definite article changes its form when it is combined with the words **a** (to), **de** (of), **em** (in) or **por** (by):

	o	a	os	as
a+	ao	à	aos	às
de+	do	da	dos	das
em+	no	na	nos	nas
por+	pelo	pela	pelos	pelas

For example:

ao lado do café	next to the cafe
está no hotel	he's in the hotel
vou à praia	I'm going to the beach
feito pelo artista	made by the artist

THE INDEFINITE ARTICLE (A, AN, SOME)

This also varies according to whether the noun is masculine or feminine, singular or plural:

	sing.	pl.
m.	um	uns
f.	uma	umas

For example:

um bolo	uns bolos	a cake (cakes *or* some cakes)
uma cama	umas camas	a bed (beds *or* some beds)

When the indefinite article is combined with **em** (in):

$$em + um \rightarrow num$$
$$em + uma \rightarrow numa$$

ADJECTIVES

Adjectives in Portuguese usually follow the noun they refer to and change their form according to whether the noun is masculine or feminine, singular or plural.

To find the feminine form:

change the masculine ending   to

-o	-a
-or	-ora

In most other cases the masculine and feminine forms are the same.

The plurals of adjectives are formed according to the rules which apply to nouns.

For example:

as garrafas pequenas	the small bottles
vestidos azuis	blue dresses

COMPARATIVES (BIGGER, BETTER etc)

Comparatives are formed by placing **mais** in front of the adjective:

bonito   nice   **mais bonito**   nicer

To say that something is 'more... than...' use **mais... do que...**:

mais caro do que o outro   more expensive than the other one

To say that something is 'as... as...' use **tão...como...**:

tão alto como o seu amigo   as big as your friend

SUPERLATIVES (BIGGEST, BEST etc)

Superlatives are formed by placing **o** or **a mais** in front of the adjective:

bonito   nice   **mais bonito**   nicer   **o mais bonito** nicest

or **a mais bonita**

Note that 'in' following a superlative in English is expressed by **de** in Portuguese:

as malas mais baratas da loja   the cheapest bags in the shop

A few adjectives have irregular comparatives and superlatives:

bom	good	**melhor**	better	**o melhor**	the best
grande	big	**maior**	bigger	**o maior**	the biggest
mau	bad	**pior**	worse	**o pior**	the worst
pequeno	small	**menor**	smaller	**o menor**	the smallest

POSSESSIVE ADJECTIVES (MY, YOUR etc)

As with other adjectives, their form depends on the gender and number of the noun they refer to. The possessive adjectives are:

	m. sing.	f. sing.	m. pl.	f. pl.
my	o meu	a minha	os meus	as minhas
your (sing. familiar)	o teu	a tua	os teus	as tuas
his/her/its; your (sing. formal)	o seu	a sua	os seus	as suas
our	o nosso	a nossa	os nossos	as nossas
your (pl. familiar and formal)	o vosso	a vossa	os vossos	as vossas
their	o seu	a sua	os seus	as suas

For example:

as tuas malas	your suitcases
o nosso apartamento	our apartment
o seu passaporte	your passport

Since **o seu** can mean 'his', 'her', 'its', 'your' or 'their', the following may be used instead, placed after the noun, to avoid confusion:

dele	his
dela	her
de você	your (sing.)
deles	their (m.)
delas	their (f.)
de vocês	your (pl.)

For example:

o amigo de você	your friend
a mala dela	her bag
o passaporte dele	his passport

DEMONSTRATIVE ADJECTIVES (THIS, THAT etc)

Demonstrative adjectives are placed before the noun, and their form also depends on the gender and number of the noun. There are three demonstrative adjectives in Portuguese:

este	this (referring to an object near the speaker)
esse	that (referring to an object near the person the speaker is addressing)
aquele	that (referring to an object distant from both the speaker and the person addressed)

The forms of the demonstrative adjectives are:

	este	esse	aquele
m. sing.	**este**	**esse**	**aquele**
f. sing.	**esta**	**essa**	**aquela**
m. pl.	**estes**	**esses**	**aqueles**
f. pl.	**estas**	**essas**	**aquelas**

For example:

este hotel	this hotel
essas raparigas	those girls
aquelas mulheres	those women

PRONOUNS

PERSONAL PRONOUNS

	subject		direct object		indirect object
eu	I	**me**	me	**me**	to me
tu	you (sing. familiar)	**te**	you	**te**	to you
ele	he	**o**	him/it	**lhe**	to him
ela	she	**a**	her/it	**lhe**	to her
você	you (sing. formal)	**o/a**	you	**lhe**	to you
nós	we	**nos**	us	**nos**	to us
vocês	you (pl. familiar)	**vos**	you	**vos**	to you
eles	they (m.)	**os**	them	**lhes**	to them
elas	they (f.)	**as**	them	**lhes**	to them
vocês	you (pl. formal)	**vos**	you	**vos**	to you

Pronouns expressing the subject are often omitted in Portuguese as the ending of the verb makes it clear who is carrying out an action. For example, **falo** can only mean 'I speak'. But when different subjects take the same ending of the verb, e.g. with the he/she/it/you form, subject pronouns may be used to avoid confusion. They are also used to place emphasis on the subject.

For example:

ela fala inglês	she speaks English
eu quero um café	*I* want a cup of coffee

Pronouns expressing the object or indirect object follow the verb and are joined to it by a hyphen, but if the verb is negative they are placed in front of it without any hyphens:

ele vê-me	he sees me
não a conheço	I don't know her

YOU

There are three common ways of expressing 'you' in Portuguese. They are:

tu   used to address friends, relatives and children, and also used
                          between young people.

você (sing.)   more formal, used to address people the speaker doesn't know
vocês (pl.)   well. Verb endings with these are **-a** or **-e** in the singular and
                          -am or **-em** in the plural.

o senhor (m.),   used to complete strangers. These take the same form of the verb
a senhora (f.)   as **você**.

For example:

tu sabes chegar lá?   do you know how to get there?
que deseja você?   what would you like?
o senhor sabe onde é?   do you know where it is?

REFLEXIVE PRONOUNS (MYSELF, YOURSELF etc)

Reflexive verbs are those with which the object is the same as the subject, e.g. I wash
(myself). The reflexive pronouns are:

me   myself
te   yourself (sing. familiar)
se   himself/herself;
                          yourself (sing. formal)
nos   ourselves
se   yourselves (pl. familiar and formal);
                          themselves

Portuguese uses many more verbs reflexively than English.
For example:

levanto-me às sete   I get up at seven
posso sentar-me aqui?   may I sit here?
ela vai deitar-se   she's going to lie down

POSSESSIVE PRONOUNS (MINE, YOURS etc)

These are identical in form to the possessive adjectives.
When they follow the verb **ser** the definite article (**o**, **a**, **os** or **as**) is dropped:

são suas   they are yours
não e o meu passaporte, e seu it isn't my passport, it's yours

DEMONSTRATIVE PRONOUNS (THIS ONE, THOSE etc)

These are identical to the demonstrative adjectives (see page 111) but a neuter form also
exists which is used when no specific noun is being referred to. The neuter form is:

isto   **isso**   **aquilo**

For example:

isso é ridículo   that's ridiculous
o que é aquilo?   what's that?

VERBS

Portuguese verbs are divided into three groups:

those ending in **-ar**	e.g. **falar** – to speak
those ending in **-er**	e.g. **comer** – to eat
those ending in **-ir**	e.g. **partir** – to leave

THE PRESENT TENSE

To form the present tense, take off the **-ar**, **-er** or **ir** endings and add the present tense endings:

falar		**comer**		**partir**	
fal-o	I speak	**com-o**	I eat	**part-o**	I leave
fal-as	you speak (sing. familiar)	**com-es**	you eat (sing. familiar)	**part-es**	you leave (sing. familiar)
fal-a	he/she/it speaks; you speak (sing. formal)	**com-e**	he/she/it eats; you eat (sing. formal)	**part-e**	he/she/it leaves; you leave (sing. formal)
fal-amos	we speak	**com-emos**	we eat	**part-imos**	we leave
fal-am	you speak (pl. familiar and formal); they speak	**com-em**	you eat (pl. familiar and formal); they eat	**part-em**	you leave (pl. familiar and formal); they leave

Most verbs are regular and follow the above pattern, but some common verbs are irregular:

ter (to have)	**dar** (to give)	**ir** (to go)	**pôr** (to put)	**vir** (to come)
tenho	**dou**	**vou**	**ponho**	**venho**
tens	**dás**	**vais**	**pões**	**vens**
tem	**dá**	**vai**	**põe**	**vem**
temos	**damos**	**vamos**	**pomos**	**vimos**
têm	**dão**	**vão**	**põem**	**vêm**

The following are irregular in the 'I' form only:

fazer	to do	**faço**
saber	to know	**sei**
dizer	to say	**digo**
pedir	to ask for	**peço**
ouvir	to hear	**oiço**
poder	to be able	**posso**

THE PAST TENSE
Two past tenses are in common use.

The IMPERFECT TENSE is used to express an action which was repeated over a period of time (like the meaning of 'used to' in English) and is formed as follows:

falar (to speak)	**comer** (to eat)	**abrir** (to open)
fal-ava	com-ia	abr-ia
fal-avas	com-ias	abr-ias
fal-ava	com-ia	abr-ia
fal-ávamos	com-íamos	abr-íamos
fal-avam	com-iam	abr-iam

The verb **ser** (to be) has the only irregular imperfect:
> era
> eras
> era
> éramos
> eram

The PRETERITE TENSE is used to express a completed action in the past and is formed as follows:

falar	**comer**	**abrir**
fal-ei	com-i	abr-i
fal-aste	com-este	abr-iste
fal-ou	com-eu	abr-iu
fal-ámos	com-emos	abr-imos
fal-aram	com-eram	abr-iram

There are a number of irregular preterites:

ser (to be)	**fazer** (to do)	**vir** (to come)	**dizer** (to say)	**ir** (to go)
fui	fiz	vim	disse	fui
foste	fizeste	vieste	disseste	foste
foi	fez	veio	disse	foi
fomos	fizemos	viemos	dissemos	fomos
foram	fizeram	vieram	disseram	foram

This tense is used to express both the idea of 'I did' and 'I have done'.

THE FUTURE TENSE
Portuguese uses two methods to express the future.

The PRESENT TENSE is used if it is clear that the future is meant:

a que horas volta você?	when will you come back?
faço isso amanhã	I'll do that tomorrow

The verb **ir** (to be going to) is also used, as in:

que vão fazer?	what will you do?
vamos falar com ele amanhã	we'll speak to him tomorrow

MAKING THE VERB NEGATIVE
By putting **não** in front of the verb, it is made negative:

não tenho calor	I am not hot
não quero ir a uma discoteca	I don't want to go to a disco

Não is also used in conjunction with other negatives:

não... nada	nothing, not... anything
não... nunca	never
não... ninguém	nobody, not... anybody
	no one, not... anyone
não... nenhum	none, not... any

For example:

não quero nada, obrigado	I don't want anything, thanks
não fumo nunca	I never smoke
não vejo ninguém	I don't see anyone
não tenho nenhum	I don't have any

THE IMPERATIVE (GIVING COMMANDS)
The forms used to people addressed as **tu** are:

fal-a	speak	**com-e**	eat	**abr-e**	open

For people addressed as **você** or **o senhor** the forms are:

	falar	**comer**	**abrir**
sing.	**fal-e**	**com-a**	**abr-a**
pl.	**fal-em**	**com-am**	**abr-am**

Verbs which are irregular in the 'I' form use the same irregularity in the imperative:

venha cá!	come here
ponha isso aqui	put that here

To make the imperative negative, **não** is placed in front of the verb. In the case of the **tu** form, **-s** is also added to the verb, a final **e** becomes an **a** and a final **a** becomes an **e**:

não falem	don't speak
não olhes	don't look
não bebas isso	don't drink that

TO BE

There are two verbs meaning 'to be' in Portuguese – **ser** and **estar.** The present tense forms of these are:

ser   **estar**

sou	I am	**estou**
és	you are (sing. familiar)	**estás**
é	he/she/it is; you are (sing. formal)	**está**
somos	we are	**estamos**
são	you are (pl. familiar) you are (pl. formal); they are	**estão**

Ser is used to express permanent position or permanent qualities. It is used with nationalities and occupations as well as with expressions of time and in impersonal expressions.

For example:

onde é a igreja?	where is the church?
Maria é alta	Maria is tall
sou inglês	I am English
você é médico?	are you a doctor?
são duas	it's 2 o'clock
é fácil	it's easy

Estar is used to express temporary position or a temporary state. When used with **a** + a verb it expresses an action actually taking place:

estás aí?	are you there?
Pedro está cansado	Peter is tired
estou a tomar banho	I'm taking a bath

TELLING THE TIME

what time is it?	que horas são? *[k-yorash sowng]*
it is ...	é ...(for one o'clock)
	são ... *[sowng]* (after one o'clock)
one o'clock	a uma *[ooma]*
seven o'clock	as sete *[set]*
one a.m.	uma hora da manhã *[ooma ora da man-yang]*
seven a.m.	as sete horas da manha *[set-yorash da man-yang]*
one p.m.	uma hora da tarde *[ooma ora da tahrd]*
seven p.m.	as sete horas da tarde *[set-yorash da tahrd]*
midday	meiodia *[mayoodee-a]*
midnight	meianoite *[may-anoh-it]*
five past eight	as oito e cinco *[oh-itoo ee seenkoo]*
five to eight	as oito menos cinco *[oh-itoo mehnoosh seenkoo]*
half past ten	as dez e meia *[dez ee may-a]*
quarter past eleven	onze horas e um quarto
	[onz-yorash ee oong kwahrtoo]
quarter to eleven	onze horas menos um quarto
	[onz-yorash mehnooz oong kwahrtoo]

CONVERSION TABLES

1. LENGTH

centimetres, centimeters
1 cm = 0.39 inches

metres, meters
1 m = 100 cm = 1000 mm
1 m = 39.37 inches = 1.09 yards

kilometres, kilometers
1 km = 1000 m
1 km = 0.62 miles = 5/8 mile

km	1	2	3	4	5	10	20	30	40	50	100
miles	0.6	1.2	1.9	2.5	3.1	6.2	12.4	18.6	24.9	31.1	62.1

inches
1 inch = 2.54 cm

feet
1 foot = 30.48 cm

yards
1 yard = 0.91 m

miles
1 mile = 1.61 km = 8/5 km

miles	1	2	3	4	5	10	20	30	40	50	100
km	1.6	3.2	4.8	6.4	8.0	16.1	32.2	48.3	64.4	80.5	161

2. WEIGHT

gram(me)s
1 g = 0.035 oz

g	100	250	500
oz	3.5	8.75	17.5 = 1.1 lb

kilos

1 kg = 1000 g
1 kg = 2.20 lb = 11/5 lb

kg	0.5	1	1.5	2	3	4	5	6	7	8	9	10
lb	1.1	2.2	3.3	4.4	6.6	8.8	11.0	13.2	15.4	17.6	19.8	22

kg	20	30	40	50	60	70	80	90	100
lb	44	66	88	110	132	154	176	198	220

tons

1 UK ton = 1018 kg
1 US ton = 909 kg

tonnes

1 tonne = 1000 kg
1 tonne = 0.98 UK tons = 1.10 US tons

ounces

1 oz = 28.35 g

pounds

1 pound = 0.45 kg = 5/11 kg

lb	1	1.5	2	3	4	5	6	7	8	9	10	20
kg	0.5	0.7	0.9	1.4	1.8	2.3	2.7	3.2	3.6	4.1	4.5	9.1

stones

1 stone = 6.35 kg

stones	1	2	3	7	8	9	10	11	12	13	14	15
kg	6.3	12.7	19	44	51	57	63	70	76	83	89	95

hundredweights

1 UK hundredweight = 50.8 kg
1 US hundredweight = 45.36 kg

3. CAPACITY

litres, liters

1 l = 7.6 UK pints = 2.13 US pints
$\frac{1}{2}$ l = 500 cl
$\frac{1}{4}$ l = 250 cl

pints
1 UK pint = 0.57 l
1 US pint = 0.47 l

quarts
1 UK quart = 1.14 l
1 US quart = 0.95 l

gallons
1 UK gallon = 4.55 l
1 US gallon = 3.79 l

4. TEMPERATURE

centigrade/Celsius
$C = (F - 32) \times 5/9$

C	−5	0	5	10	15	18	20	25	30	37	38
F	23	32	41	50	59	64	68	77	86	98.4	100.4

Fahrenheit
$F = (C \times 9/5) + 32$

F	23	32	40	50	60	65	70	80	85	98.4	101
C	−5	0	4	10	16	20	21	27	30	37	38.3

Numbers

NUMBERS

0 zero *[zairoo]*
1 um *[oong]*   1st primeiro *[preemayroo]*
2 dois *[doh-ish]*   2nd segundo *[sigoondoo]*
3 três *[trehsh]*   3rd terceiro *[tirsayroo]*
4 quatro *[kwahtroo]*   4th quarto *[kwahrtoo]*
5 cinco *[seenkoo]*   5th quinto *[keentoo]*
6 seis *[saysh]*   6th sexto *[sehshtoo]*
7 sete *[set]*   7th sétimo *[seteemoo]*
8 oito *[oh-itoo]*   8th oitavo *[oh-itahvoo]*
9 nove *[nov]*   9th nono *[nohnoo]*
10 dez *[desh]*   10th décimo *[deseemoo]*
11 onze *[onz]*
12 doze *[dohz]*
13 treze *[trehz]*
14 catorze *[katohrz]*
15 quinze *[keenz]*
16 dezasseis *[dizasaysh]*
17 dezasete *[dizaset]*
18 dezoito *[dizoh-itoo]*
19 dezanove *[dizanov]*
20 vinte *[veent]*
21 vinte e um
22 vint e dois
23 vinte e três
etc

30 trinta *[treenta]*
40 quarenta *[kwarenta]*
50 cinquenta *[seenkwenta]*
60 sessenta *[sisenta]*
70 setenta *[sitenta]*
80 oitenta *[oh-itenta]*
90 noventa *[nooventa]*
100 cem *[saing]*
101 cento e um *[sentoo]*
200 duzentos *[doozentoosh]*
300 trezentos *[trizentoosh]*
400 quatrocentos
500 quinhentos *[keen-yentoosh]*
600 seiscentos
700 setecentos
800 oitocentos
900 novecentos
1000 mil *[meel]*
1987 mil novecentos oitenta e sete *[meel novsentoosh oh-itenta ee set]*

2000 dois mil